LATINO COMMUNITIES

EMERGING VOICES
POLITICAL, SOCIAL, CULTURAL, AND LEGAL ISSUES

edited by

ANTOINETTE SEDILLO LOPEZ
UNIVERSITY OF NEW MEXICO

A GARLAND SERIES

LATINO FICTION AND THE MODERNIST IMAGINATION

LITERATURE OF THE BORDERLANDS

JOHN S. CHRISTIE

LONDON AND NEW YORK

First published 1998 by GARLAND PUBLISHING, Inc.

Published 2014 by Routledge
2 Park Square, Milton Park, Abingdon, Oxfordshire OX14 4RN
711 Third Avenue, New York, NY 10017

Routledge is an imprint of the Taylor and Francis Group, an informa business

Library of Congress Cataloging-in-Publication Data

Christie, John S.,, 1954–
Latino fiction and the modernist imagination : literature of the borderlands / John S. Christie.
p. cm. — (Latino communities)
Includes bibliographical references and index.
ISBN 978-0-8153-3246-6 (hbk)
ISBN 978-1-138-00180-0 (pbk)
1. American fiction—Hispanic American authors—History and criticism. 2. American fiction—Latin American influences. 3. American fiction—European influences. 4. Hispanic Americans—Intellectual life. 5. Modernism (Literature)—United States. 6. Mexican Americans in literature. 7. Cuban Americans in literature. 8. Puerto Ricans in literature. 9. Ethnicity in literature. 10. Narration (Rhetoric) 11. Literary form. I. Title. II. Series.
PS153.H56C49 1998
813'.5409868—dc21

98-31294

To my mother, Dorothy Sexton Christie

Contents

Acknowledgments

No part of this study would have ever been completed or even conceived of without the support of two people: my wife Lucía who gave me the time to work and all the Latino stuff that's in me, and my friend and teacher, Gina Barreca, who has somehow kept me laughing the whole way through.

I owe thanks as well to my colleagues for their comments, advice and encouragement: Evelyn Farbman, Charlie Darling, Ron Pepin, Nancy Caddigan, Barbara Douglass and Mary Ann Affleck.

Introduction

From a general perspective, the growth of Latino literature is a fairly recent phenomenon. Sometime in the early 1980's, perhaps with the publication of Sandra Cisneros's *The House on Mango Street* (1983) or Oscar Hijuelos's *Our House in the Last World* (1983) or Richard Rodriguez's *Hunger of Memory* (1982), it dawned on the mainstream book industry and parts of the reading public that there existed a body of literature written in English by U.S. writers of Latin American descent. Over the last decade or so, encouraged at first by small, independent publishers, readers have begun to turn their attention to a collection of novels and stories which give voice to the lives of U.S. citizens living within the bicultural/bilingual borderlands of this country. Obviously, Latino fiction had been around long before this period of recognition (not to mention the Latino poetic tradition which lies outside the scope of this study), but by the late 1980's and early 1990's, works by writers like Arias, Pineda, Islas, Chávez, and Viramontes began to appear on the shelves of bookstores outside the Southwest. The few established Latino writers, nearly all of them Chicanos (Rechy, Anaya, Villarreal, Paredes, Hinojosa, Rivera)—those whose popularity arose after the 1960's Chicano political movement – now gained credibility as elder statesmen for a younger generation of novelists and storytellers. In the eastern U.S., the autobiographical *Down These Mean Streets* by Piri Thomas (in the wake of Claude Brown's *Manchild in the Promised Land*) resurfaced as one model for the urban "autofiction" of writers like Judith Ortiz Cofer, Abraham Rodriguez, Esmeralda Santiago, and Junot Díaz. Cuban-American writers like Hijuelos, Cristina Garcia and Roberto G. Fernandez (writing in English) established the beginnings of Cuban-American prose as a force distinct from the island's rich literary heritage. There appeared more frequent reviews of stories and novels in English by writers with Latin American cultural connections to the Dominican Republic (Alvarez, Díaz) or Central and South America (Goldman, Manrique). The result of this increasing public attention is an extensive body of Latino literature which, it is now fair to say, constitutes a particular subgenre of American literature. The list of fiction writers grows daily as publishers release new anthologies in their constant search for the next best-selling "ethnic" voice: Castillo, Véa, Sáenz, Goldman, Benítez, Agüeros, Abella, Alcalá, and Gilb.

Scholars are not far behind this explosion of creativity: courses in Latino literature abound throughout the academic world, and there are numerous projects currently underway at universities throughout the U.S. to categorize and document the contributions made by Latinos to American letters. So far, the results are impressive in the particulars, but also fragmented. For those interested in Chicano/a writing, journals offer an extensive amount of criticism that is expanded upon daily as perspectives change and literary works are rediscovered. Chicana feminists are especially active in scholarship directed toward the lives of southwestern Latinas. At the same time, individual critics investigate the literary contributions of Latino writers with cultural roots in the islands of Puerto Rico, the Dominican Republic, and Cuba, and thereby contribute to the larger field of post-colonial studies. Yet most Latino critics have primarily focused either upon individual, separate ethnic groups (mainland Puerto Ricans, Chicano/as, or Cuban- Americans) or analyzed a limited selection of texts, often by a single writer whose work might mesh with a specific critical approach. For example, influential works by the first of New York's Puerto Rican immigrant writers, Bernardo Vega and Jesus Colon have reappeared through the efforts of scholars like Juan Flores and Hunter College's Centro de Estudios Puertorriqueños whose mission is decidedly focussed upon a single group. The important scholarly works of feminists like Roberta Fernández, Tey Rebolledo, Gloria Anzaldúa, and Eliana Rivero concentrate solely on the woman writer, while the Jameson-influenced cultural studies of Chicano writing by José David Saldívar and Ramón Saldívar omit the urban Puerto Rican and Cuban-American authors. Scholars like Rosaura Sánchez, Genaro Padilla or Nicolás Kanellos have turned their attention to literary history, especially to Spanish texts from the Chicano past in order to showcase a Latino historical literary tradition. Emily Hicks has begun to establish a theoretical base for "Border Writing," and Debra Castillo a case for Latin American feminist theory, but both studies emphasize Latin American literature and leave little space for close readings of Latino fiction.

The aim of this book is to approach Latino fiction from a wider perspective, and to cross the standard critical boundaries between Latino groups in order to focus upon the literary language of a collection of complicated novels and stories. My goal here is to provide a detailed and informative examination of a wide range of texts, believing that an emphasis upon the formal aspects of Latino fiction will neither detract from the writer's depictions of sociological situations, nor deny the heterogeneity among distinct Latino ethnic groups. I assume from the start that readers will understand the problematic nature of the term "Latino" (or "Hispanic" which I have chosen for the most part to avoid), and that they naturally recognize the extensive cultural diversity of people who fall under such a nebulous label. In fact, I will argue that the close readings in this book help to foreground each individual author's political, ethnic, and racial uniqueness by recognizing and celebrating the narrative elegance with which cultural issues are presented. Since language and culture are inseparable, readers who overlook the vibrant literary creativity in these novels and stories often underestimate the Latino writer's expertise, and may therefore misinterpret the strength of a writer's social convictions. At present, many scholars and teachers from a variety of academic fields outside literature use these literary texts to illustrate social issues impacting on Latino life. While this may be a valid practice, Latino fiction, as a consequence, is somewhat ghettoized and distanced from a literary association, as the reader's attention is steered toward socio-political issues arising mainly in the plot and character of the texts. As writers, Latinos are seen less as artists than as commentators. The point stressed in these pages is that sophisticated manipulation of language (i.e. subtleties of linguistic design, structural patterns, mixtures of Spanish and English) in no way hinders a writer's capacity to convey his or her cultural critiques of the hybrid Latino world. The bulk of this study, therefore, explores in detail how Latino writers use narrative and linguistic innovation in order to celebrate and question the details and dilemmas of their own hybridity.

No less than any other group of American writers, Latino storytellers have literary connections to the modernist techniques that have shaped the prose of twentieth-century writers. I use modernism therefore as a theoretical framework for a number of reasons. To begin with, it allows me to narrow the focus of the book; I can exclude, for instance, most fiction written in a realist mode – in particular the great many straightforward Latino autobiographical texts. Investigating the formal aspects of Latino fiction means privileging the language and style of the texts considered, and thus carries my critical attention across cultures in a productive, if random, way. The study remains contained, yet there is no need for limiting explications to one particular Latino population. Comparisons, for example, between a young Chicana heroine like the narrator of Cisneros's "One Holy Night," and a newly arrived Cuban adolescent like Delores in Hijuelos's *The Mambo Kings Play Songs of Love* strike me as valid and interesting. The fragmentation of points of view in works by Viramontes (a west coast Chicana) and Ed Vega (a mainland Puerto Rican) present relationships between two writers otherwise disconnected and dissimilar. Yet both, like their counterparts discussed throughout this book, are U.S. writers of Latino fiction, and they deserve to be studied in a literary context as contributors to twentieth-century American literature.

Latino writers, like most mainstream American writers, are aware of European literary traditions. Yet they are also enriched by the flavors of a Latin American literary heritage, and by oral, folkloric cultures. They maintain an outsider's bicultural perspective on life in this country and cannot help but struggle with the need to express that duality. The confrontation of influences from Europe and Latin America generates in Latino works a special, imaginative quality, a playful fictional fusion that is both powerful and inventive.

The closer Latino writers are to the multicultural, "ajiaco" (stew) of U.S. Latino life, the more apt they are to complicate their fictional narrative. Those historical novels written about Latin America (i.e. Abella's *The Great American* or Ferré's family sagas like *The House on the Lagoon*), and even those works merely half-focussed on events outside the U.S. like Goldman's *The Long Night of White Chickens* or Santiago's *America's Dream* steer their creators for some reason toward traditional realist presentation. Montserrat Fontes's portrayal of northern Mexico, *Dreams of the Centaur*, is a realist work. So too is Pico Iyer's depiction of modern Cuba: *Cuba and the Night.* Similarly, Kathleen Alcalá's *Spirits of the Ordinary* and its sequel, both set in northern Mexico, despite elements of magical realism, are written in straightforward, narrative modes. And yet, for her stories, set in an indistinct borderland between California and Mexico, she employs modernist switches of points of view and non-linear chronologies. For the Latino writer, the amalgamation of cultural life in the U.S. seems almost to necessitate more fractured narrative structures and stylistic finesse.

As we follow characters of Latino fiction outside the predicaments and problems of U.S. Latino life, we find narratives that read faster, but perhaps challenge us less as readers. Turn in the opposite direction – into the urban centers of Chicago, East LA, Miami, or New York for example – or, for that matter, toward the dusty South Texas border towns in Sáenz, Cisneros or Gilb, and the tangles of borderland life (of identity, prejudice and language) complicate the prose and perhaps *require* the characteristics we associate with modernism. The U.S., according to a character in a recent Cormac McCarthy novel, "totters upon an unspoken labyrinth of questions." For some of the writers emphasized in this study, questions of cultural hybridity transcend geographical borders, pervading, for instance, novels set in Cuba by Cristina Garcia, in Mexico by Ana Castillo, and in Peru, Brazil and Java by Cecile Pineda. Those Latino writers most interested in the frictions of U.S. Latino life set their novels and stories within complex, polyphonic narratives where literal geography gives way to metaphorical borders, and readers are forced to understand something of alienation, a bit about crossing over, and the vitality and advantages of living on the fringes, between worlds. My intention throughout this work is to explore how the techniques of modernism furnish Latino writers with a series of methods for voicing their hybrid identities, authenticating their bicultural worlds and establishing their own visions of Latino self-awareness.

Latino Fiction and the Modernist Imagination

CHAPTER ONE

The Narrative Techniques of the Border

At the end of Tomás Rivera's classic novel *Y no se lo tragó la tierra*, the narrator defined what may be the central task for U.S. Latinos: "to discover and rediscover and piece things together. This to this, that to that, all with all. That was everything" (152). To form an identity out of a mixture of cultural ingredients, to recognize oneself as a sort of "stew" or "ajiaco" (to use Pérez Firmat's idea), this is both the problem and the source of creativity for Latino writers. What "thrills" Rivera's narrator, however, is not success in forging a clear identity out of a rediscovered past, or in reviving that past, but rather the knowledge that the process of remembering and understanding and retelling constitutes a reason to exist. Latino writers are engaged in connecting the pieces of their complicated hybrid lives, not necessarily for the purpose of bringing to life some distant ancestral tradition, some mythic truth to live by, but in order to make sense out of the complexity of their own identities spread out in fragments before them. The subsequent attempt on the part of Latinos to adjust their lives to the impossibility of wholeness, of totally belonging to something clear and certain, constitutes the central tension in their fiction, and it is that tension that can only be partially resolved in an acceptance of permanent "dualness," of hybridity. For the critic Bruce-Novoa, Chicano literary "space" (central to all his critical theory) lies between Mexican and North American culture, and between U.S. and Latin American literary influence. This "retrospace" exploits the "inter cultural possibilities" of that "nothingness" between the two (*Retrospace* 98), "the space created by the tensions" of the interrelations of both worlds. Chicana critic Gloria Anzaldúa speaks of the writing from "cracked spaces," from a position between cultures, from the fringes of society. Chicana poet, Pat Mora, titles her non-fiction collection of essays *Nepantla*, an Aztec word meaning "one torn between two ways" (*Borderlands* 78). Modern Latino writers willingly inhabit and write about a border state, a liminal territory signaled by any number of catchy phrases from "Life on the Hyphen" to "Cultural Schizophrenia."

While some Latino writers (both men and women) use their fiction, poetry and essays to express their "border state" directly—in, for example, an autobiographical mode—it is certainly true that others communicate the flavor and atmosphere of their liminal world through fictional artifice and that the literary devices they employ enhance rather than hinder an expression of Latino life. Further, the scope of Latino creativity manifests itself in a variety of narrative techniques, at the same time Latino critiques of U.S. culture and inversions of accepted stereotypes (and other practices common to writers outside the margins of power) are displayed on both a literal and narrative level, both in the content and in the form. Though Sandra Cisneros lamented the fact that the people she knew about (urban Latinos) were not represented in mainstream literature or in the academic discourse of the University of Iowa's Writers workshop,[1] it becomes increasingly clear with each of her new books that she has borrowed stylistic methods and techniques of craft from her literary precursors, adjusting them to tell her own stories of Chicanas in Chicago and Texas. In fact, it is reasonable to conclude that any Latino writer, when traveling through the U.S. University system, would necessarily pick up the same canonical basis for their art as any mainstream writer would. To deny this is to ignore or underestimate the Latino writer's expertise in narrative skill. It has been argued that Chicana writers, and by inference other Latina writers as well, have only recently begun to shed taboos and to directly state what is on their minds regarding questions of sexuality, gender and ethnicity, whereas before such writers were handicapped by literary conventions and the academy's expectations for formal aspects of creative writing.[2] Yet since the artistic forms of fiction, because of the demands they put upon the reader, often generate the power of literary prose, an exploration of the narrative modes with which Latino and Latina writers experiment should reveal the depth and vitality of the craft and consequently, the ideas within the stories. It is in part the purpose of this study to explore those formal narrative techniques and demonstrate precisely how they encourage readers to share in the complexities and dualities of the Latino labyrinth.

The British modernists, confronted with the overt discontinuity of World War I, industrialization and the explosion of accepted ideals, sought to portray their world in fragmentary systems of narrative. Their effort to put together, juxtapose or balance the "heap of broken images" bears similarities to the intentions of Latino writers today. Much of the cinematic quality—Pound saw the change from rural to urban mirrored in a shift from narrative to cinematic glimpse—what Kenner calls the "aesthetic of glimpses" (69) finds its way into Latino fiction especially in the collage work of Roberto G. Fernández (in some ways an oral Dos Passos) or the "estampas" of Rolando Hinojosa (reminiscent of Faulkner's "postage stamp" Yoknapatawpha) or in the collected snippets of conversation and narrative in Rivera's . . . *Y no se lo tragó, la tierra,* the understanding and ordering of which constitutes the narrator's key to psychological survival. As Pound saw the use of fragmentary lines (in Sappho's poetry) as valid in conveying a sense of memory and bits of the past, so Latino writers use this "aesthetics of glimpses" to communicate their own momentary laments at lost pieces of non-European American life: culture, food, music, and oral language. Ed Vega, for instance, expresses his Nuyorican oral culture via what he calls "amusing anecdotes" (*Mendoza's* 15) incorporating a Puerto Rican story telling tradition into his literary technique. If these short, "funny stories . . . with a meaning" as J. L. Torres in the story "My Father's Flag" (265) calls them are typical of Puerto Rico, their use coincides with the methods of modernist prose. Vega's *Mendoza's Dreams*, a novel built of interconnecting tall tales, is a clear example of fragmented, multi-voiced fiction that exemplifies Latino modernist craft. Sandra Cisneros's very short modernist "lyrical sketches" echo the influential Uruguayan writer José Enrique Rodó's "parables" (Monegal *Borzoi* Vol. I 340) and the Guatemalan Augusto Monterroso's "art of compression," in his "microcuentos" or micro stories (Lindstrom 4). Both these early twentieth-century Latin American writers began the century profoundly influenced by the aesthetics of "modernismo," just as Cisneros and Vega (in the closing decades of the same century), would be guided in their craftsmanship by the modernist imagination.

British modernist thought resulted from various kinds of historical collapses, artistic changes, world events and the influx of individuals who viewed the existing traditions and circumstances through the eyes of the marginal outsider. As James, Pound, Joyce, Eliot, and Conrad privileged their peripheral viewpoints in order to attack and critique the dullness of what they found in turn-of-the-century English literature, so do modern Latino writers take aim at severe political, economic, and sociological complexities inherent in cross cultural life within the U.S. today. They poise themselves between cultural and geographical borders in a position with unique perspective.

E. M. Forster's complaint with the modernists and their distance from economic reality (James's characters who exist without economic or language problems in unreal settings—who bounce from garden to garden in Europe) points directly at a major difference between "high" British modernists (Woolf, Pound, Eliot, Joyce) and current Latino writers. It was the opinion of William Carlos Williams (whose undervalued Puerto Rican background is just now coming to light[3] that "The Waste Land" had set back poetry because it called for attention to the "classroom" rather than to "the locality" which "should give . . . fruit" to "the essence of a new art form" (Bradbury 55). Following their Latin American counterparts (busy pursuing, since mid-century what Carlos Fuentes called "La nueva novela hispanoamericana"), Latino writers center their work upon the fruit of Latino existence which lies outside formal education (the classroom), and is deeply embedded in the reality Forster missed in the characters of Henry James. William's "fruit," an apt word if one considers the Edenic and tropical quality of Latin America in fiction, refers to the lives and cultures of the underestimated Americas whom Williams saw as the subject of a truly "new" art. Though toward the end of his life, Pound was to speak eloquently of gathering "from the air, a live tradition or from a fine old eye, the unconquered flame," around that famous year of 1910 when "human character changed" (Woolf "Mr. Bennet" 96), King Edward died, and the first post-Impressionism exhibition hit London), he was calling for a rigorously academic pursuit, a journey down obscure and distant scholarly channels. Williams, on the other hand, was examining (literally) the detailed world around him in its most practical and obvious manifestations. The difference is not important because individual poets chose distinct subjects, but rather because the impact of those subjects upon the sensibility of the poets was so dramatically different. Williams's eye turned toward the bare simplicity of the ordinary object, while the modernists tended to highlight the past, the unconscious, and thereby distance the poet from reality, creating a literature filled with connotations of alienation, despair, "bleakness, darkness and disintegration" (Bradbury 26). Juxtaposed against the ordered past and the lofty traditions of European culture, everyday reality of industrialization and urbanization of life in England seemed morbidly decayed and destitute.

The modernists' portrayal of a barren reality and their emphasis upon the isolated and ineffectual individual in society vividly contrasts with the exuberance of first Latin American writers and later Latino writers as they approach the reality of their worlds. The reasons for this difference lie in the fact that the institutions and traditions lauded by an Eliot weren't necessarily esteemed by those literary figures outside the margins of control. To those within the walls of "Oxbridge" things looked gloomy as traditions and values appeared to be crumbling, but for those, like Virginia Woolf, having been denied access to education because of those very traditions, who now watched the "crisis" from university lawns, the changes in society must have been more welcome. Something similar in U.S. academia is certainly happening presently as those who mourn the passing of "cultural literacy" and the breakdown of the dominance of the English language stand on one side while minority, multi-cultural, post-colonial writers and scholars stand on the other.

At the time of British modernism's peak (impossible to determine exactly but regarded as roughly between 1910 and 1925 , the same anti-nostalgia was part of those writers even further distanced from European tradition, namely, Latin Americans, and it is certainly true today for their U.S. descendants and counterparts: Latino writers. World War I may have loomed in Europe by 1910, but the date for Latinos, especially Chicanos is more closely tied to the height of the Mexican revolution when Porfirio Díaz and all he represented (U.S. oil companies, wealthy landowners etc.) first began to fall. Virginia Woolf could not have been the only person to notice that 1910 was to change relationships between "masters and servants, husbands and wives, parents and children" or to conclude that such change, though radical, presented positive aspects for those previously deprived in diverse ways. Mexican writers were not afforded the luxury of separating themselves so drastically from a political reality as British modernists were and while experimental techniques eventually were handed down, the spiritual desolation of alienated individuals was less a factor. U.S. troops occupied Cuba off and on through the heyday of modernism (1898-1902, 1906-1909, 1912, and 1917-1922) which helped shape Cuban twentieth-century fiction in a naturalistic, social and political mode, following the direction of José Martí. It wasn't until the 1930's that modernist narrative patterns become noticeable in the works of Carpentier and Lydia Cabrera—among other exiles. In Puerto Rico, the change from Spanish to United States domination led literary figures to see in modernism, not its themes of alienation and the unconscious, but "the new ideas it contained about literature and culture" which allowed Latin Americans like José Martí to see "national culture as an artificial construct, laboriously put together by an intellectual elite" (Foster 565).

A commitment on the part of twentieth-century writers of fiction to the political realities of Latin America grew out of what was perhaps a more removed form of modernism in Latin America than was the case in Europe. Scholars of Spanish America refer to modernismo as a distinctly separate and different literary movement from the modernism associated with Joyce and Pound. Modernismo arrived in the New World from Europe (France particularly) roughly between 1890 and 1893, years before high British modernism took hold in London. It brought, especially to its chief disciple, Rubén Darío, its familiar characteristics of fore-grounding language over content, "violations of accepted expression" and the use of personas (Davidson 1). It opened the way for explorations into inner thoughts and mental conditions like boredom, depression, anguish, obsession, and emphasized the use of embellished, mannered and decorated language. Modernismo represented a "quest for distinction and artistic uniqueness." It rejected sentimentality, naturalism, and the romantic "outpouring of spontaneous emotion" (1-6). Though one could argue with the general theme in Lukács attack on modernism (1963), Latin America's primary modernist was certainly an example of one removed from his society (he wrote practically nothing of his native Nicaragua), and his work was isolated from common life. He was bent on capturing individual sense experiences, and perhaps it is because of his self-conscious search for stylistic perfection that the backlash toward socially committed fiction in Latin America was stronger than in Europe. Where Woolf and Pound were social creatures and the modernism of Joyce was never that distant from his own Dublin political reality, Darío "and the modernistas became intoxicated with France" (González Echevarría 29), pushing poetic language to its symbolic, metaphorical extreme and distinctly separating their art from certain "American" realities. For women, the exoticism of modernismo provided a rallying point around which to argue in a different and vitally political direction. Sylvia Molloy has argued that modernismo excluded woman by speaking of her solely as "subject matter," as "passive recipient," as "commodity," and as "the most valuable piece in its museum" (Castro Klarén 109). One could not make the same argument for European modernism as readily since the writings of Virginia Woolf, Kathryn Mansfield, Rebecca Webb, Stevie Smith, Jean Rhys and Gertrude Stein are so integral to the modernist movement. Neither was it as necessary to combat modernism's "homosocial and homoerotic characteristics" (109) in Europe as it was for Latin American women writers like Castellanos, Garro, Mistral, and Victoria Ocampo. Methods, therefore, of "writing the body" provided these writers with the means to rewrite or reassemble themselves in order to confront the biased "machismo" of Latin American culture, in part because of the restrictive facets of modernismo. As a reaction to the confines of pure style (in search of the universal truth), Latin American women attempted to legitimize the individual and the particular.

By the time the classic works of British modernism had made an impact upon writers in Latin America, during the 20's and 30's, modernismo had given way to Realism and Naturalism and the purely aesthetic modes of writing had been to some extent politicized. Led by the example of Rodó's famous essay, *Ariel*, in which Shakespeare's Caliban is cast as the materialistic U.S. and Ariel embodies the lofty spirituality of Latin America, the innovative writers of the 1930's—writers of the Avant Garde—combined experimental, formal innovations (derived from both types of modernism) with a vivid enthusiasm for their own American world. It is this group that Lindstrom sees as being most closely associated with the modernism of London and the Parisian Latin Corner (8).

Still, in terms of narrative technique, the similarities between modernismo and European modernism need to be mentioned because Latino writers, poised between both strands of aesthetic influence, could very well have drawn their artistic expertise from either side. Both forms of modernism made use of other embedded languages, de-emphasized plot, and concentrated on "the vital rhythmic qualities to prose" (13)—Pound's avoidance of the metronome, his "absolute rhythm." Where the movements differ and where the Avant Garde writers followed the European trends was with regard to the now famous dictates of brevity and clarity and specific images put forward in Pound's "Imagist doctrine," and exemplified in Eliot's precise, unmannered descriptions. The embellishments of Latin American modernismo gave way to avant-garde simplicity and exactitude—"no superfluous word"—while fragmentation, irony and the distortions inherent in the use of personas replaced the aesthetic whole. This "second phase" of modernism (for some called "vanguardismo" or vanguardism), in Latin America challenged the aesthetics of elegance and distance, creating a refined style with a new emphasis upon an escape from Spanish (and European) culture and an interest in a Latin American "cosmopolitan spirit" (Davidson 24).

Fernando Alegría writes in his *Nueva historia de la novela hispanoamericana* that the avant-garde writers "escaped" toward Western culture while remaining conscious of their "American social reality," and therefore looked for narrative flexibility to reflect that reality (108). The first "new" novels, according to the critic Eduardo Camacho Guizado, were *Al filo del agua* by Agustín Yáñez (1950) and *Pedro Páramo* by Juan Rulfo (1955). These writers, building on modernist experimentation consciously blended American subjects with European style, melding "a regional subject with subjective modern aesthetics (Alegría 108). Alejo Carpentier had questioned "how to write in a European language—with its Western systems of thought—- about realities and thought structures never seen in Europe" (J. D. Saldívar 92), and later Latin American writers of the so-called "Boom" generation would expand upon the narrative techniques of modernism in order to further confront this problem. The result of this questioning was to become "The new novel" ("La nueva novela latinoamericano"), the dominant characteristic of which is "magic realism."[4]

Writers like Rulfo and García Márquez were concerned not just with the reality that confronted them in its bizarreness (butterflies, myths, legends, folk tales, superstitions), but with the formal portrayal of these things for Europeans. From the early 1920's on, Latin American writers did not cut themselves off from their immediate reality; they were "exotistas, preciosistas, alegoricos" in one novel and "realist revolutionaries in the next" (Alegría 110). They were politically aware, and struggling to record "the marvelous in the real" that surrounded them and that had been consistently distorted and misrepresented in European texts. It is this desire to recreate, rewrite, or renarrate existing cultural realities that Latino writers share with their Latin American counterparts. The tools of the trade, it seems, come from modernist craft, and are geared toward the altering of Eurocentric perception and the sensitizing of readers.

If the postmodernism spirit has something to do with understanding that a "logocentric" truth is an illusion, that universalism must always give way to relativeness, many Latino writers are postmodernist.[5] Yet, Rosaura Sánchez is certainly correct in recognizing that Chicano fiction (and Latino fiction as a whole) is only "tangentially" postmodernist ("Postmodernism" 12) because, despite its use of modernist/postmodernist narrative techniques, it does not deny entirely humanist subjectivity, or historical representation. There is a strong sense of particularity and specific time and place. Often, as post-colonialist critics are quick to point out, the drive toward finding the universal, the global truth in human characters thinly disguises a way to impose one's own limited understanding upon others by declaring something to be true overall. Latino writers incorporate a technically advanced storytelling mode, one that allows (even demands) multiperspective, polyphonic understanding on the part of writer and reader.[6] Where realism and its authoritative, omniscient narrator lends itself to conclusive writing, and where early modernist works like *Ulysses* hinted at a controlling writer behind the scenes (paring his fingernails) even while the text itself fractured into complex, broken images, Latino writers excel at using modernist methods to wrench the text away from any conclusive, one-dimensional interpretation. Fragmentation in Latino fiction underlines the essentiality of shifting, relative perspectives, of multifaceted characters with complicated identities. It helps the Latino writer, as Akers points out in his discussion of Chicano fiction, to "expand his [or her] narrative scope" (133). At the same time, fragmented texts resemble the first New World Chronicles and this formal allusion to what Nieto reminds us were the first examples of "European literary documentation in America (241) often points to the flaws and misconceptions buried in European narratives of historical "truths." Latino fiction's modernist twists of point of view, frames and metaframes, and stories within stories both emphasize the work's fictionality and simultaneously portray the multivoiced Latino world without implying total denial of practical historical reality.

Critics have argued before that minority groups have always felt the sense of alienation and fragmentation that postmodernism often highlights.[7] The techniques of fracturing narrative point of view which innovators like Faulkner utilized extensively and which seem such a crucial aspect of recent Latino fiction reflect a decentered experience common to marginalized people which is also, as Harper says, a "constituent of the postmodern condition" (Harper 8). Where the modernist focused upon the "alienation" of the subject, the postmodernist's concern is the "fragmented condition of the human subject" (23). Writing mostly about Latin American literature, Emily Hicks speaks of "Border Writing," categorized by "fragmentation in cultural, linguistic, and political deterritorialization" (Intro xxiv), and much of Latino fiction falls under her label by dwelling on the "differences in reference codes between two or more cultures" (xxv).

The freedom of modernist and postmodernist narrative styles allows Latino writers to explore the ambiguities of a complex reality. The complexity and variety of their discourse therefore mirrors the multifarious Latino world. This is not to say that autobiographical (or testimonial) fiction is somehow flawed, but neither can one agree with Gloria Anzaldúa, the co-editor of *This Bridge Called My Back,* in her essay "Speaking in Tongues" or in the preface to her anthology of women's writing *Making Face, Making Soul: Haciendo Caras*. Her denouncing of what she calls the "pseudo-intellectualizing" (*Bridge* 165) of academic writers, her rejection of "abstraction and the academic learning, the rules" (173) and her conviction that "academic language" with its "theoretical babble" (*Making Face* Intro xxiii) and "esoteric bullshit" (*Bridge 1*65) is a tool of the colonizer demonstrate a somewhat counterproductive argument. A creative writer's attention to the "sacred bull, form," far from being restrictive, can often enhance a fictional work by doing exactly what Anzaldúa advocates: shock readers "into new ways of perceiving the world" (172). It is the use of "frames and metaframes" in a novel like Cecile Pineda's *Face*, and the twisted chronologies of action or swings of narrative point of view in writers like Viramontes and Vega that truly distort and alter perspective, that communicate the "discontinued and incomplete discourse" (*Making Face* Intro xvii) Anzaldúa desires. Earl Shorris, author of *Latinos,* whose notions of language are often debatable ("Spanish is not a good language to be spoken by women" 119), argues that the Latino sense of time is somehow linked to the Spanish subjunctive tense which "hesitates, ponders, questions" where English pronounces with clarity and emphasis (116). This could surely be a factor in Latino fiction which attempts to convey via non-linear, non-chronological narrative framework some sense of the Latino's ambiguity and tendency to reject "universals." Thus, the thinking behind a modernist story like Woolf's "The Mark on the Wall" which highlights the haziness of logocentric truths would hold special importance to Latino writers; the formal devices of the modernists would therefore serve them well, as we see in works like Ron Arias's *Road* or Pineda's *Face.*

In his final "Drafts and Fragments" of his Cantos, Pound speaks of his inability to "make it cohere," of a "tangle of words unfinished" (CXVI). A similar sense of futility underlies the fiction of Latino writers to some extent. "To make Cosmos—," Pound writes, cutting the sentence off as if to confirm the impossibility of making order from Chaos, to reconcile the bits and pieces of one's life into a sensible whole, to gather together in coherent design the "broken images." It is almost as if modern Latino writers begin with Eliot's "I can connect nothing with nothing," and what changes is not the vehemence of the endeavor, but the attitude toward a necessary failure. At times there is even delight in the absurdity of the attempt. In some works there is fragmentation because the notion of concrete wholes and one-dimensional positivism is purposely being questioned. A character such as José Rafa may be destroyed by fear as the familiar traditions he abides by crumble around him, but some Latino writers and their protagonists delight in the inconclusiveness of their lives. The need to make everything "connect" is less a dilemma than an opportunity to explore the multiple characteristics of Latino hybridity. We never know, for instance, whether Felicia in *Dreaming in Cuban* actually pushes her lover/husband from a roller coaster, or merely dreams it, or whether Celia's son Javier dies or not, or whether Pilar and her mother are finally reconciled. There is a sense of open-ended "writing beyond the ending." Even more suggestive of this point is the convoluted, "telenovela" plot of Castillo's *So Far From God* where the author never makes it clear what happens in the end. It seems that Francisco, out of jealousy, abducts (using words) Esmeralda, because he is in love with Caridad who shares a special relationship with the kidnapped victim. He takes her off in his pickup and murders her in the desert (213), an incident foreshadowed by an episode with a gun-wielding terrorist on a highway northeast of Santa Fé. She returns as a ghost and Caridad and Esperanza go to the Indian pueblo ruins at Acoma where Esmeralda sees Francisco and runs off the cliff, taking Caridad with her (like a kite) and neither are found again. But nothing in these convoluted events is absolutely clear, nor is it meant to be. The playful changes of tone, and experiments in language (there is a war of clichés at one point) outrank the need for consistency of plot or thematic closure.

Latino writers take hold of modernist narrative devices flexible enough to demand that readers share their sense of incertitude. This is not to say that all Latino fiction incorporating some form of stylistic experimentation is inherently polyphonic. Margarita Engle's *Singing to Cuba* is a case in point. The narrative alternation Engle imposes upon her story of Castro's "secret war" merely shifts from a first person journalistic narrator to a third person realist account of her uncle's fate at the hands of the Cuban government. The result is a didactic novel written to expose a political condition ("the Captive Towns") on the island, and nowhere is the reader encouraged to entertain more than one perspective or feel sympathetic toward characters with differing views. Guy Garcia attempts to complicate his novel *Obsidian Sky* by incorporating the journals of a sixteenth-century Aztec shaman within his modern day mystery of a Chicano anthropologist in Mexico City. While this text within a text clarifies Aztec mythology, the narrative is otherwise straightforward and the novel's thematic concerns entirely unambiguous. A bit more inventive is the title story in Virgil Suárez's *Welcome to the Oasis* about a "marielito" refugee which is broken into twenty sections of a page or two in length. These divisions, at first seemingly unnecessary, actually enhance the story by mimicking the sort of fractured vision, and dangerously confined perspective the Cuban refugee has of his new environment. His momentary glimpses of people coming in and out of the "Oasis Apartments" where he has been employed are paralleled in Suárez's cinematic images, choppy prose, and present tense descriptions. The breaks between events, by denying causality, emphasize the innocent painter's unjustified murder.

Cecile Pineda divides her novel *Frieze* into 120 sections, narratively paralleling the 120 sections of the carvings of Borobudur in Java,[8] but her lyrical first novel *Face* is a work even more firmly based on this kind of playful aesthetic as opposed to linear plot structure. The main character, Helio Cara (translated as "face" in both Spanish and Portuguese), a poor Brazilian, is left literally faceless as the result of a fall which occurs one rainy night in a Rio "favela." Pieces of his story are revealed in short imagistic glimpses—a style that mimics Helio's own reconstruction of the events that led to his fall and his "recovery." These "loose fragments," as Bruce-Novoa notes, provoke in the reader a sense of disorientation similar to the main character's ("Deconstructing" 77). As Helio (like the "half-man, Half beast" face in his old boss's pictures) makes himself whole, the reader gathers together fragments of his story. Pineda's fleeting objective descriptions, devoid of authorial commentary, parallel Helio's glimpses of the world as he regains consciousness after the accident. The entire novel is framed by a prologue spoken by a plastic surgeon, and is therefore an attempt by the doctor to reconstruct Helio's life just as the reader will in the process of reading the book. The narrative structure therefore is an essential part of the novel, for without the frame, or without the at times cryptic (and poetic) delivery of pieces of the story (i.e. fragmented dreams and memories), the novel would be deprived of any meaning beyond the particular Brazilian slum. As Gonzales-Berry claims, the disjointed, scattered events of the first part are replaced in Part II by a more or less chronological pattern, thus mirroring Helio's moving from chaos to order (Review 107). Helio himself reads a text on the practice of plastic surgery, and like the reader, uses language to reconstruct himself. According to Bruce-Novoa, his is a "journey of self-discovery through suffering, degradation, renunciation and disciplined work" ("Deconstructing" 76). From the corrupted capital to the town's central plaza of Bomfim (Good End) in the "Hinterlands," Helio journeys toward his natural origin (his mother's home) where he confronts the reality of his individual capacities and rebuilds his face/identity/life. Planting trees rather than styling hair in a barbershop, he is forced to discard the superficiality of inorganic city values. He throws away the handkerchief he hides beneath (when a gunman tries to kill him) and, finally and most importantly, he confronts the repressed memory of his father's murder by a man in "black, polished leather shoes" (186) which, the reader remembers belong to his dandyish stepfather, Julião Cara. His father "smelled of earth," Julião of "toilet water" (131). Pineda follows the description of the shoes with an allusion to another avenger, Orestes (Oreste the butcher—132). The reader must connect the "luminous details" buried in fragments in order to understand Helio's reasons for leaving his mother's farmland to begin with (escaping such a stepfather and possibly the betrayal of his adulterous mother), as well as the extent of his psychological recovery. [9]

A second example of narrative fragmentation is Cristina Garcia's *Dreaming in Cuban,* in which the protagonist Pilar (named after Hemingway's boat, the character maintains—220—although one suspects Garcia has more the Spanish republican in *For Whom the Bell Tolls* in mind) is confronted with the task of reuniting herself with her Cuban heritage. Divided into three sections ("Ordinary Seductions," "Imagining Winter," and "The Languages Lost"), the disjointed narrative moves through three general time periods (1972, 1974 and

1980), and is told from multiple points of view. Interestingly, the younger generation Cubans reveal their thoughts and ideas through first person narrative while sections devoted to the older generation are written in third person. As in *Face*, the reader's task parallels that of the protagonist's, in this case, Pilar, as she pieces together the events and personalities that shape her identity. She reads her grandmother's fragmentary lyrical letters and juggles her divided family's multiple perspectives. It is a process that her grandmother goes through in order to understand the reasons for her son's delirium, as she "pieces together his story" (156), and one that her aunt Felicia attempts when she "awakens" from her amnesiac carnival life and must "assemble bits and pieces of her past" (154). Like Celia's piano playing, "each note distinct from the others yet part of the whole," Pilar's life is a collection of conflicting and confusing cultural memories and beliefs, and along with the reader who gathers in the individual sections of the book, she constructs her own identity as she sifts through her family's past. Pilar, as an artist, recreates herself in similar fashion to the narrator of Rivera's . . . *Y no se lo tragó la tierra* where, according to Bruce-Novoa, "the need to display the loose images in a coherent manner, relating them and unifying them, is thematically central" (Bruce-Novoa *Retrospace* 108). The result for both characters is an "intercultural state [that] negates the unacceptable extremes and affirms the synthesis process (117).

The formal stylistics of modernist works often prompt readers to reevaluate the way they read and to consciously monitor the systems they use to interpret the world around them. Much of the high modernist emphasis upon the education of the reader exists in Latino works as well, yet it is interesting that some of the most didactic Latino literature displays the least affiliation with a modernist style. Eliot's and Pound's complexity (accompanied by overtly didactic essays and instructional guides like *The ABC of Reading*) were intended to steer literature away from what they considered to be simplistic romance geared toward a female audience. In Latino fiction, however, the most formally complex works are often those by woman and also, in the sense that they offer ambiguous truths, the least overtly sententious. At the same time, the most blatantly didactic Latino works are also by women, but written in either a realist mode (i.e. Mary Helen Ponce, Graciela Limón), slightly disguised autobiography (i.e. Judith Ortiz Cofer), semi-realist style (Alma Villanueva, Margarita Engle) or straight polemical essay (i.e. Cherríe Moraga, Gloria Anzaldúa).

If Gilbert and Gubar are correct in arguing that "a male-female sexual dialectic impelled the construction of what we have traditionally understood as modernism" because alternative perspectives on life made sense to marginalized women ("Female Imagination"), it seems clear that such a "dialectic" is equally important to recent modernist Latino/a fiction. Latinas continue to find modernist experiments valuable in their "reeducation" of the reader. It would be fruitless to argue that Latinos tend to preach more than Latinas, just as it would be to claim that Latinas experiment more in their narratives, yet the role of gender, as one component of fiction that revolves around the conflict of oppositions (of class, race, ethnicity etc.), is certainly a dominant force in literary creativity. Considered from non-gender perspectives, one can conclude that the most innovative Latino writers, men and women, tend to preach the least, and that rebelliousness of thought often parallels stylistic innovation. Given the extent of nostalgic desire to reach the island paradise of old, to reconnect oneself with a lost tradition and comprehensible order, one can easily see a connection between many male Latino writers (like Hijuelos or Candelaria for example) and what Ellen Friedman argues is a predominant characteristic of male modernist/postmodernist fiction in general. Women writers, Friedman claims, "look forward, often beyond culture, beyond patriarchy, into the unknown, the outlawed" (244) and rely less upon either the Oedipus "master narrative" of a search for the missing father/identity/origin (i.e. Rodriguez's *Spidertown)* or its variation: a preoccupation with the loss that the futility of that search creates (Martínez's *Voice-Haunted Journey*). Having recognized the flaws of male society in the past and present, liberated women writers would necessarily lean toward, at least partially, removing themselves from the traditions of the past. In Latina literature, one must be attuned to the Latina writer's difficulty in both recognizing her past, her "culturally constructed self" and moving "beyond the border of culture" for a sense of individuality and self worth (Friedman 243). In this way, Latino fiction exemplifies Friedman's point. Nostalgia for past order and the security of tradition is less a preoccupation for the modernist imagination of Latina writers than it is for Latinos. One could point to characters like Cesar and Nestor Castillo in *Mambo* or Mickey Acuña in Gilb's *The Last Known Residence of Mickey Acuña*, or many of the men and women who inhabit the stories of Jack Agüeros who long for the simpler days of radio broadcasts, new singer sewing machines and trips to Woolworths. Consider any of the women in the works of Ana Castillo and notice the male writer's attention to the demons of nostalgia and the Latina writer's search for something quite different. In any case, beneath this important divergence, lies the modernist quest to, as González Echevarría puts it, "search for a vision of the world different from, if not opposed to, that provided by Western culture" (117).

Though all fiction, it can be argued, teaches something, a general trend in recent Latino fiction suggests that the more varied and subtle (and stylistically sophisticated) the prose, the less conclusive the argument and the more pluralistic and polyphonic the work. The realism of a Piri Thomas has given way to the metafictional playfulness of Ed Vega just as the obvious borderland themes and linear, chronological narratives in Chicano writing of the 60's and 70's have been replaced by the lyrical sketches of Sandra Cisneros and the narrative fragmentation of Helena Viramontes, writers whose works establish their cohesiveness through associations and juxtapositions as modernist fiction does. This could signal a decline of the Latino writer as spokesperson for a particular ethnic community (The Chicano writer, the Cuban-American writer, etc.) and, in fact, does suggest that Latino writers are simply becoming more versatile U.S. writers. It may just as well indicate that, as the spaces for creative expression widen for Latinos, those that choose to tell the stories of their lives are doing so in purely autobiographical forms while others are taking advantage of the multi-dimensional possibilities of fiction. Whatever the reasons, their experiments with fractured authorial point of view, ellipses and gaps connected in the mind of the reader by allusion and symbol, and non-linear, non-chronological plot lines present an intricate view of space and time which is decipherable only through a recursive process of discourse analysis.

Compare, for example, Viramontes's short story "The Cariboo Café" and Graciela Limón's novel *In Search of Bernabé.* Both contain mothers searching for lost sons, and revolve around the fractured lives of war torn El Salvador during the 1980's. At one point, Limón gives an extended explication of how Bernabé's memory of Picasso's "Guernica" painting relates to the panicking survivors of a right wing death squad attack: "As Bernabé marched in the cortege, [following the death of Archbishop Romero], he realized that these people around him were really fragmented: faces, eyes, cheeks, and arms. They were broken pieces just like in Picasso's disjointed painting" (22). Viramontes achieves an even more powerful sense of fear and loss and disjointedness through her narrative fragmentation where the reader shares with the frightened characters the struggle to connect illogical events as he or she balances the three intersecting pieces of the story and imagines the contents of the gaps between them. Characters see each other in pieces. The cook characterizes Delia's by her "unique titties," one larger than the other (*Moths* 65) and Sonya by her "poking eyes" (66) while the Salvadorian woman sees the cook as little more than "shrunken cheeks" and "hands of a mechanic" (72). Their fragmented perspectives of each other leave these "displaced people" in a maze of tragic misunderstandings, a "zero zero place," what Debra Castillo labels "that quintessential symbol of negativity" (93). For Limón, the fragmented lives of innocent people might well be repaired if only the horrors of civil war were to end. For Viramontes, the situation is more complex (the war is in the past, the psychological effects remain in the woman's mind, the racial prejudice exists) and certainly more disconcerting, partly because of her refusal to shape the story into a monological argument. Hearing the voices of these marginal individuals, the reader's sympathy goes out in various directions, toward the cook who has lost his son Jojo (note the double zeros), toward the lost children of illegal aliens, and toward the devastated mother who has also lost her son (again, two lost sons, two zeros) to the Salvadorian military.

The modernist distrust of language manifested itself especially in the use of multiple narrative points of view. There are traces of Woolf's *The Waves* or Faulkner's *Sound and the Fury* or *As I Lay Dying* in those Latino stories and novels which deny authoritative conclusiveness by fracturing the reader's perspective with multiple narrators. Several of Helen Viramontes's stories alternate from first to third person narration, sometimes, as in "The Long Reconciliation" or "Birthday" slipping back and forth without warning. Similarly, Cisneros switches unexpectedly into a gossipy first person narrative voice in her story "Woman Hollering Creek." Cleófila's thinking, at first revealed from without, gradually takes over and we are inside her head, hearing her enthusiastic summary of a favorite telenovela: "Did you see Lucía Mendez . . . " (*Women* 44-45). All the episodes which make up Ed Vega's *Mendoza's Dreams* need to be filtered through the distorting mirror of the central narrator, a man visited by "The Three Stooges." Dominican-American writer, Julia Alvarez divides her three novels into chapters which reflect the perspectives (directly or indirectly) of the character named at the onset, encouraging the reader to understand each daughter as an individual. This is especially important in *In the Time of the Butterflies* where Alvarez is combating the reader's tendency to lump the Mirabal sisters together as mere victims of Trujillo's sadism. Instead, her switches from first to third person, her shifts of focus from the revolutionary Minerva to the religious Patria or the girlish María Teresa immerses us in the complications of their lives and the tragedy of their deaths. The writer, in a sense, creates a mosaic of voices which tell the story piecemeal, a technique which further accents the notions of flexibility and ambiguity that underlie Latino fiction.

Though in a different way, narrative point of view is equally complex in a novel like Ana Castillo's *So Far From God* since the single narrative voice casually swings in and out of limited omniscience. Castillo's narrator sounds at times like the Brazilian writer Jorge Amado's, sympathetic, but distanced and authoritative. At other times, folksy Chicana twang rings loud and clear. The long discursive chapter titles remind us of those in Amado's *Tieta* which recall in turn those in Fielding's *Tom Jones*. Chapter fifteen for example is entitled (described) as follows: "La Loca Santa Returns to the World via Albuquerque Before Her Transcendental Departure; and a Few Random Political Remarks from the Highly Opinionated Narrator." Despite the authoritative tone of these titles, it isn't long before the narrator's folksy speech takes over, complete with strings of clichés, double negatives, fillers and asides like "well," "so to speak" or "come to think of it" (46). At some points our code-switching narrator slips in a bit of Caló or Chicano slang as in "just outside *ese* [this] village" (121) or "like *esa* Hamlet said" (124), but elsewhere sounds like a preachy storyteller: "But there are still those for whom there is no kindness in their hearts for a young woman who has enjoyed life, so to speak" (33). Castillo creates an informal and jumbled perspective. At another point someone, unnamed, but labeled the "comadre," seems to take over the story. One passage that begins describing Sofi's feelings turns in on itself so that Sofi herself might be speaking to us directly:

> In fact, Sofi seemed a little absentminded about things like that lately, you know? Like she actually forgot to charge the comadre last month for her purchases at the carnecería [meat market]. For years, the comadre had been buying every week from la Sofi and because times were sometimes a little harder than others and they were comadres and one never knows when she'll need her troca [truck] jumped some cold early morning and the compadre down the road never minds too much being woken up to give it a jump, or you might find your

> comadre's grown daughter with the child's mind wandering down by the acequia [ditch or sewer] barefoot in the snow, so you run to tell her where she is and things like that happen between neighbors all the time, it all evens out. (131)

By incorporating interlingual slang ("troca")[10] and Spanish vocabulary until the English structure nearly deteriorates, Castillo produces an oral quality to her prose, and her story is free to reveal a Latino world of obscure, unexplainable fragments and complications. The unofficial, the gossipy and the outcasts are highlighted, and the logical causal elements of life (i.e. the plot, the grammar) dismissed. She insinuates here that Chicano life cannot be told in a coherent and rational manner, that prose must be distorted by a chatty, agrammatical, anecdotal voice if the vitality of the Chicana folk world is to be communicated.

Such polyphonic fiction, according to David Lodge, as a result of its "indeterminacy of meaning leads to an increase of meaning, because it demands more interpretative effort by the reader than does traditional narrative" (*Bakhtin* 143). As the reader works harder to decipher who speaks, through whose mind the information must be filtered, the possibilities for meaning increase. Take for example, Mickey Acuña, in Gilb's novel, *The Last Residence of Mickey Acuña* whose story is seemingly told from an omniscient point of view. Yet Gilb manipulates the reader by filling the narrative with phrases like "Mickey would say" and "Mickey said" indicating that the narrator could be merely retelling the story from Mickey's version of events. Despite the occasional conversational tone, we never know the narrator to be a character within the novel. We sense gaps in the speaker's omniscience, and like Mickey himself, we begin to doubt the difference between reality and illusion. At times, we are certain the events are Mickey's inventions. The problem of distinguishing reality from fabrication, truth from illusion, or what genuinely occurs and what is *said* to occur permeates the work. No one in this claustrophobic YMCA setting (similar in many ways to Harry Hope's saloon and rooming house in O'Neill's *Iceman Cometh*),[11] is straight with anyone else, and each degenerate has a tale to tell. None can speak clearly: the beer drinking Butch talks so softly Mickey hardly ever hears him; the drunken Omar screams so loudly about his lost love, Lucy, that everyone dismisses him as harmless until his violent side reveals itself in the barroom scene and his duplicity becomes clear when he steals a car loaded with Butch's gifts for his children. Fred the desk clerk refuses to confide in anyone, Charles

Towne mumbles constantly and macho John Hooper regards himself above all the crazies. There is no communication here, and everyone, including Mickey, is waiting for mail that never arrives. One blind man dies and no one knows how long he's been dead, and the psychotic Blind Jimmy, desperate for a sex change, is carried away by men in suits. Preachers are violent, and the boss, known as "Big Ears" never listens to anyone. Adding to this dysfunctional world, this halfway house of dreamers and losers is a narrative form that precludes definitive understanding of the actions and characters. We never know who is responsible for Mr. Fuller's death: Charles, who gets blamed for it, the sleazy New Yorker Mafia men who might have been looking for Mickey, or Mickey himself who has at this point lost contact with the difference between "true and real things" (209) and his own memories, dreams and "Wild West" visions.

Polyphonic fiction parallels Rachel Duplessis notion of an insider/outsider position where the writer's "double consciousness" refuses to allow a reliance upon dualities, and while she speaks of women's writing, it is clear that Latino works by both men and women, by combating the simplicity of a monological view, and by embracing the nonauthoritative voice "incorporate contradiction and nonlinear movement into the heart of the text" (78). One notices a tolerance for multiple types of characters, and a generosity and sympathy toward them in works as different as *Dreaming in Cuban* and *Bless me, Ultima.* As an example, one could cite the refusal on the part of both Garcia and Anaya to narrowly confine their characters by judging their folk oriented spirituality. Just as important, neither writer exalts the mystical at the expense of a rational view of life; rather the two views exist at once.

The trend toward polyphonic fiction is a fairly recent one among Latino storytellers. For example, the Chicana writer Portillo-Trambley attempts to complicate her work when she puts stories into her overall narratives in order to divide perspective. In her novel *Trini*, however, the effect is minimal since the voices of distinct storytellers all sound the same. Her stories within the story only tighten authoritative control. Rather than relish what Jay Clayton refers to as the "pleasures of Babel," the multifaceted thrill of a country as a "babel of competing cultures" (101), Portillo-Trambley flattens out perspective into a single voice. For example, when Sebastiana tells Trini about Sabochi's killing of Hector the rapist (*Trini* 120-122), the voice is indistinguishable from the narrator we have heard throughout. The same is true for a later embedded story, told by a character known as Tio Pancho using an identical tone. Similarly, Helen Ponce (*Taking Control)* and Alma Villanueva (*The Ultraviolet Sky*) rely almost exclusively on a monological point of view in which the voice of the implied author clearly dominates whatever alternative positions exist. Their characterizations tend to reduce minor figures into mere "blocking" characters (to use Frye's term) or one-dimensional obstacles to their heroines' quests. Villanueva rarely allows her reader into the minds of minor characters, except at those moments when their ideas and beliefs fully concur with Rosa Luján's, the protagonist's, and thus merely echo the authority of the writer. In Ponce's stories, the flashback narrative device only adds to her intrusive didacticism which deprives her writing of the complexity her plot situations deserve. To some extent, Portillo-Trambley, Ponce and Villanueva, have succumbed to what William Carlos Williams warned against: devoted themselves too much to subject matter over form (*Essays* 288). Intent upon revealing the plight of Chicana women, they ignore the stylistic finesse necessary to make their women interesting enough for a reader to care about. Their stories, because they lack narrative complexity, tend to cram their characters into one-dimensional traps where readers can do little but pity their situations.[12] One need only think of Cisneros's Cleófilas from "Women Hollering Creek," or Viramontes's Arlene from "Miss Clairol" and "Tears on my Pillow" to be reminded how Chicana women's complicated lives can be portrayed in such a way to engender vital interest and sympathy. For these types of portrayals, the reader must turn to texts that probe those lives with variation and creativity.

Among Latino fiction writers, not only Chicana writers are capable of didactic prose. Margarita Engle's *Singing to Cuba* and J. Joaquín Fraxedas's *The Lonely Crossing of Juan Cabrera* both present a highly distorted picture of Cuba from the reactionary, right-wing, political perspective. Though Engle divides her story into present events interspersed with pieces of a continuous flashback (unnecessarily printed in boldfaced type), the uncomplicated plot is consistent with her conservative views. Fraxedas's simplistic view of recent Cuban history has Castro, a man eating shark (described in shark guidebook vocabulary—65), and the "crossing" to Florida in a rubber raft a journey from "darkness to light, from death to life" (69). Cuba is nothing more than "a suffocating blackness" (26). The cliché ridden prose—"the harsh light from the bare bulb . . . two of his teeth were missing, had got in the way of a rifle butt" (12)—and bits and pieces that sound like a Florida Keys Travel Guide make this condescending work sound like a double parody of *The Old Man and the Sea* and *Jaws.* By sacrificing the dialogic potential of innovative, modernist, narrative technique, both novels disintegrate into one-dimensional simplifications of modern Cuba vis-à-vis the United States. The obvious contrast to these Cuban-American novels would be Cristina Garcia's *Dreaming in Cuban* where the reader is never allowed to judge any character solely on the basis of political stance. Lourdes, for example, in spite of the harshness of her anti-Castro rhetoric, is still a multifaceted woman, both practical and "tacky," tortured by a horrific past, wronged by her adulterous husband, hated and loved by her rebel daughter, caught between two cultures, and absorbed by her loyalty to her father's ghost. Unlike Fraxedas who inexplicably feels the need to explain at length an allusion to Icarus (146), Garcia's subtle references to Lorca, for instance, suggest the connection between her characters' feelings and the things she describes, a dreamy relationship between inner and outer reality important in Lorca's emotional poetry. Lorca, like Pilar's abuela is a poet of the moon, sadness, solitude and death, and his poems are quoted throughout the novel. In "Gacela de la Huida," the poet surely speaks for Celia:

> me he perdido muchas veces por el mar.
> Ignorante del agua, voy buscando
> una muerte de luz que me consuma.
> [I have lost myself in the sea many times.
> Ignorant of the water I go seeking
> a death full of light to consume me.
> (trans. Stephen Spender and J.L. Gili).

Celia's daughter Felicia learns a "florid language," words strung "together like laundry on a line, connecting ideas and descriptions she couldn't have planned" from her mother when they'd sit on the porch reciting poems and the sea "had *metered* their intertwined thoughts" (110). Her lyrical letters even fall into iambic pentameter (51), so strong is the poetic element in her being, just as art will be for her granddaughter. Garcia's narrative subtleties and complexities, like those of the other writers to be considered in this study, stretch her novel beyond editorial comment into imaginative, polyphonic literary art. And it is this Latino writing, with its roots in modernist craft, that will take us into the richness and vitality of the Latino borderlands.

In 1958, Chicano writer Américo Paredes set down an important pattern of narrative reconstruction with his influential, anthropological exploration into the life of the renown turn-of-the-century outlaw, Gregorio Cortez Lira: *With his Pistol in His Hand.* Gathering fragments of oral border ballads ("Corridos"), Paredes pieced together the man's life, the narrative stylistics of the ballads that kept his memory active, and the lives of the people who sang and remembered him.[13] His story of the outlaw pointed out the ruthlessness of the "heroic" Texas Rangers, but perhaps more importantly it documented and authenticated a narrative style that would seep into the writings of Chicano fiction to come. In numerous Latino stories we see a similar ethnographic investigation of old pictures, and family histories: the "snapshots" of an elderly lady in the Viramontes story of that name, or a Tejano family's photo albums in Roberta Fernández's *Intaglio*, or the Cuban family pictures in Oscar Hijuelos's novels. The displaying of pictures and pieces of the Latino past is, in the words of the Chicana critic, Rosaura Sánchez, "an effort to recuperate oral texts, memories and recollections of past events that have long been ignored, erased, denied and dismissed" ("Discourses" 74). In grainy black and white photos, lives of people, otherwise forgotten can be reevaluated and lessons learned from remembering.[14]

Hererra-Sobek and Viramontes, introducing Denise Chávez's collection "Novena Narrativas y Ofrendas Nuevomexicanas" (a work which splices together a crowd of Chicana voices into a series of dramatic monologues) mention that her work was influenced by the cultural traditional of "ofrendas," the collections of pictures, cards, clay figures and other objects assembled in shrine-like fashion for the purpose of honoring the deceased (Hererra-Sobek 85). Chávez's narrative style, here and in *The Last of the Menu Girls*, is meant to mirror these mosaics, to capture piecemeal the essence of the people of her cultural past. No wonder then that modernist fiction's tendency toward a discourse of fragments connected by pattern, allusion, image or symbol occupies such a central position in Latino fiction, as it did in the fiction of James, Conrad, Joyce or Woolf when the British modernists first experimented with French Symbolist poetry.

Certain Latino writers employ multiple perspectives and odd chronologies not as mere literary devices, but because they often wish to present the Latino world nonjudgementally in all its complexity. Monological prose becomes as destructive as any stereotypical reduction, because it demands a uniform discourse which many Latino writers adamantly oppose. The movement toward displaying the liveliness of the Latino community's vicissitudes and intricacies sometimes leads Latino writers toward a piecemeal narrative design which results in specific structures.

One group of works, which would include Alfredo Véa, Jr.'s *La Maravilla,* John Rechy's *The Miraculous Day of Amalia Gomez,* Roberto Fernandez's *Raining Backwards*, or less successfully, Louie García Robinson's *The Devil, Delfina Varela and the Used Chevy*, depicts a marginal community glimpsed through the course of a short period (a day or a week), where the reader experiences (almost as voyeur) the "fringe dwellers" who reside there. This somewhat cinematic technique (cf. Spike Lee's films or John Sayles' "City of Hope") permits numerous personalities and interconnecting relationships and establishes a multi-dimensional mosaic of the community. The opening image of Robinson's book, for example, is of a church scene while the author/camera pans the congregation, introducing the characters one at a time. The chapter breaks neatly mirror TV commercials. This panoramic portrayal of a diverse cross-section of Latino life allows the writer to zero in at any particular point, upon any specific character, and still maintain for the reader a sensation that he or she is entering a much larger and more complicated world of opinions and actions. The sheer number of characters leaves the reader with more a sense of indeterminacy and variety than any conclusive conviction.

An alternative pattern common to Latino fiction is the use of interconnected short stories which combine to form a subgenre of the novel. Perhaps first used by Sherwood Anderson in *Winesburg, Ohio*, the best examples of this narrative format are those of writers directly under Anderson's influence: Faulkner's *The Unvanquished* and Hemingway's *In Our Time.* More recent works include Jamaica Kincaid's *Annie John,* and *Lucy*, and Alice Munro's *The Beggar Maid* while, in Latin American, the pattern was used for Azuela's classic Mexican novel, *Los de Abajo* [*The Underdogs*]. In this type of fiction, as in *Portrait of the Artist as a Young Man*, the prose often develops along side the consciousness of the central character, and each story intertextually depends upon another. As subsequent events shed light upon previous ones, the reader goes through a necessary process of re-reading, and re-understanding. Kenner saw this process part of the modernist "aesthetics of delay." Lodge explains it as a style that "plunges [the reader] into a flowing stream of experience with which we gradually familiarize ourselves by a process of inference and association." Gina Valdés's hard to find 1981 novel *There are no Madmen Here* is perhaps the first experiment of this kind in Latino fiction. Beginning with three seemingly unrelated short episodes, the novel's fourth section—the story of the central protagonist, Maria Portillo—ties the people and events together. The design, therefore, neatly emphasizes Maria's importance to her family.[15] Despite Valdés's novel,[16] it is Tomás Rivera's highly acclaimed . . . *Y no se lo tragó la tierra* which is usually held responsible for influencing later fiction molded on a similar narrative pattern, works like Roberta Fernández's *Intaglio* and Sandra Cisneros's *The House on Mango Street.* The latter work, reminiscent especially of Joyce, has been criticized by Shorris because of its simplicity and the childlike voice of its narrator, which is as ludicrous as condemning Faulkner for his Bengi, or Joyce for the moocow (Shorris 390). Cisneros's narrative builds toward a sophistication that goes deeply into the class and gender realities of urban Chicano life and presents it in a narrative that, while seen through the eyes of a young girl coming of age, breaks down the stereotypes Shorris accuses her of prolonging. In both Rivera and Cisneros, it is the reader's job to splice together the vignettes. In other works, the action is similarly broken into segments, as in the case of Virgil Suárez's *Welcome to the Oasis* or Pineda's first two novels. Here the sections are cohesively progressive and dependent upon each other to form a continuous narrative. For Viramontes and Cristina Garcia, the gaps and ellipses between sections are deliberately obtrusive, forcing the reader to juxtapose events from distinctly opposite points of view. The gaps between chapters of Fernández's *Intaglia* create what Chapman sees as a narrative discontinuity that can only be reconciled by the reader as he or she meanders through complex family trees and bits and pieces of family history (71). Denise Chávez in *The Last of the Menu Girls* splices seven stories together with one central writer/narrator, Rocío Esquibel. Slightly more involved is Sandra Benítez's *A Place Where the Sea Remembers*, which ties together various stories from the small Mexican coastal town of Santiago and intersperses lyrical vignettes which center upon the rituals and powers of a curandera [healer] figure named Remedios.[17] It is her centrality in the work which melds the various characters into a community, her "remedies" which at least partially unite a pair of feuding sisters. That the shape of her vignettes was suggested to Benítez by Hemingway's *In Our Time* is perhaps confirmed by the striking stylistic similarity between *The Old Man and*

Sea and the segment about the widower Pescador and his young son, Beto.

> Out on the boat, the sea was leaden. There were times when the sea was very blue and the water was silky to the touch and it gleamed and you could look down into it, seeing quite clearly the fishing nets ballooning down into the deep, seeing the schools of haddock or sea bass or dogfish heading in the silent rush for the nets. But today the north wind threatened, and the sea was dense, and you could not look past its surface. (93)

Beneath the simplicity of the description, the exactitude of information (haddock or seabass or dogfish), one senses a deeper level of significance, something unsaid, a glimpse of the "dignity of movement of an iceberg" (Hemingway *Death in the Afternoon* 192). As with *Intaglio,* and Julia Alvarez's novels, each chapter of *A Place Where the Sea Remembers* follows the character named in its title in the pattern of Faulkner's *As I lay Dying* and the network of family and personalities crisscrosses the interconnecting stories, purposely forcing the reader to reconstruct the whole. What is missing from the Benítez novel, and what is central to Faulkner novels is the change of language as we shift from person to person or as we progress in the chronological sequence of the plot. This is mostly the result of Benítez's consistent third person point of view. Though the perspective shifts as we view La Curandera, El Ensaladero, El Fotógrafo, La Recamarera etc., none of these characters is given an individual voice. Unlike in Faulkner or Joyce or Cisneros or Alvarez, there is no change in narrative style which might signal a character's psychological disintegration (as with Darl) or some sort of maturation (as with Stephen Dedalus or Esperanza of *The House on Mango Street*). For *In the Time of the Butterflies*, Julia Alvarez even invents a picture filled diary for the youngest Mirabal sister in order to suggest her youthful creativity, sensibility and linguistic inarticulation. Yet the lyrical nature of the individual stories in the Benítez novel keeps her characters static. Though told in the third person, the stories are filtered through the mind of the central figure, the curandera. Unlike with another central narrator/storyteller, Ed Vega's highly opinionated and fallible Mendoza, we never doubt the truthfulness of this woman for Benítez equates her with the constancy of the ocean, the element which figures in all the stories and holds the people of Santiago together. Remedios listens to the people and recounts their tales. She's a mystical "earth woman," a "sea-woman" to whom everyone returns in search of solutions to the complications of life. She is the visionary healer, "she who knows" (23). The result of such reliability, however, smoothes out Benítez's story, sacrificing something of the possible medley of styles and voices.

Julia Alvarez's third novel stretches narrative mode much further. Though a novel, the book is actually a series of interconnected short stories, and like Faulkner in *The Sound and the Fury*, the author tells each section from a different perspective (in varying points of view), yet she centers each chapter around the central figure of herself: Yolanda Garcia, "Yo" [I]. Bringing back the Garcia sisters of her first novel, here Alvarez takes "autofiction" a step beyond the norm. The frame for the work, the opening interactions among the writer's sisters, confuses fiction and reality in a postmodernist, playful way as family members vent their frustration at being turned into fictional characters by a sibling who knows the intimate details of their lives. As the work progresses, the personalities who have come into contact with the novelist get a chance to tell their individual stories, each in a fairly distinct, if conversational style and voice.

Helena Viramontes is particularly good at sliding from one narrative point of view to another as she complicates the situations her characters find themselves in. The reader is pulled closer and closer to their individual thinking by the gradual movement of perspective. The vision of the reader is paramount in her novel *Under the Feet of Jesus* where we begin watching the migrants in their Chevy Capri station wagon from afar, as if circling above them, and as the novel progresses and the action of plot slows, we gradually enter their minds. Sometimes Viramontes discards omniscience entirely and we enter a stream of consciousness or interior monologue. For instance, this is true in the short story "Snapshots" or in "Birthday" though in the latter, Viramontes slips away from the first person for a paragraph or two. "Birthday" is an interesting twist on Elizabeth Bishop's poem "The Waiting Room" about a young girl in a dentist's office and her epiphanic recognition (via National Geographic) of her own individuality and sexuality. The waiting room of the story is some sort of makeshift abortion clinic and Alice, the young pregnant woman, is struggling not with the recognition of her sexuality, but with the dramatic decision to forgo motherhood. Alice's monologue proceeds like Stephen Dedalus's in *Ulysses*, in David Lodge's words, "by perceived similarities and substitutions" (*Bradbury 485*). Her mind moves from thinking "the room was probably a kitchen before" to a previous conversation in a kitchen. Where Bishop writes: "But I felt: you are an I / you are an Elizabeth / you are one of them," Alice begins her monologue with "At the moment, there are only two things I am sure of: my name is Alice . . . "(*Moths* 41). The name is repeated numerous times in the short story suggesting the confusion of Lewis Carroll's Alice and a young girl's attempt to make sense of what she doesn't understand. Yet, paradoxically, the repetition of the name reinforces the character's own desire to remain who she is ("Would I like to stay Alice, or become a "mama"?—41), and convince herself that she is right to make the decision herself ("The decision was ultimately hers"—42), and therefore maintain her individuality.

Latino writers, especially those who are also poets Alvarez, Cisneros, Rios, Sáenz, Cofer), because of their modernist concerns for the form and sound of their prose, employ certain systems of incantatory repetition in syntax and vocabulary. These musical experiments—repetitions of rhythmical prose with only slight variations—owe something to the innovations of Gertrude Stein. As in her fiction, such techniques tease readers into a continuous search for meaning that keeps escaping, constantly moving further and further ahead, word by word. We find that Cisneros's stories, for example, rely heavily upon this type of lyrical musicality. The counting in Spanish in her story "Tepeyac" produces this effect: the young girl climbs the stairs, the years go by. In a much more obvious example, Margarita Engle's novel *Singing to Cuba* has the phrase "On the morning of his arrest" to begin each section of Gabriel's story. While Engle varies the phrase slightly as the story progresses, it is difficult to know what purpose the repetition accomplishes. Perhaps the intention is to suggest the oral nature of this Cuban tale in that, like a classical, storytelling pneumonic device, the phrase keys the speaker's memory. Certainly, the central narrator is gathering her information from an unwritten history, from unofficial sources.

One rather involved example will demonstrate this kind of modernist contribution to Latino fiction. In the highly fragmented postmodernist novel *Voice-haunted Journey*, for example, Eliud Martínez uses repetition rather than explicit explanation to draw the reader into an active response to his work. The novel opens with the corpse of Alejandro Velásquez (the narrator's brother), sitting up and smiling and laughing. Martínez's weaves certain repetitions into his opening paragraphs: Alejandro was "smiling . . . a beautiful smile . . .

He was smiling . . . tossed his head back and laughed . . . laughed joyfully . . . playful spirit . . . the gift of laughter . . . he would laugh . . . he saw and smiled . . . his brother's smile . . . to be playful and mischievous . . . his brother's laughter . . . his brother's laughter . . . the gift of laughter" (4-5). The extent of this musical iteration suggests the book's dominant thematic and stylistic difficulties by requiring the reader to question reality as the narrator reveals it. Is the man really dead (the novel's magic realism will be dealt with later), or is the scene an imagined memory ("Only Miguel heard his brother's laughter" -5)? The stylistic shift emphasizes a need to juxtapose, at the level of character, the authenticity of the narrator with the actual memory, while at the level of discourse we contrast the death and sadness (and the family mourners), of the opening paragraphs with this joy and laughter present somewhere, if only in the mind of the narrator. The pounding incantatory emphasis upon the "laughter," following so closely the scene of death and crying, presents the contrasts that reverberate throughout the book: that of life and death, memory and fact, fiction and reality. *Voice-haunted Journey* blurs the line between memory and reality by confusing what is memory with what is fiction. This particular repetition furthermore presents a thematic motif central to Miguel Velásquez's psyche. He is not a funny man, and his dead brother was. Much of the novel captures the dour, humorless solemnity of its narrator (or at least Miguel's obsessive side since the entire book is ostensibly his own), though we see, through irony and metafictional twists, that Martínez has intentionally deprived his novelist narrator of an ability to see the humor in his world. "You gotta get a little humor into it" says one particular voice in the penultimate chapter (243), and we recall the dead brother laughing. It is again the opening repetition that is in part responsible, for it signals to the reader the importance of humor and comic deflation (i.e. the burro eating his grandfather's ponderous notebooks, his father arguing that reading will make him go crazy) that will follow. Alejandro Velásquez's "playful spirit" (even in his coffin) mirrors the playful narrative of this self-reflexive novel.

Modernist techniques of personas and individual voices, each telling separate, but related versions of the same story suit writers whose oral culture surpasses their written records. Because the voices of, for example, Cristina Garcia's novel are individualized, each contributing a different sort of color to the entire picture, the resulting mosaic exemplifies the borderland's (and North America's) "plural, syncretic, sometimes conflictual nature" (Clayton 109). Latino writers who self-consciously divide their works into multiple personas reflect the vitality of such a complicated world.

Dagoberto Gilb's collection of stories *The Magic of Blood* establishes his ability to genuinely sympathize (in a way reminiscent of Raymond Carver) with working class people, in this case southwestern Chicanos. The down-and-out protagonist of "Look On the Bright Side," for instance, is so optimistic that his decline toward homelessness becomes logical, justifiable and somehow commendable, until that is, the reader considers the narrative device of persona and calculates Gilb's irony. In "Nancy Flores" the voice of a boy "thirteen years old going on fourteen" (*Magic* 31) comes clearly in the prose: "Nancy Flores was the most beautiful girl I or anyone else had ever seen—and she *really* was, really she was, it was true, it was *true*, and nothing I did or thought or imagined could possibly not include her" (31). One feels the youthful persistence amid the idealistic and naive notion that he alone, child of a wandering working class mother, can experience superlative love. He sees things in sports terms—her words to him are "strong, deep tosses that landed close and loud" (30). The story traces how a working class boy from a dysfunctional single parent household can win out over time in the battle for the girl. Matched against the high school hero, the "preppy" Trey, whose reputation "soared skyward like a God's" (41), Richie's persistence is rewarded, not with the girl, Nancy Flores (who, after dumping the narrator for Trey, disappears from the story), but with the knowledge that Trey's post high school career had faltered, that his school status once as "heroic as a TV star's" has been tarnished. Built on the age-old tradition of town-gown rivalry, the story celebrates the "common" Chicano's victory over privileged rival Trey. Trey, a sort of hare to the narrator's tortoise, winds up a pimply faced stockboy, his hair showing "only the greasy residue of its heroic gloss" (47).

Gilb's first person narrative voices echo the sensitive intelligence and humility of a Raymond Carver character, as well as the cynical objectivity of a Hemingway male.[18] The driver at the mercy of a peculiar uncommunicative mechanic in "Al, in Phoenix" is savvy and capable about cars even as he slowly loses control of the situation. He walks into a bar thinking: "It's not much of a place, a hangout for real unattractive people who wouldn't think that about themselves" (86). The construction worker "churchgoers" in the story of that name, comes to us through the eyes of an accomplished "tradesman" with years of experience building high-rises and a vocabulary to match:

"The men weren't speechless, but sentences faltered, words spilled like nails when a man tried to grab too many" (116).

The most elaborate persona in Latino fiction to date might be the Mendoza character/narrator of Ed Vega's novel *Mendoza's Dreams.* Mendoza sets out to tell the "dreams" of his Puerto Rican friends and acquaintances up and down Manhattan's Spanish Harlem. Stories within stories and frames around frames issue from the mind of this teller of "amusing anecdotes," a Chaucerian jokester and comedian whose author, like Chaucer himself, accepts not a particle of responsibility. The opened-ended indecipherability could be said to reflect the complex nature of multidimensional, "divided" Nuyorican identity. Beyond that, such a device allows Vega to ridicule and satirize, not only the high society of New York, but the marginal Puerto Rican population as well. His long novel *The Comeback* which mocks the prototypical Puerto Rican inner city bildungsroman (i.e. Thomas's *Down These Mean Streets*) is perhaps the reason Vega's works seem to carry so little weight among Latino critics; this despite Vega's formal expertise and humor. In order to avoid the attacks from righteous organizations, Vega turned to the Mendoza persona and the complicated frames of the book.

In a postmodernist mode, one could cite the frame that surrounds Eliud Martínez's *Voice-Haunted Journey.* Billed as the first of a series called "The Notebooks of Miguel Velásquez" (2), the novel is thus framed as a would-be fiction writer's fragmented collection of ideas. Yet the story begins with a third person narrative explaining a passenger named Miguel Velásquez on a plane recalling the death of his brother, a perspective clearly separate from Miguel Velásquez's own point of view. The story gets increasingly self-reflective as we learn that this character, Miguel is creating a novel based upon the events of his own life. We see these events in a montage of glimpses as either actions Miguel will use in his book or as his own inventions. We are never sure which is which. Whatever he thinks becomes material for the autobiographical novel he has been writing for years, turning fact into fiction (166). His main protagonist is a surrealist painter named Lorenzo Correa most of whose characteristics are derived from Miguel. Yet Miguel attributes "his own introspective discoveries to his fictional character" (26). What Miguel dreams or invents (mentally transforms into language) blends with his memories, so that what actually happened and what is his fiction is unclear. The reader is reading a novel about a novelist creating the same novel. No wonder that Martínez uses so often the phrase "wending in and out" (25.50.83,167,233) for a work whose interwoven stories, dreams, and events resemble a fictional mobius strip, intertwining and becoming each other. It is clear by the end that there will be no sequel since this is mere wishful thinking on the part of the protagonist, and no trilogy could suffice to please its creator.

Cecile Pineda's third novel, *The Love Queen of the Amazon,* takes its reader on a similar journey between fiction and reality. Pineda's heroine, Ana Magdalena, is married to a novelist who is writing a book based upon the events of his life. His work has the same title as the novel we are reading. As a result, the entire story becomes a part of one character's imagination, and the reader is left pondering the borders between reality and art.

Critics such as Ray Gonzalez have begun to disparage what they see as overuse of narrative fragmentation in Latino fiction[19] which creates, in his words, "novels . . . shaped by so many quick jumps" (101), but in the hands of Pineda or Cisneros or Islas, such a technique is key. The momentary images and the patterns that develop as they are flashed in front of the reader distinguishes these works as reflective of the modernist narrative mode, and it is through such a style that many Latino writers reveal their creative imagination. If Rebolledo and Rivero are correct in detecting a move toward more straight forward realist Chicana writing, toward essay and autobiography,[20] there is just as certainly a need for Latino writers to continue experimenting with narratives devices. It is a sign that the themes and ideas may reflect the Latino experience, but the form may finds its roots in Cortázar or Vonnegut or Joyce.

NOTES

1. Quoted in an interview printed in *Partial Autobiographies: Interviews with Twenty Chicano Poets*, Wolfgang Binder, ed. Erlangen: Verlag, Palm & Enke, 1985.

2. See the introductory chapter to the anthology *Infinite Divisions* by Rebolledo and Rivero or the introduction to Gloria Anzaldúa's anthology *Making Face, Making Soul: Haciendo Caras.*

3. See the Puerto Rican poet, Julio Marzán's book *The Puerto Rican Roots of William Carlos Williams.*

4. See Chapter Two.

5. See Rosaura Sánchez's article on "Postmodernism" for the debate about what the word means.

6. According to Jay Clayton, storytelling can be "empowering" because stories help people "escape disciplinary control" (*The Pleasures of Babel* 96-97). They "preserve the memory of successful tactics" (97), link people to the oral past, and "create community" (106). As the curandera Remedios in Sandra Benítez's *A Place Where the Sea Remembers* knows: storytelling means remembering in the "heart, where nothing dies away because it is remembered" (142).

7. Phillip Brian Harper makes this case in *Framing the Margins: The Social Logic of Postmodern Culture.* Oxford University Press, 1994.

8. In *Frieze*, the powers and forces of cyclical nature overtake the workings of man. Thematically, the novel has several parallels to Carpentier's *The Kingdom of this World*, not the least of which would be the building of a monumental structure for the glorification of a selfish ruler at the expense of the poor. In both works, what is sacrificed is the voice of the people, and what Bruce-Novoa calls, their "vernacular history." In both works, the monuments crumble into ruins as the natural world triumphs.

9. David Johnson, in his article "Face Value (An Essay on Cecile Pineda's *Face*)" has argued a somewhat different interpretation of the book, claiming that Helio's recovery is paradoxical, since the face he constructs is ultimately "unremarkable" and "perfectly institutional" (82). Rather than recovered his humanity, his identity, Helio, Johnson claims, has merely learned to play the game, has made himself "faceless" (and therefore acceptable to "technological" society which "takes as [its] goal the reduction of the human to the inhuman—82). Despite the power of this argument, Helio does grow in a positive way—especially in his coming to terms with his memory. That he "reinscribes himself within society" is both constructive because he as an individual accomplishes the task, resurrects himself despite society's obstacles, and deconstructive because he must lose his unique (albeit grotesque) appearance in order to do so. The novel reads both ways, precisely as a result of the pluralistic narrative structure.

10. For more on "interlingualism" see Chapter Four.

11. The novel could be compared to other works as well, most notably Kesey's *One Flew Over the Cuckoo's Nest*, or the more violent and disturbing play *Short Eyes* by the Puerto Rican playwright Miguel Piñero. Guatemalan – American writer Francisco Goldman's second novel *The Ordinary Seaman* sets up a similar situation where a group of sailors are trapped on a boat in a Brooklyn harbor though, unlike the works above, this novel inexplicably steers clear of the powerful tensions between the men.

12. It should be mentioned here that these particular writers may show more stylistic versatility in genres other than fiction. In fact, Portillo Trambley's central work is dramatic, Ponce is now working in the fields of autobiography and Children's literature, and Villanueva's central focus is poetry.

13. For the most detailed and involved discussion of Paredes's book, see Ramón Saldivar's critical work *Chicano Discourse* (1990), 26-42.

14. This accounts for the devastating betrayal of the migrant workers in Rivera's work when a con-artist "borrows" the only existing photographs of their sons killed in Korea and then reneges on his promise to have them enlarged and elaborately framed. When the ruined pictures are later discovered in a ditch, the reader senses the migrants' frustration in maintaining a connection to those lives undocumented elsewhere.

15. My interpretation here depends upon a reading of *There are No Madmen Here* as a novel divided into four parts. This is how Latino bibliographer Marc Zimmerman and critic Kay Thurston see the book. An earlier essay, however, by Rosaura Sánchez, explains that Valdés wrote the novela *María Portillo* (the fourth part) in 1976 and that the three stories are separate, later works which simply revolve around the same characters ("Chicana Prose Writers" 64-66). Sánchez's familiarity with Gina Valdés's career indicates this to be true, but the book is published without reference to any stories and thus encourages the reader to tie the segments together.

16. That this small, innovative novel continues to be ignored by readers is a source of frustration to critics like Kay Thurston. See her article "Barriers to the Self-Definition of the Chicana: Gina Valdés and *There are no Madmen Here.*"

17. Numerous Chicano scholars have discussed the importance of the curanderas in southwestern and Mexican culture. See Rebolledo's *Woman Singing in the Snow*.

18. Gilb has also acknowledged a debt to Cormac McCarthy's works which should point critics toward the interesting issue of the relationship between Latino writers and the Anglo writers who write (using Spanish and English) of the borderlands normally associated with the Latino writers.

19. See his review of Luis Alberto Urrea's *In Search of Snow* in *The Nation* July 18, 1994.

20. Autobiographical accounts of Latino women in general do seem to be published with more and more frequency. Gabriella De Ferrari's *Gringa Latina* (1995), Esmeralda Santiago's *When I was Puerto Rican* (1994) Pat Mora's book of essays *Nepantla* (1993) are some examples and the list is growing.

CHAPTER TWO

The "Magic" of Influence upon Latino Narrative

The poet and short story writer, Benjamin Alire Sáenz, in an essay entitled "I Want to Write an American Poem," argues cogently that it is inaccurate for literary scholars to assume that Chicanos are "*necessarily and by definition* working in the Anglo-American tradition" (525). Claiming that "there are many literary and cultural traditions that coexist in America," Sáenz seeks to disassociate himself from Anglo-American literature (Pope and Eliot, Frost and Stevens) and lay claim to a space related to writers like James Baldwin, Eduardo Galeano, Langston Hughes, and James Joyce. The aesthetic traditions of British literature alone provide insufficient criteria in exploring the cultural heritage of U.S. Latino art. By even suggesting narrative literary influences upon Latino writers, the critic then falls into the trap Sáenz wishes to avoid. That is, by connecting works intertextually (highlighting allusions for example, or marking traces of stylistic similarities between writers), we might reduce Latino literature to a product belonging solely to the "society of the academy," where it is often judged on purely aesthetic grounds and, according to Sáenz, detached from native cultural and historical realities. Yet, while Sáenz doesn't see himself as a "true heir" of Walt Whitman or of William Carlos Williams, their ideas have been filtered through his thought: he searches, like Williams for "an American idiom . . . not merely North American but *pan* American" (535) and like Whitman he wants to "sing himself into America" (536). What Sáenz seems to be saying is that to focus exclusively on literary influence is to ignore political and historical realities, and that to dogmatically assert that an Anglo-American tradition is somehow responsible for the literature coming out of the U.S. is ridiculous. Because he wishes to document the lives of the people he knows and values, he sees an acceptance of this Anglo-American tradition as one more means of keeping Latinos "mortgaged to European culture and European standards" (535), of maintaining a state of "cultural and historical amnesia" (534), when in fact the history of English political influence upon the Americas is partly a record of destruction and genocide.

It becomes the task of the critic, therefore, to trace and discuss influences upon Latino fiction with both an understanding of European narrative traditions and a willingness to recognize Latin American and indigenous cultural and literary contributions. The criteria used to evaluate Latino writers needs to be expanded beyond documented European trends. In this way, readers can perceive not only the aesthetic ties between Latino fiction and past canonical writers (British or not), but also those qualities of the writings that remain unconnected and unique, those for example that refer to indigenous Indian populations in the Southwest or Mexico or the African traditions of the Caribbean. Thus while one cannot deny, for example, the influence of Virginia Woolf upon García Márquez, to overemphasize this tie is to run the risk of simultaneously overlooking something distinctly Latino (often a political factor) and subordinating Latino fiction to a sub category of European literature. Like Latino writers themselves, the critics that explore their works for influences must cross cultural borders just as readily.

José David Saldívar has used the term "double-voiced writing" to describe how Latino writers borrow and learn from both Latin Americans and European Americans, and that this range of influence creates a "cross-cultural hybridization." He looks at the works of Arturo Islas, for example, whose novels contain links to various writers across the spectrum of the Americas stretching from Faulkner, to Stevens (in his anti-religion themes), to Rulfo, Cather, Stegner, García Márquez, and even Maxine Hong Kingston (108). In addition, Islas's novel *The Rain God* refers to the Aztec god Tláloc, the Mayan Chác, and thus Islas's cultural heritage is extended into the non-European realms as well. Latino artists are often vehement about denying an exclusive allegiance to either Latin American or European American literary traditions. In a 1980 interview with critic Juan Bruce-Novoa, Chicano writer Ron Arias pointed out that the Mexican novelist Juan Rulfo was not the only novelist to which Arias felt a literary debt, and he cited a list of writers including Faulkner, B. Travern and Dostoevski as all impacting his "style and substance" (245)[1]

Once the door is opened to allow non-European artistic traditions to exert their influence upon Latino writers, the possibilities become endless. First of all, the thematic and stylistic roots of Latino writers depend upon their own individual, emotional, and political relationships with various traditions. That the connections reach across the borders of first and third world countries makes for a complicated network of influences. It would seem impossible and unnecessary to determine conclusively all the influences upon any given writer, let alone upon a group as broad as the one covered by this study. It may be that most modern literature reflects a hybrid influence as the world's creative works become more and more accessible, but Latino writers especially, because of their dual cultural backgrounds, require some degree of cross-referencing. What is possible is to suggest linkages and similarities between individual writers which could then become the focus of subsequent, less general approaches. Secondly, the critic must first narrow his or her focus in hopes of discovering a chain of influence of particular importance upon specific writers. The narrative mode known as *magical realism* (for the moment, loosely defined as a mixture of the fantastic and the real), serves as one broad, overarching area of intersection between Latino fiction and preceding works, both inside and outside the Anglo-American tradition. Because it concerns the straddling of borders between cultures and the blurring of distinctions in reality, *magical realism* easily accommodates the essentially hybrid quality of Latino fiction, becoming, for this reason, a valuable starting point in a discussion of influence.

The earlier comparison of European modernism and its Latin American counterpart, modernismo, emphasized stylistic and formal similarities between both literary movements. Yet, as Naomi Lindstrom has explained, among the modernistas, there also existed an interest in the bizarre, in, for example, "the transmigration of souls and mystically perfect numbers and vibrations" (Lindstrom 21). Though both European and Latin American modernism "ransacked the cultural past in search of reusable and adaptable themes and forms . . . " (22), the mystical interests of the modernistas, influenced no doubt by their exotic natural world and their alien indigenous cultures, would help steer Latin American writers away from European tradition, toward a new form of literary expression.

Magical realism has been called the central characteristic of Latin American fiction since the publication of Rulfo's *Pedro Paramo.* Though not all Latino writers of fiction use its narrative techniques (many in fact do not), it would be impossible to dismiss its importance for a number of reasons which can be more effectively detailed after a closer look at what is meant by the term. Of special importance as well, is the fact that *magical realism* encourages us to apply a dual, non Anglo-American perspective for our study, since in itself, the technique reflects a mixture of European and Latin American literary energies.

Tzvetan Todorov's discussion of the fantastic literary genre predates most references to the term *magical realism*, yet his categories often coincide with those aspects of *magical realism* relevant to Latino works.[2] Todorov's claim that the fantastic "occupies the duration of . . . [an] uncertainty" (25) where the reader "hesitates" between "types of natural causes and supernatural causes" (26) is not substantially different from Angel Flores's definition of "Magic Realism" as an "amalgamation of realism and fantasy" (189) in which, as Young and Hollaman explain, the "domination of any one way of looking at things is, at least temporarily, placed in jeopardy" (2). Examining Todorov's narrative grid (Todorov 44), we find, on one side, the "Uncanny" (or merely "strange") which, because it ultimately presents rational solutions for supernatural occurrences, corresponds to "the real." On the other side, Todorov's "marvelous" which ultimately denies rational explanation thus parallels the "magical" (or "marvelous" if we retain Alejo Carpentier's term). In this schema, *magical realism* coincides with Todorov's "fantastic," the border (a potent term for Latinos) between and overlapping into this pair of narrative classes. Todorov argues extensively that the fantastic exists in works like James' *The Turn of the Screw,* where the reader is left with ambiguous events unresolved, (is it dream or reality, a ghost or madness?). The fantastic, he states, is "a particular case of the more general category of the 'ambiguous vision'" (33). Young and Hollaman claim a similar criteria for *magical realism* since in it there must be an "irreducible element, something that cannot be explained by logic" (4). They refer to *magical realism* as "a hybrid [form of narrative] that somehow manages to combine the 'truthful' and 'verifiable' aspects of realism with the magical effects we associate with myth, folktale, [and] tall story (2). As Chanady explains, this is to consider *magical realism* a "narrative mode" and not as a genre or attitude toward the world (2). One finds, for example, the use of *magical realism* throughout literature in writers such as Sterne, Poe, or Kafka, and in works like Gogol's "The Nose" or Virginia Woolf's *Orlando*. The bizarreness of supernatural elements is, in these works, grounded in concrete realism as magical events (a nose going out in search of its face, a man/woman living hundreds of years) coexist with the plausible and are left unexplained. Though Gregory Samsa's transformation is fantastic, the details of his environment are believable to the point of being mundane. Todorov relates the Uncanny (the Real) with the knowable past, the marvelous with the unknowable future, and the fantastic with the "pure limit between the past and the future:" the present. The "strange interlude," between real and unreal, between past and future, leaves the reader questioning, and this open-ended, polyphonic quality of magical realist narratives accounts, in part, for their popularity among Latin American (and subsequently Latino) writers. Employed as a tool with which to examine the conflicting truths of "New World"/"Old World" concepts, *magical realism* becomes essential, so much so that critics since the 1960's have seen it as the principle characteristic of twentieth-century Latin American fiction.

Early magic realists, like Miguel Angel Asturias, combined the stylistic devices of European modernism with an interest in ethnology or the study of human races and their relations. While Asturias portrayed the Mayan farmers of Guatemala in the 1930's, a decade later Lydia Cabrera composed her "Transpositions" (the name she gave to her compilations of Afro-Cuban folk tales). In the late 1940's and early 1950's, Alejo Carpentier traced the cultural and political lives of ex-slave Africans in the Caribbean in works like *The Kingdom of this World*. Throughout the region, Latin American writers expressed interest in *indigenismo*, the study of Native American indigenous cultures,[3] one component of their gradual shift in emphasis away from the self, often apolitical absorption of European modernist thought toward the cross-cultural dimensions of a New World environment.

As Latin American writers continued to express their own vision of the world around them, the literature began to reflect a focus upon an "interior reality" as opposed to the outer (Martínez "Ron Arias" 12). Veering away from realism, but concerned with the political and cultural vitality of their environments, the "Boom" generation of writers worked within a "New American Reality." According to critics in the mid 1950's, *La nueva novela hispanoamericana* (The New Hispanic American Novel) came about with the publication of Juan Rulfo's *Pedro Páramo* and Agustín Yáñez's *Al filo del agua* (Guizado

135). As Fuentes's book makes clear, the New Hispanic American Novel also owes a debt to European critical thinking, specifically to Robbe-Grillet.

Robbe-Grillet saw the "new novel" as one that visually describes and measures characters and objects without instilling the objects with human meanings, or the characters with morality. The writing is therefore a scientific, objective approach which, (while never completely possible) makes objects and people "real" again; that is, uncontrolled by the author's borders or interpretations, unbiased by his or her traditions and perspectives. Such writing serves to "free us from our own conventions" (Robbe-Grillet 468—470). Presenting characters, objects, or gestures as they are, without interpretation or moral judgment makes them newly "real," because to instill meaning in every object is to make only the significance of that object important and thus the object itself disappears. Hence, the "new reality" and a "new novel," less involved with "passion." In poetry, Pound's Imagist doctrine calling for the "direct treatment of the thing" in order to "make it new" parallels Robbe-Grillet's idea. The distinction being that for Pound, the object becomes "the adequate symbol," the "luminous detail" while Robbe-Grillet dismisses the significance or symbolic level entirely. This sort of attention to scientific detail, coupled with the modernist desire to avoid what Flores calls "mawkish sentimentalism," or what Pound labeled "poppy-cock . . . emotional slither" (*Essays* 12) and a general appeal to a sophisticated reader "versed in subtleties" became central to mid-twentieth-century Latin American fiction (A. Flores 191).

The "modernist" generations of early and mid twentieth-century Latin American writers (Borges, Carpentier, Asturias), were reacting in part to the limits of nineteenth-century realism, regionalism (novels of the land) and criollismo (Chilean regionalism about people born in the Americas of Spanish descent) that preceded them in the works of writers like Güiraldes, Azuela, Gallegos, or José Eustasio Rivera (Giordano 127). Since modernist thought in psychology, anthropology and sociology had altered conceptions of reality, emphasis upon the magical served as a method to connect with the mythical past (as Joyce and Pound and Eliot used western myth). Yet in Latin America, writers reached out to non-western indigenous worlds and a truly "Latin American cultural inheritance" (Martínez "Ron Arias" 10). They looked for new mythical origins in order to center *their own* world, and make sense of their own changing reality. After 1935, with the publication of Borges's stories and translations of Kafka, (and especially during the decade of the 1940's), a large group of writers Angel Flores describes as magical realists ("Magical Realism" 190) began to instill in objects of reality a "magical" meaning, by emphasizing the unexplainable, celebrating the unknown of the "new world," and presenting the fantastic literally (Giordano 129). As Flores explains, *magical realism* in narrative had existed for years in the diaries of Columbus, and the writings of New World chroniclers, and had only "entered the literary mainstream during modernism" (189). Borges's influential 1932 article "Narrative Art and Magic" advocated the use of detailed, convincing depictions of the magic where "every detail is an omen and a cause" as the route where the "only possible integrity" for the novel lies since the "natural" is "an incessant result of endless, uncontrollable processes" (38). In the works of European modernists, the myth was used to juxtapose a shabby, drab reality with a glorious golden age. For the Latin American modernists the myth was more vital and necessary as it connected one to the essence of Latin America, nature and the exotic.

The next generation of Latin American writers (the "boom" generation of the 1950's and 1960's) was to declare the mythical journey back to the ancestors and origins irrelevant; the magical events and objects remain but they no longer provide epiphanic connections with the world. We find still the dreamy, irrational aspects of otherworldly events and actions, but the mystical is not necessarily a means toward salvation or path toward perfection (Giordano 131). Instead, the focus of writers like Rulfo, Sábato, Cortázar, Puig, or García Márquez is upon an objective depiction of the "New World," one without sentimentality and nostalgia. To avoid comparing their Latin American realities with the European known, the "new" novelists sought a "different treatment of the external" (Young and Hollaman 5), and perhaps their desire was best accommodated by Carpentier's earlier notion of "the Marvelous in the Real." This turned their attentions toward their unique surroundings and away from the introspection common to their modernist predecessors. Whereas earlier writers had desired to identify with Indian myths and gods, the "Boom" generation was comfortable on the periphery, existing somewhere between the indigenous vitality of Latin America and the creative literary forces of Western Europe.

As Chanady notes, *magical realism* is a blending of a "rational and an irrational worldview," a synthesis of the coherent supernatural codes of primitive Americans and logical European thought (*Magical Realism* 21). That the outside world (that of Indian and African beliefs etc.) was unknown led to utilizing the magical to portray it. Incorporating modernist literary methods, writers concerned themselves with the decentering of western perspective, so that cause and effect are "shuffled" and the world is not ordered logically. As Camacho Guizado has written, more flexible literary techniques were necessary to capture the complexity of the magical within reality (135), and the use of *magical realism* as a "literary mode" (Chanady *Magical Realism* 21) became an essential narrative apparatus in accomplishing this.

To emphasize the unrecognized New World meant to question the written and the known, that is, European, metropolitan norms. Consequently Latin American writers were attracted to a narrative form which permitted "an unexpected alteration of reality (a miracle)" and "an amplification of the measures and categories of reality" (Carpentier Prologue iv). To put the reader in a "limit state" (or liminal state) of "faith," Carpentier says, required deviating from standards of verisimilitude in order to capture "the marvelous in the real," the foreign and the exotic so strange to the European, but sometimes verifiable to the Latin American. Among other things, *magical realism* allowed writers to capture "the marvelous" flowing "freely from a reality precise in all its details" (viii). It is this aspect of *magical realism*—the freedom it gives to explore, non-judgmentally, the exotic and unscientifically proven that exists within reality—which attracts Latino writers. Because they position themselves between what U.S. society accepts and everything else on the borders, *magical realism* offers them a wealth of possibilities for overturning the status quo, satirizing notions of the "proper" and for upsetting destructive stereotypes.

Magical realism depicts the point where too different realities come together in much the way advocated by Gloria Anzaldúa, in calling for her "hybrid, malleable, mutable" Chicana, in short her "new mestisa consciousness" with its "tolerance for ambiguity" (*Borderlands* 77). *Magical realism* reflects the duality of reality and fantasy, the borderland synthesis of things concrete and rational and things fantastic and otherworldly. The reader cannot accept the work as pure fantasy and therefore dismiss it as, Todorov explains, Science fiction, Ghost stories, Fantasy, or other "marvelous" narrative forms. Neither can the seemingly irrational be explained and legitimized as in most of Poe[4] (who deals with human extremes, yet often qualifies the supernatural with rational explanations) or in detective or mystery stories where the unknown is finally clarified and the mystery solved (Todorov 48-50).[5]

Equating *magical realism* with Todorov's fantastic is not, however, entirely justified, since *magical realism* often includes narrative elements which he labels "hyperbolic marvelous" and "exotic marvelous" (55). In magical realist fiction, we frequently find both types, though Todorov argues that they fall between the fantastic and the Marvelous. Embellishment, particularly, is a key factor in magical realist political critiques where the texts push reality one step beyond plausibility. Like García Márquez, Cecile Pineda often use the "hyperbolic marvelous" to accent the ridiculousness of one limited perception of the world. In *The Love Queen of the Amazon*, for instance, after a suitor has sent thousands of flowers to his young love, swarms of bees soon make the room uninhabitable (63). The extension is not entirely unrealistic, simply overstated enough to call attention to the quirks of a romantic custom. Alfredo Véa describes the strange story of a woman named Boydeen who stabs to death an abusive partner named Hiawatha Carson. Damaged both physically and emotionally, she retreats into a mute, quasi-catatonic state. Véa pushes the limits of verisimilitude when Boydeen takes up residence beneath the front porch of a small general store where she becomes a sort of invisible stenographer, scribbling verbatim every conversation she hears from above. She speaks only in what Véa calls "readback" while the porch becomes an unofficial town hall where "desperate mothers" record their prayers, and "young black nobodies from nowhere . . . say words to marry each other in writing, on this fringe of life" (184). Discussing the Cuban-American writer Roberto G, Fernández, Mary Velásquez argues that this sort of "imaginative reach outside the structures of time and space" can be regarded as linked to the fantasizing of the Cuban exile, as the natural imaginative extension of his or her longing and dreams ("Fantastic" 75). It seems, however, that bending the limits of plausibility in Latino fiction has as many purposes as there are examples.

The magical realist text doesn't rely upon the first person point of view as often as the fantastic does. In a first person narrative, the confusion and bewilderment the reader feels is filtered through an equally mystified narrator who experiences the bizarre. Removing this personae, magical realists characteristically employ the third person (Todorov's "non-represented" narrator), which, Todorov argues, is clearly associated with the marvelous where the "supernatural universe is not intended to awaken doubts" (83). *Magical realism* questions both the magical and the real because the reader has no intermediary in his confrontation with the strange. Unlike certain examples of the fantastic, there are few lexical or syntactical clues in *magical realism* to draw attention to the fiction's ambiguity. Todorov cites the uses of words like "seemed" and "believed" and the indistinct temporal quality of the imperfect tense. The absence of these "modalizing formulas" (Todorov 80) in modern *magical realism* can only further obscure certainty in the text. Neither does magical realist fiction depend upon a linear narrative, as does Todorov's fantastic. The magical quality is simply presented rather than carefully prepared for with foreshadowing and suspense. In a scene reminiscent of García Márquez's short story "The Saint," Ana Castillo's "La Loca" sits up in her coffin when the lid is removed at the funeral, then flies up on to the roof (*So Far from God* 22-23). Later in the same book, "La Loca's" beautiful and "selfless" sister Caridad is maimed and left for dead by the side of the road, only to wander off one night "whole and once again beautiful" dressed in a wedding gown (37). There is no preparation and no explanation for these sorts of miraculous occurrences, and no one gapes in awe when they occur. The narrator is not necessarily unreliable, and the reader is left to find a symbolic significance in the events. In this case, Castillo is perhaps suggesting women's unfortunate need to escape an abusive world. La Loca explains that she flies to the roof top to escape the "smell" of humans, and Caridad becomes a sort of disconnected phantom, gliding away, dazed and unreachable like Mary Tyrone in O'Neill's play. More importantly, the absence of conclusive explanation brings the reader's understanding of events to a level identical to that held by the townspeople in the book. We are compelled for a moment to share in the beliefs of rural southwestern, Chicano, folk culture, where miracles play a genuine role in determining spiritual convictions. When García Márquez's "very old man with enormous wings" somehow falls out of the sky, the reader must similarly experience the reactions of poor, coastal Colombians with some of their own confusion and disbelief, and understand the methods of their coping with the otherworldly.[6] We are perhaps more soundly tied to the roots of their myth making. With this narrative trick in the hands of writers like Castillo, the bizarre and implausible become the means of guiding the reader toward the vivid cultural realities of characters.

These distinguishing characteristics of *magical realism* suggest that Chanady is correct in asserting that, while sharing qualities of the fantastic, *magical realism* differs from it in the manner of its portrayal since "in *magical realism*, the supernatural is *not* presented as problematic" (emphasis mine 23). *Magical realism*, because of its characteristic "authorial reticence," the withholding of explanation, "naturalizes the supernatural and the strange world view presented in the text" (Chanady 149). Moreover, *magical realism* (like the fantastic) cannot be reduced (and excused) by allegorical interpretation. The term implies "borders" by mixing opposites. One needs to see *magical realism* as a name for fiction that throws worlds (cultural, metaphysical, or political) together in such a way as to disrupt and disturb the status quo. Thus, a reader is made aware, as Edward Said has claimed, of "the dense interwoven strands of a history that mock linear narrative, easily recuperated 'essences,' and the dogmatic mimesis of 'pure' representation" (276). What grounds *magical realism*, and despite its affinity with aspects of Todorov's fantastic, is its realism.

Whether or not the critical label *magical realism* is sufficient or should be replaced with "mestizo consciousness" or "border writing," it is true that the fiction the term refers to suggests a blending of two worlds and obligates the reader to manage both simultaneously—thus creating the necessity of a dual (multi) perspective. Hicks has suggested a "multidimensional" perspective she compares with the image of a hologram (Intro xxviii—xxix), which nicely incorporates the notion of each perspective creating an apparent whole, yet that whole being the shifting assemblage of fragments rather than a solid reality. One's cultural vision seems complete, but once altered by experience, is shown to be inadequate and in a constant state of change. Once aware of the magical in the reality of Afro-Cuban religion, for example, the reader must embrace a dual perspective. A bicultural vision becomes necessary. Where escape into the purely marvelous can disconnect a reader from socio-economic reality, *magical realism*, like metafiction in general, tricks the reader by creating a recognizable situation and then "shattering" the "fictional illusion" (Alexander 3-4). The writers of the new Hispanic American novel destabilize their own works and consequently question the nature of reality and not simply the modernist idea of questioning how we perceive reality (Alexander 22).[7]

Magical realism provides a formal release from the restrictions of realism, without the ultimate escapism and disconnection of fantasy or the purely marvelous. The verisimilitude of the opening scenes of Cecile Pineda's *The Love Queen of the Amazon* is firmly established by the believable representation of a Catholic institution, its rituals and restrictions. Yet the heroine of the novel is born to a mother sleeping in a bathtub, mythically born "swimming vigorously . . . and entirely covered with downy black hair" (4). Three pages into the story, the reader feels the tension between a mythic birth that augers a future "singularly free of virginal modesty or unnecessary chastity" and the concrete reality of a convent with no "plumbing facilities" that teaches the "feminine arts" that "make a woman a woman." This is the first instance of how reality in the story will be adjusted to fit the life of the novel's heroine. She is Ana (after a maternal grandmother), but also Magdalena (after a "deceased maiden aunt); she lives in a marvelous world beneath the surface of reality. Where realism uses language to create recognizable worlds, the "new language" (in the tradition of modernism), defamiliarizes the world in language that draws attention to itself (Alexander 6). Pineda begins her book with a magical, unconventional birth which sets the stage for the unconventional acts the heroine will undertake throughout the story. Unafraid of water, she'll rescue a drowning girl. Unafraid of societal etiquette, she'll establish a brothel in her husband's mansion.

As were the magical realists of the 40's and 50's, Latino writers are appealing to an audience, in Angel Flores's words, "not merely initiated in aesthetic mysteries but versed in subtleties" (191). In their rejection of stereotypical views and popular attitudes toward Latinos in the U.S., they are naturally inclined to embrace a mode of narrative that questions and deconstructs the dominant society's accepted standards, rules and beliefs. Specifically, whether or not their works include the overtly fantastic, because of *magical realism*, they are free to emphasize the oral nature of human communication, the vernacular component to their cultures. This narrative mode legitimizes the stories and tall tales of the Latino's ancestors and families. Empowered with this distinctly Latin American, postmodernist mode, writers can twist their tales in startling ways in order to upset conventions. They can exaggerate whatever they want and escape the narrow confines of autobiographical prose.

Ed Vega, for instance, in a typical example of his outrageous mocking of conventional attitudes about sex, describes a prostitute's reaction to seeing the enormity of one Filiberto Casablancas's penis:

> . . . the night was pierced by the most horrifying scream he had ever heard. Within the scream there was an eerie whistling which set dogs howling and cocks crowing as if it were morning. The next day the

> hibiscuses, roses, marguerites, jasmines and lilies in all the gardens of the town had wilted and earthworms appeared everywhere as if they had poured from the heavens despite it not having rained the previous night. (*Mendoza* 30)

Exaggeration here serves, not only to embellish a humorous story, to mythologize an exceptional character, but to satirize predictable reactions of readers and townsfolk alike. Like Vega, Latino writers in this way can creatively reflect upon themselves and their writing with irony and humor, calling attention to the absurdity of social custom and taboo. Moreover, the release from realism serves their purpose of revealing the uncertainties of Latinos struggling between cultural systems. *Magical realism* stretches the borders and accounts for those in the liminal ground between. It doesn't require that the reader maintain a judgmental distance from the bizarre, so writers may portray their marginal community in all its strangeness, from within without the necessity of abandoning or critiquing it. For these reasons *magical realism* has, as Homi Bhabha asserts, become "the literary language of the emergent colonial world" (7).

Arturo Islas, in his second novel, *Migrant Souls,* mentions a wedding cake from the "Aracataca Bakery" (97). Ed Vega jokes about comparing pen size (among other things) with his good friend Gabo in a short story from *Mendoza's Dreams* (23). Ron Arias reworks the short story "The Handsomest Drowned Man in the World" for his novel *The Road to Tomazunchale.* Directly or indirectly, many Latino writers display the influence of García Márquez. José David Saldívar perhaps overgeneralizes when he states that García Márquez more than any other writer "has most shaped the course of U.S. minority discourses in the 1970's and 1980's," yet García Márquez surely has had a hand in guiding "the new narrative from Our America" (23). He has "set out to create a Native American tradition . . . on the aesthetic grounds prepared by Cervantes, Kafka, Borges, and Faulkner" (24). The "discovery" of García Márquez's *100 Years of Solitude* forced European critics to recognize the existence of South and Central American literature, and appreciate certain qualities of it. The magnitude of the book's critical and popular success surely accounts for the abundance of allusions to it and its creator in fiction all over the world. Of course, García Márquez had roots in Faulkner, in Carpentier, and in Virginia Woolf, but there was a newness in Macondo that refused to allow literary scholars to follow their accustomed trail of influence back through European tradition, or at least to branch off that path momentarily, and therefore, once having deviated, never quite being capable of falling back in line. Hugh Kenner, discussing how the cave paintings on the walls of Altamira helped shape the modernist perspective of time, explains that by virtue of their existence, they proved that art lived outside of time and beyond existing strategies of decipherment and accepted methods of judgment (30). It can be argued that García Márquez's writing has had a similar impact upon writing in the Americas, especially among Latinos.

The reasons for the Colombian writer's influence are many. First of all, it is with his work that the concept of *magical realism* enters the mainstream literary dialogue. Critical acclaim for García Márquez broke down regional restrictions and nourished a global perspective. As José David Saldívar has noted, García Márquez's brand of *magical realism* emphasized the "oral expressions" of Third World cultures and so accented the collective voice of the folk world, the unofficial, the anti-official (*Dialectics* 94-95). Prior magical realists (predominately during the 1940's and 1950's, up to the time of Angel Flores's famous essay), while suggesting an alternative to the written reality of European history, were only marginally concerned with communicating something of the folk world and its beliefs in their attempt to disrupt status quo versions of reality. In authenticating the oral, the storyteller, the mythic Indian peasant's version of reality, García Márquez was helping to invent a language for those on the periphery of the literary world. As Fuentes has claimed, "to invent a language is to say all that history has silenced" (30).

Magical realism nourishes the writer's imaginative questioning of certain irrational, but genuine, features of the folk culture he or she portrays. García Márquez has the freedom to discuss a "very old man with enormous wings" or a beautiful girl's ascent into the air, and in so doing develops a method of critiquing a psychological characteristic of Latin Americans: a tendency to believe in an external locus of control. Partly a product of Roman Catholicism, the notion holds that what happens in life is often the result of something other than one's own actions. The Spanish language incorporates the idea into its own grammatical structures: "Se me olvidó," "Se me pasó," "Se me perdió" (literally "It forgot itself on me"). When Ariel Dorfman and Arland Mattelart attack the U.S. Government and the Disney Corporation for their Donald Duck cartoons, they are rebelling against what they deem propaganda which purports the correctness of such a system of thought. As Donald Duck wanders through his numerous futile attempts to better his life—a pattern they label "suffrenture" ("suffering coated with adventure" 43)[8]—readers are led to believe that nothing can be done, that human action (like working, rebelling, striking) is irrelevant, that fate and accident determine all, and that money (like children) arrives magically. Folk tales throughout Latino fiction are filled with this particular concept of understanding the world and its relationship to oneself. One need only check the frequency of words like "milagro" (miracle), or destino (fate) in Latin American and Latino fiction for confirmation. Fernando Alegría recognized this metaphysical perspective in Alejo Carpentier's sense of "a peculiar Latin American consciousness devoid of self-reflexiveness and inclined to faith; a consciousness that allows Latin Americans to live immersed in culture and to feel history not as a causal process that can be analyzed rationally and intellectually, but as destiny" (González Echevarría 125-126). "What can you do?" asks a character in a story by Junot Díaz, "Life smacks everybody around" (*Drown* 174).

With the freedom of a narrative system that incorporates the folk voice, where fantasy and reality are not entirely incongruous, the stories of previously silent grandmothers, now legitimized as both subjects and conveyers of fiction, could be told. Gustavo Gardeazábal could recount the story of a "Mafioso" (during the period of "La Violencia" in Colombia), from tall tales and "rumors."[9] Isabel Allende could depict her uncle's Chile from a woman's perspective, and her work surely sparked Cristina Garcia's. Latino writers follow in this path, weaving the "orality of culture" with the written (Kanellos 121), privileging the "cuentistas" by valuing their spoken words. Eliana Ortega in her article "Poetic Discourse of the Puerto Rican Woman in the U.S.: New Voices of Anacaonian Liberation" explains how the mythic Indian rebel, Anacaona, is given voice as "oral discourse is superimposed over the exclusively literary one that belongs to the intellectual elite (122-123). For Chicanos, Paredes's famous anthropological study of folk hero Gregorio Cortez, *With his Pistol in His Hand*, exemplified how the valorization of oral folk culture authenticates an integral part of Chicano identity just as the Afro-Cuban folk tales compiled by Lydia Cabrera served a similar purpose for Cuban and Cuban-American culture. The Latino focus upon an oral tradition, and therefore the accenting of the "bizarre" landscape (to Western readers anyway) of legends and tall tales will impact Latino fiction in ways to be explored in a later chapter, but the idea must be introduced at this point in order to fully appreciate García Márquez's influence. By privileging the folk voice of his Colombian community, he legitimized a writer's attempt to treat "the commonplace as if were exceptional and the exceptional as if it were commonplace" (Brushwood 10).

We see the beginnings of García Márquez inspired narrative innovation in Chicana writers like Portillo-Trambley in her novel, and Helen Ponce in short stories like "El Marxista" or "The Playgoers," who borrow a system of flashback used in the individual chapters of *100 Years of Solitude*. Each chapter begins with a climax of sorts and the reader reconstructs the sequence of causes bit by bit as the chapter progresses. While such a circular technique can become repetitious (as in Ponce's writing), it helped García Márquez convey his cyclical rendition of time. As Julio Ortega has explained, the famous opening sentence of *One Hundred Years of Solitude*:

> Many years later, as he faced the firing squad, Colonel Aureliano Buendia was to remember that distant afternoon when his father took him to discover ice. (1)

recalls the fairy tale opening "Había una vez" [Once upon a time] and establishes a mythical timelessness that frames the entire novel.[10] This "tiempo fabuloso" [fable time], both "tenso" and "calmo" [tense and calm] where "todo el pasado pertenece ya al futuro" [all the past belongs already to the future] (139) forces a reader to follow sequences of chronological time, and, simultaneously, to read through a veil of nostalgic memory. The timeless storybook opening infuses the prose with a feel of universality and importance, and makes it "mas resonante, más tangible, un tiempo que es duración ay transición" [more resonant, more tangible, a time that is duration and transition"]. Perhaps most importantly, the opening sentence connects the written word to the "orality of culture," substantiating the validity of folk tales and signaling a mythic adventure unimpeded by the restrictions of realist writing.

Non-realist, Latino writers, frequently borrow the phrase "many years later" with varying results. Eliud Martínez's second sentence in *Voice-Haunted Journey* reads: "Years later Alejandro's older brother would not remember how many people were there, sitting in the funeral chapel in Austin, Texas . . . " In this novel of jumbled time and metafictional game playing, the opening sets the stage for a non-linear narrative that bounces from past to present to future. The phrase ruptures the narrative of *The Rain God* at one point so that Jaunita's reactions to her father's death are juxtaposed with her reactions to her nephew's and the narrative is jolted into the future (44). The second paragraph of Judith Cofer's *The Line of the Sun* reads: "Many years later, after Guzmán disappeared into the New York City subway system, Papá Pepe dared to say at the dinner table that it was his wife's prenatal violence that had made Guzmán the runaway he would always be" (1). Cofer's "tiempo fabuloso" soon changes, however, to purely linear time as the novel continues (mysteries are solved) and the mythical quality is grounded when historical dates (i.e. the year 1951) and events (the Korean War) begin to fill the narrative. Cofer may begin with the energy of a fable, but her Nuyorican experience growing up during the 1950's in a New Jersey "barrio" guides her toward a more realistic narrative. This is why the opening lines are tied to Guzmán, the exotic outcast with "the face of a wise harlequin" (191) whose carnivalesque persona will fade as the narrator copes with the traumas of an urban housing project. It is as if the reader moves from story to reality, from mythic universality to concrete specific.

Roberto Fernández uses the phrase in an early scene of *Raining Backwards* to broaden the meaning of a particular situation. The young Cuban-American, Eloy, frequently visits his neighbor in order to hear her nostalgic glorifications of Cuba's beaches. In return for her stories, he washes her back. "Eloy commenced lathering the sponge without realizing that *many years later* he would forbid his wife to use a sponge to do the dishes, much less bathe the kids. This strange spongephobia would last throughout his life" (15). The stretching of time pulls us away from a voyeuristic view of a sexual scene between the boy and the nostalgic Mirta by directing our attention into the future and toward the long lasting effects of the incident. We are meant to laugh at the "spongephobia," and asked to grasp Eloy's disgust as we distance ourselves from the event. The consequence of the event, not the description of the event as it happens or Eloy's reflection upon the event—since his opinion is never directly given—communicates the boy's displeasure with Mirta, and, by inference, a displeasure for the dreamy reminiscences of exiled Cubans. The phrase joins the past, present and future in such a way as to comment upon the destructive consequences of nostalgic revelry.

Cecile Pineda self-consciously uses the line both to open *The Love Queen of the Amazon*, as well as to open the novel within the novel being written by one of her characters (of the same name and about the heroine of the novel). Pineda begins her novel:

> Many years later when there was little doubt left, people still marveled how Ana Magdalena as a young girl at least had possessed all the qualities you would expect in a young girl of good but impoverished family. 'Who could have imagined,' they said, 'that one day she would become known as a succubus?'

The phrase "many years later" encourages the reader to see events in terms of their consequences. Simultaneously provided with Ana's story and people's future attitudes toward her (people "still" marveling), the reader can only assume that these types of attitudes remain, that society's views of the proper are very much a part of the present. To the mythic establishment of non-time, as in García Márquez, Pineda adds her own touch of sarcastic wit. Later in the novel, she openly parodies *One Hundred Years of Solitude* as well as its author. The flowery prose of Ana's comical husband, the "illustrious Federico Orgaz y Orgaz," should seem familiar:

> Many years later, when she appeared before the town fathers, Ostencia Candelaria remembered when her mother had first showed her lace maker's bobbins. It was a time when the world was first conceived, and nothing, not even vice, had been invented. There were no words for things like overhead, or commissions, or money, and people went about trading things for other things, or sometimes favors for other favors, and they worked only when they needed something or when they felt like it . . . (138-139).

Orgaz y Orgaz himself is described as a "world-renowned fabulist who, rumor had it, was soon to be nominated for an internationally prestigious literary prize; an extraordinary man of letters, the first from the New World to achieve an international reputation on a par with that of the many very superior writers of Europe . . . " Allusions to other writers abound in Pineda's parodic novel: there is even a salon scene in which Ana is stifled by the stuffy air of literary conversation the way Woolf's Orlando is by the wisdom of eighteenth-century English male writers. Ana has "trouble breathing" while listening to "the matinee idol novelist and perennial presidential also-ran, Vacio-Llares" (59), a reference to Peruvian writer Mario Vargas Llosa though here his name could be translated "empty pot-hanger" according to *Cassell's Spanish Dictionary.*[11] Though the novel is filled with moments of magical realism, their mystical attraction is often comically deflated. Such is the case when the famous Orgaz sends flowers to Ana, phallic flowers "a lion tamer might favor." He sends so many that "the bees began arriving," in an "invasion" that rivals the storms of butterflies in *Cien Años*. It is just one of what Pineda in a comment surely meant for the devotees of García Márquez's style, offhandedly refers to as "another in a long and tiresome string of miracles" (123). Later in the novel, Clemencia begins to ascend into the air like García Márquez's famous Remedios the Beauty. In Pineda, however, she hovers below the ceiling and her servant has to feed her "by extending a pole to which she had affixed a fork" (165). After the floating woman manages to kick out the window casement, and the wind catches her, she is blown upward "over the rooftops" like the "Very Old Man with Enormous Wings." Somehow the majestic and miraculous beauty of Remedios's death is reduced here to a merely awkward and humorous incident. She floats because she is too nostalgic and her ascent is no more than "an embarrassing abnormality of her behavior" (144). Pineda's parody usually revolves around gender and it is Orgaz's belief that history is all about great men which comes under fiercest attack. Though he gets his subject matter and creative impulse from women (specifically his madam wife and her bordello downstairs) while he hides like Willa Cather's professor in a locked room above it all, detached, he really only wants the "fame, and considerable fortune, which might even place him in line for international acclaim and the coveted "gunpowder prize" (150).

At one point, Federico Orgaz y Orgaz reads a section of his dialogue in which three Cardinals (Cardinal Gorgonzola, Cardinal Provolone, and Cardinal Parmigiano) discuss what is to be done with the "succubus" madam in the Amazon. Pineda is mimicking García Márquez's humorous swipes at the officialdom of the Catholic Church, and this too is something practiced elsewhere among Latino writers. There are many instances where organized religion comes under attack. Tomás Rivera blasts the Protestant priests who arrive to teach the poor migrant farmers carpentry and wind up teaching them nothing. In fact they don't even come out of their trailer (107). The scene (which echoes one in *Chronicle of a Death Foretold* where the bishop bypasses a Colombian town despite the day's festivities in his honor) is central to Rivera's novel because it lies between (and separates) the key chapters in which the narrator's religious doubt is confirmed and he is, as Ramón Saldívar's argues, liberated from passive acceptance of his lowly state in life. Recognizing that the earth will not devour him, he can curse God and resolve "not to believe and hence not to be bought and sold like an animal or like the fields that he works" (Saldívar 85).

One further example may sufficiently demonstrate the benefits of examining Latino fiction with one eye cast toward the work of García Márquez. The central matriarch of Arturo Islas's *The Rain God* is named Mama Chona, but she instructs her kin to call her Mama Grande. Two pages into his novel, Islas is here surely alluding to the well known story "Big Mama's Funeral," and the effect is to immediately instill in the reader a sense of doubt concerning Mama Chona, Encarnacion Olmeca de Angel, and the authority she represents. The García Márquez story mocks everything Mama Chona stands for and celebrates all the extremes of life that she rejects. The carnival of the funeral—Big mama's "monumental buttocks," her last final "loud belch" (192)—counters Mama Chona's desires of perfect Catholic spirituality, her obsession with avoiding "impurity." The oral nature of the narrative (a sort of carnival barker hyperbole) counteracts Mama Chona's preference for the formal, written Castillian Spanish which in the story becomes mere "words, words, words," or "historic blahblahblah" (195). Her preference for "silence . . . like Teotihuacan pyramids" (*Rain God* 27) gives way to the clamorous noise of festival and noise. With García Márquez in mind, Islas opens his novel by suggesting the death of the matronly Catholic traditions embodied in Mama Chona. Islas wishes to foreshadow how the authoritarian rules and rigid moral codes the woman endorses will be undermined by later events in the story. The García Márquez story is about power and Islas's novel will go on to question the matriarch's power over her complicated family.

The mark of García Márquez's narrative craftsmanship on Latino writers extends beyond allusion. We find, for example, the use of extensive and involved family genealogies (certainly something García Márquez borrowed from Faulkner) in writers as different as Oscar Hijuelos and Arturo Islas. This repetition of family names relates to the notions of cyclical time, of the inheritance of patriarchal power and incestual decay—ideas that tie Hawthorne's "sins of the father" themes to Faulkner, to García Márquez to Islas. In Latino fiction, especially Chicano, family trees carry Catholic guilt and an obsession with the dead.

Roberta Fernández's *Intaglia* is strengthened by such a technique, not only because, as in Faulkner, extended family trees allow characters to stretch beyond the boundaries of their fictional communities (individual stories or novels), nor, as Rebolledo and Rivero explain, because the family names document the existence of marginal lives and cultures, and compel the reader to sense a Latino "cultural memory" (18), but also because the linking together of family members and the prioritizing of each female member's contribution and connection is both the central job of the reader and the essential reason for the protagonist's (Nenita's) maturity. As we tie the family together, so does Nenita tie herself to her past and her heritage, finding in her glimpses of family the continuity she needs to confront the challenges in her life. In Candelaria, in Martínez, and in Islas, the repetition of paternal family names—the names like José Rafa, Miguel Velásquez, and Miguel Angel are passed down through two, even three generations—and one is reminded of the Buendia family line which in turn carries echoes of the Compsons, the Sartoris's, the McCaslins and the Snopes. Certain particular parallels are even more exact, as is true for Martínez's Miguel Velásquez's soldier grandfather who bears a resemblance to García Márquez's mythic hero Colonel Aureliano Buendia, himself an echo of Colonel Sartoris astride his mythic horse, Jupiter in *The Unvanquished*. As with the Fernández novel, the reader's attention in these works is focused upon the generational conflicts of family heritage. In Faulkner's novels, family name relates to class, reputation and identity, and these issues carry extra weight in Latino family contexts. Echoing a stereotypical sentiment, one Dagoberto Gilb character remarks: "Wanting to be with your family is as Mexican as having babies" (213).[12]

William Faulkner's novels are in part responsible for the coming together of U.S. and Latin American literature in twentieth-century Latino fiction. Like Poe's work in the 1800's, Faulkner's impact on writing extended beyond the boundaries of North America. His influence on García Márquez has been documented in numerous studies[13] and the extent of his literary prominence goes far beyond the purpose of this study. Nevertheless, there is a need to establish the link with Latino literature and Faulkner, not for the purpose of regaling the old master but rather for demonstrating how modernist Latino prose synthesizes U.S. and Latin American narrative influences. As discussed earlier, modernist narrative strategies from Latin America and from Europe combined to allow Latino writers a certain flexibility in portraying their worlds. Faulkner's works would serve as models, particularly for alternative, fragmented perspectives of life in the U.S. Yet Latino fiction is closer to Faulkner's writing than in mere structural design. This can be evidenced by noting similarities of imagery and connecting the thematic issues certain images suggest. Though numerous equally interesting facets of Faulkner's imagery would suffice, let's take, for instance, his use of "dust." Usually, dust in Faulkner implies the decay of society, of wealth, of tradition, and of moral codes of conduct as in the story "Dry September." The image resurfaces in the "dead village" (6) of Comala in Rulfo's *Pedro Paramo*, and in García Márquez's Colombian coastal streets. Examining "dust" therefore brings forth a rich comparison between Jefferson, Comala and Macondo (one that might include tyrants like Pedro Paramo and his similarities to Sutpen, or to the dying Patriarch; or one centering upon incest like the couple in Rulfo's novel). Tracing these similarities, extensive as such an exercise might be, would point critics eventually toward Latino works, and at the same time establish the salient interaction of influence shaping Latino fiction. We see the dust in Pineda's comic portrayal of decaying oligarchy in the "house of Orgaz, the most illustrious—and dusty—family of all." Come spring, "the prestige of each house could be gauged by the volume of dust raised by the vehicle" that the "great houses still chose to affect" in the streets of Malyerba (*Love Queen* 21) while peasants ("The common people were about, but they are always about in any case, and deserve no great attention here."—22), avoid the "dusty onslaught" of wealth and power. In Islas's *The Rain God*, characters fight the "pestilential dust" of the desert (162) that traps old people in their beds (148), buries kitchens (57), and fills the eyes of the dying (48). "Romantic dreams" vanish into the desert evening" (56). Judith Cofer writes about a lifeless Puerto Rican town known as "El Polvorín" [the "dustdevil"] coming alive during carnival (*Line* 106). For Anaya, there is mythical evil in summer dust storms of the llano: "The dust devils of the llano are numerous. They come from nowhere, made by the heat of hell they carry with them the evil spirit of a devil . . . " (*Bless Me, Ultima* 51).

Faulkner's imagery stresses how the dust of decay absorbs the "eternal verities," the principles of the Ante-bellum south, and leaves a world of connivers and materialists, a wasteland void of tradition. For Chicanos, the western sand becomes an image of hopelessness and the Latino's futility in trying to regain the golden age of Aztlán, and the purity of times prior to Western contamination.

Faulkner's sense of deterioration carries into Chicano fiction as writers watch a consumer driven society eat away at ethnic traditions. Hawkshaw's attempt in "Dry September" to rescue the innocent black man from a gang of KKK murderers fails when he jumps from the car and the car is "swallowed" by the dust (74). Often the superficiality of North American culture threatens and even swallows the native traditions of the rural Chicano (and of all immigrant groups), in much the same way. This, in part, accounts for the multiple versions in Latino fiction of Faulkner's famous character, Emily Grierson or variations of her like Rosa Coldfield and Joanna Burden. She stands for people who cannot cope with the overwhelming practical need to change opinions and beliefs. We see her type in the unnamed woman narrator in García Márquez's story "Bitterness for Three Strangers" or in Rebeca of *One Hundred Years of Solitude* and even in the patriarch of *The Autumn of the Patriarch.* Pineda's Andreina is like Emily, concerned with societal position over all, and "mummified in her flannel nightgown" (*Love Queen* 38). So too is the elderly "Senhora" who gives Helio a job in her garden in *Face.* He imagines her and her sisters "in their starched lace, eternally propped in their straight-backed chairs, waiting there for a suitor who had never come" (141-143). A grandmother living in a bedroom "filled with her past" (*Flowers* 125) in the story "The Idol Worshippers" by Sáenz declares that "Reputations always matter" (140). Mrs. Rentería in Arias's *Road* wants to sleep with the attractive corpse of David, a "mojado" found in a dry riverbed. For Latino writers, Emily is a twentieth-century parallel to an older tradition of the woman who lives by rules and codes no longer applicable. Rolando Hinojosa has noted the parallels between Faulkner's Civil War and the Mexican Revolution's importance to the rural Chicano's modern world (Hernández 86). Where the Civil War has dislocated Faulkner's southern high society ladies, the status of exile or cultural disruption has uprooted and marred certain elements of the Latino character. Nearly archetypal, this figure of the lonely, older woman bent on maintaining an obsolete tradition in the face of modern times occurs frequently. Islas's matriarch, Mama Chona, carries a strong allegiance to a rigid Roman Catholic purity, advocating "pure bodiless intellect. No shit, no piss, no blood—a perfect astronaut" (8, 164). She struggles in vain to uphold the family name of Angel, preaching a "Spanish conquistador snobbery that refused to associate itself with anything Mexican or Indian because it was somehow impure" (27). This "highborn Spanish" woman now living in Mexico (141) is fossilized in her beliefs, claiming that "angels" are "better than the illiterate riffraff from across the river" (15), and that Castillian Spanish is better than Mexican. Faulkner's emphasis upon the futility of the struggle to maintain a dying tradition, and upon the consequences of miscegenation and sexual taboos has obvious relevance to recent fiction in general and the frequent allusions to his writing among writers like Pineda, Islas, or Arias attests to that fact.

If Faulkner's dust imagery can so easily lead to the heart of his writing, it is because he focused intensely upon the problems of U.S. society in all its misshappened manifestations, and the dysfunctional, marginal family became for him a microcosm of larger societal decline, a movement from slow, solid order toward speed and fragmentation. García Márquez saw a similar decaying of old world order in coastal Colombia following the departure of The United Fruit Company, and he populated his town with characters bearing striking similarities to those of Faulkner's. Faulkner's "community building," his creation of Jefferson and its "myriad" inhabitants helped him convey this sense of loss, change and deterioration by centering his focus upon people coping with such destructive environments. As with García Márquez, such a narrative, structural framework accommodates an exploration into fringe communities of people whose lives have been previously neglected by recorded history. William Kennedy's Albany novels or the works of Carolyn Chute demonstrate the potential of exploring the domains of the underclass, and many Latino writers have adapted this blueprint for their portrayals of Latino fringe dwellers—those in barrios (on Mango Street, in East LA or in Patterson, NJ), in rural slums, in the camps of migrant workers, in prisons (as in Piñero's *Short Eyes*), in YMCA's (as in Gilb's novel), or trapped on decaying ghost ships in a Brooklyn harbor (as in Goldman's).

Faulkner's family motifs of revenge, lineage, inheritance, betrayal and mysterious genealogy become examples for Latino writers exploring their own complicated communal heritages. The problematic question of race explored in his works is increasingly a factor in Latino fiction as the writers confront North American stereotypes and prejudice. One thinks of the Cuban, Dominican and Puerto Rican writers/characters who, immediately upon arrival in the U.S., are categorized by Anglos as blacks and discriminated against accordingly. There is a Faulkner flavor in the story of Vernetta's past (a flashback within Véa's *La Maravilla*) which details the brutal murder of her black boyfriend by the KKK in Arkansas: "the evidence had to be preserved for an investigation that would lead nowhere and an arrest that would never be made" (129). Vernetta (who had she been a boy would have been given the Snopsian name of "Vern") escapes her house by sliding out the window like Caddy Compson. Faulkner began to tell the stories of people of mixed Caribbean heritage as well as those descended from Native Americans (usually the Chickasaw Indians) and writers like Ana Castillo continue that tradition. We see the thematic concerns he raised become the focal points in works by one Latino writer after another: racial and cultural prejudice in Viramontes, Junot Díaz and Pineda; the trials of blue collar folks in Gilb and Sáenz; the politics of cultural barriers in Mohr and Cofer, of sexual taboo and religious friction in Cisneros and Rechy, and of large societal change in Véa and Anaya.

The case can be made that Faulkner's influence upon Latino fiction overshadows that of any other twentieth-century North American novelist, and that García Márquez rivals any other Latin American source of inspiration. But to say this is hardly surprising since the two are directly related and both have had an impact on nearly all fiction of the Americas written over the last 40 to 50 years. Latino writers owe their allegiances to a mixture of their influence and to various others as well. We see for example the obvious debt owed to Julio Cortázar by Ana Castillo in her epistolary novel, *The Mixquiahuala Letters.* Like *Hopscotch,* her novel forces the reader to actively construct his or her own text by choosing the order of the chapters. Manuel Puig's dramatic movie summaries in *Kiss of the Spider Woman* have something in common with the vivid dream sequences in Martínez's *Voice-Haunted Journey* (50), not only in their style and content, but in the way they meander or, to use a phrase Martínez uses throughout his novel, "wend in and out" of the plot. In a larger sense, this is an example of how storytelling, so vital to Faulkner and to Latin American writers impacts Latino fiction and privileges the oral tradition over the written. Where historical records have distorted much of the Latino past, the Latino's unofficial folklore can only be recorded in the voices of storytellers. Faulkner's example of a polyvocal literature that incorporates the folk tale, the exaggerated tall tale, and the spoken legend or myth serves as a reference point from which the Latino writer can document the voices of his or her own cultural past.

Some Latino writers fit neatly within a particular canonical sequence, as is the case with Dagoberto Gilb who sometimes speaks with the cool objective authority of Hemingway. A passage, for example, from "Winners on the Pass Line" echoes the analytical expertise of the Hemingway's narratives on Bullfighting. Here the subject is Craps:

> Ray bet on her pass with certainty and when she had a point he took as many come and odds bets as he could get, and she shot lots of numbers. Sylvia let Ray's pass line money ride and made her point three more times in a row, which multiplied into winnings of four thousand dollars. (*Magic* 221).

To the uninitiated outsider, only the amount of money won in the game makes sense, but, like Hemingway, Gilb obliges the reader to accept the minds of his protagonists on their own terms, unedited and undiluted by narrative judgment. Hemingway's candid prose would serve Raymond Carver as a means of communicating without sentimentality the traumas of working class life, and Carver's subjects, in turn, would pave the way for Gilb's Chicano world in all its domestic and blue-collar vitality. From wars and bullfighting to alcohol and divorce to prejudice and construction work, the three writers form a generational chain of American male writers suggestive of this century's larger literary patterns of development from emphasizing Europe to the U.S. to Ethnic writing, from tough, to sympathetic male voices, from north to south, and from white Anglo-Saxons, to Latinos.

The writings of Rosario Castellanos have certainly had an impact upon Latina writers. Her early novel *Balún-Canán* [*The Nine Guardians*] and her first collection of short stories *Ciudad Real* [*City of Kings*] both concern the plight of Indians and women in the 1930's and 1940's in southern rural Mexico (where tensions still exist today) under the Presidency of Populist Lázaro Cárdenas. Castellanos's "Chiapas Cycle " (which also includes another novel *Oficio de tinieblas* [*Office of Tenebrae*] and another short story collection *Los convidados de agosto* [*The Guests of August*] constitutes her effort to portray the injustices committed against indigenous peoples ("the originals" *Nine Guardians* 180) and the complexities of race, class and gender among people, like herself, of mixed blood. It is this interest, combined with the parallels she saw between the state of women and that of the Indians (Foster 417) that resonates in the works of the Chicana writers Anna Castillo and Sandra Cisneros, among others. Her concern for the folk spirituality of storytelling Indian women becomes a central focus in Latino writing and the relationship between a young girl and her "Nana" in *Nine Guardians,* bears similarities to numerous Latino stories including curanderas and grandmothers. Castellanos was one of the earliest post World War II, Latin American women to openly confront what some critics refer to as "Marianismo" [Marianism] or "the idealization of female values, the Catholic cult of the Virgin Mother Mary" (Castro-Klarén 10-11).[14] Her deconstruction of the ideal Virgin Mother previews how Chicana writers privilege "malinchismo" (from "La Malinche" or woman rebel, woman of power, traitor of men)[15] over institutionalized domestic roles for women. Her indictment of the "domestic orbit" (in her poem "Foreign Woman") is mirrored in the one-dimensional feminist writings of Alma Villanueva. The famous story, "Culinary Lesson," has many descendants, including "Snapshots," by Viramontes, where an older divorced woman, Olga, could be Castellanos's young housewife, years later. Writers like Viramontes follow Castellanos's lead in revealing the restrictions of traditional gender roles and in attempting to give voice to women previously silent. One can at least partially credit Castellanos for what Debra Castillo calls an "official unsilencing" of Latina thought occurring now as more and more Latina works are published (77).[16]

In addition to ideological ties between Latina writers and Castellanos's feminist work (which exist as well with other Mexican writers like Elena Garro and Elena Poniatowska), there is also an influence in craft. Helena Viramontes's technique of what the critic Debra Castillo has called "unheard parallel monologues" owes something to Castellanos as well. In *The Nine Guardians*, various characters speak to themselves in two to three page monologues. The patrón, Cesar, speechifies (190-192), planning strategy (171-174) while his wife Zoraida grouses over her social condition (87-90). Mathilde fades into a romantic daydream (115), and the doomed Ernesto drunkenly rants to his Indian students (153-154) then later fantasizes a meeting with the president (196-199). In each case, no one hears, or understands, what the monologues convey. The speaker/dreamer is usually startled by interruption (someone asks a question, a bullet is fired). These confessional passages (multiple dramatic monologues really) serve to separate the protagonists from each other as each, in his own way, deteriorates toward selfishness and isolation, which in turn, reflects the disintegration of aristocratic classist society in the author's southern Mexico. Viramontes borrows the technique for "Cariboo Cafe" where three individuals tell a story from three very distinct perspectives. As in Faulkner's *As I Lay Dying*, or the novels of Alvarez, the multiple perspectives are never reconciled, and some, like

Vardaman's or Darl's, or Ernesto's, or the Central American woman's, become incoherent lapses of people hovering between rationality and psychosis. Viramontes's "The Long Reconciliation" displays a variation of this split point of view (reminiscent of Joyce's story "Boarding House"). Here the three protagonists: adulterous wife, husband and wealthy Patrón—whose memories and desires are revealed in fragments—bare similarities to Castellanos's families with regard to the outside pressures of Mexican politics and class conflicts, their own inability to communicate with each other, and, perhaps more importantly for Viramontes, the incapacity of some women to survive once forced beyond traditional domestic patterns. With the gossiping women from church condemning her infertility ("so young, so useless"—84), the wife, Amanda, rejects her role as mother, aborts her child and subsequently loses her husband's love. The ironic "reconciliation" takes place only in Chato's mind, 58 years later while he lies dying in a Texas hospital.

It would be a mistake however to see Castellanos, or any other writer as any more influential or important to Pineda's or Viramontes's work than are the American and European writers who influenced Castellanos or most of her Latin American counterparts. The chain of influence goes back as far as Cervantes and Chaucer, as Ed Vega's work makes clear. In his parody of the Puerto Rican autobiographical novel (still the most common narrative genre for mainland Puerto Rican writers), *The Comeback*, Vega employs conversational, explanatory prefaces and remarks in the tradition of *Tom Jones* or *Tristram Shandy*, then summarizes chapters in the manner of Cervantes while his narrator meets face to face with Miguel de Unamuno.[17] The point here is that the links of influence cross cultural boundaries and straddle literary traditions in interesting ways yet to be sufficiently explored.

The interaction of European and Latin American influences upon Latino fiction results in dramatic mixtures of subject and style which then generates a dynamic, hybrid quality in the books. This quality in turn accents what Judith Cofer refers to as "cultural schizophrenia" (*Line* 171). Some Latino writers reveal links of influence through allusions and others through style or content, and while Bejamin Alire Sáenz is surely correct in condemning the judgment of the "indigenous peoples of the Americas by the poetic standards of English culture," the critic's exploration of influence upon Latino work can be rewarding as long as he or she is willing to look both east and south for the connections. It is the mixtures of influence, from Joyce to "The

Chronicles" or from Virginia Woolf to Juan Rulfo that fill Latino fiction with a unique energy and power where opposite cultures are meshed and languages combined, where magic is discovered in the real and celebrated without restraint.

NOTES

1. Eva Margarita Nieto has claimed that influences upon Arias's writing extend back to Don Quixote and the episodic character of the picaresque novel and the novel of chivalry. See "The Dialectics of Textual Interpolation in Ron Arias' *The Road to Tamazunchale*" in Lattin, Vernon E., ed. *Contemporary Chicano Fiction: A Critical Survey.* Binghamton, NY: Bilingual Press / Editorial Bilingüe, 1986.

2. Critical debate over the nature of magic realism has been going on for over 20 years among scholars like Flores and Luis Leal in Latin America and in the US. The debate is perhaps most succinctly summarized and explained in Amaryll Beatrice Chanady's *Magical Realism and the Fantastic: Resolved Versus Unresolved Antinomy.* New York & London: Garland Pub. Co., 1985.

3. Concerning Cabrera's work, see Rosa Valdez-Cruz's article "The Short Stories of Lydia Cabrera: Transpositions or Creations? in *Latin American Women Writers: Yesterday and Today,* Latin American Literary Review Press, Miller and Tatum eds. 1977.

4. Poe's influence (by way of France) throughout Latin American is a subject outside the scope of this study, but the use in Latino fiction of what Todorov calls the "uncanny bordering on the fantastic" has its roots in tales like "The House of Usher" or "The Cask of Amontillado" (Todorov *Fantastic* 47). Poe's influence is felt strongly in the distortion of the fixed lines between life and death. In addition, Latino writers owe a debt to Poe's attention to the importance of sleeping, waking, dreaming, and envisioning, in short, his rejection of objective reality and embracing of ghosts and the supernatural. See Chapter Six.

5. Though at least one critic has questioned the value of the term, magical realist writings have fairly dramatic effects on the reader, many of them substantially political. Emily Hicks has argued that the term "depoliticizes" the Latin American Text (*Border Writing* Intro xxvi). Though some critics may focus upon the magical oddities in a given work, or may rigidly contrast the "magical realism" with the "real," thereby squeezing out the all important borderland between binary opposites—and, in Hicks words, ignoring "important issues such as narrative non-linearity, the decentered dimensional perspective"(xxvii)—the term itself suggests the opposite.

6. Wendy Kolmar cites similar narrative factors where "supernatural elements exist undifferentiated from the "present," "the past," "the natural," where "characters and readers do not confront them as *other,* they are simply part of the experience of life and of the text" ("Dialectics of Connectedness" 238). While she attributes these qualities to women's supernatural fiction, and to women writers' efforts at establishing what Rachel Duplessis called their "double consciousness," it is clear what she is talking about is related more to the tradition of *magical realism* than it is to gender. This is especially true regarding her notion that the storyteller's "use of the supernatural is one essential way in which . . . texts recover the past" (248) as will be clear when García Márquez's works are discussed below.

7. Carlos Fuentes argues as much in *La nueva novela hispanoamericana (The New Hispanic American Novel)* by claiming that one needs linguistic renovation to portray "a new language," "a language of ambiguity, a plurality of meanings" (31).

8. Dorfman's book, published in Chile during the Allende years, offers a fascinating, if one sided, view of the importance of Disney's negative cultural impact upon the people of Chile.

9. See his novel *Condores no entierran todas los dias* (1984).

10. Ron Arias remarked to Juan Bruce-Novoa that the line "transformed, *deepened* reality in so many of its aspects" and instilled in him a "wonder and fascination" (*Chicano Authors: Inquiry by Interview.* Austin & London: University of Texas Press, 1980, p 248)

11. Pineda is not the only Latino writer to parody Vargas-Llosa. Jorge Febles (1992) discusses the comical allusions to Vargas-Llosa's novel *Who Killed Palomino Molero* in Roberto G. Fernández's *Raining Backwards.*

12. Gilb is certainly aware that the somewhat stereotypical view that all Latino fiction displays some aspect of a strong familial bond is a view becoming increasingly unjustified. Writers like Gilb (whose characters frequently come from dysfunctional families or broken homes) or Abraham Rodriguez, Jr. and Luis Alberto Urrea (both of whom depict urban life) should make critics at least question this rather general notion. Rebolledo and Rivera in the introductory chapters of their anthology *Infinite Divisions* emphasize the importance of family to Chicana writers, which is surely true, but family is vital to most writers which makes pointing out general characteristics of Chicana mothers, daughters, sons and fathers (as Rebolledo and Rivera do) more or less irrelevant since the opposite characteristics are equally true somewhere else.

13. See Jose Luis Ramos Escobar's "Desde Yoknapatawpha a Macondo: Un estudio comparado de William Faulkner y García Márquez," and Susan Snell's "William Faulkner, un guía a la ficción de García Márquez." in Ana

María Hernández de López's 1985 collection of critical articles *En el punto de mira: Gabriel García Márquez.* Madrid: Editorial Pliegos. See also Harley D. Oberhelmann's article "William Faulkner and Gabriel García Márquez: Two Nobel Laureates," in McMurray's *Critical Essays on Gabriel García Márquez: New Readings. Cambridge: Cambridge University Press, 1987* and his book *The Presence of William Faulkner in the Writings of García Márquez.* Lubbock: Texas Tech Press, 1980.

14. See also Evelyn Stevens article "Marianismo, the Other Face of Machismo in Latin America" in *Female and Male in Latin America*, ed. Ann Pescatello (Pittsburgh: University of Pittsburgh Press, 1973).

15. See the following chapter for a further discussion of "La Malinche" and her importance to Latino fiction.

16. In *Talking Back*, Castillo perceptively traces the "silent" characters in Viramontes's short story, "Cariboo Cafe" (77-95) in order to show how committed Latina writers narratively explore the worlds of people readers don't usually come in contact with, and it is this type of political, feminist focus that demonstrates the connection between Castellanos and Viramontes.

17. See Nicolás Kanellos's discussion of Vega in Hispanic American Biographies (337-339).

CHAPTER THREE

Latino Voices and "English con Salsa"[1]

As Ashcroft, Griffiths and Tiffin have argued, a prominent concern for post-colonialist critics is how writers manipulate the dominant language of the center metropolis. The "project of post-colonial writing [is] to interrogate European discourse . . . from [a] position within and between two worlds" (196). Because Latino writers thrive in diglossic societies where "bilingualism has become an enduring societal arrangement" (Ashcroft 38), they, like post-colonialists throughout the third world, are involved in a continuous process of abrogating the metropolitan power over the means of communication and appropriating the dominant language in ways that force it to "bear the burden" of their own cultural experience (*Empire* 38). Disruption of linguistic dominance becomes both an expression of literary imagination and a means of questioning and challenging traditional, institutional power. For the Latino writers of this study who write mainly in English, the English language (with its obvious ties to Anglocentric thought, history and culture) is challenged and manipulated as it is forced to carry the cultural essence of Latinos living on the borders and the fringes of U.S. society. The principle resource available for accomplishing this task is the Spanish language, and as a consequence, the essence of Latino fiction can be found in the contact between the two languages.

In order to examine the complex usage of languages in Latino fiction, it will be necessary to look at the Latino writer's attitudes toward both English and Spanish. If, as post-colonialists argue, a distinction is needed between English (referring to the standard language of the center) and englishes (referring to the variants of English used throughout the world) then one is also necessary between Spanish (Castillian) and spanishes (spoken throughout Latin America and the U.S.). The levels of complexity are doubled to begin with, as there are, in essence, two centers from which Latino writers consciously deviate. Just as they modify English in order to create other englishes (the dialects with which Latinos communicate), they alter Spanish for the same reason, and in so doing reveal the cultural limitations of both standardized languages. While any form of Spanish may serve to distort the dominant English, Castillian Spanish may also, like English, convey the same Eurocentric values and prejudices often exposed by Latino works. Standing in the margins, the Latino writer feels a conflicting need to dismantle and critique two dominant languages at the same time since both are saturated with Anglo-European perspectives on life. Disturbing two centers of power at once thus creates a particular sort of energized revolt unique to Latino literature and open to multiple interpretations. For instance, to use a word like "la marketa" is to disturb standard Spanish, the violation being in adapting an English word into a Spanish grammatical system. The closer one gets to the Spanish Academy, the more grievous such an error becomes. In turn, the same word placed in an English structure is equally irregular, the difference depending only upon which set of purists is offended. To the Nuyorican writer, however, the word may connote exactly the sort of cultural hybridity he or she wishes to represent, and neither "market," "mercado," "store," nor "bodega" will function as well. Chicano critic, Bruce-Novoa coined the term "interlingualism" to describe such linguistic interchanges, and their importance to Latino aesthetics must be recognized (*Retrospace* 50).

English is the language of the center in Latino fiction, and generally points to the United States. Because Latino stories and novels most often—though not always—take place within North America, Latinos therefore rely on a variant of Spanish (any one of numerous spanishes) to disturb the dominant linguistic codes of North American English. The title to Coco Fusco's collection of essays, *English is Broken Here*, is more than a description of the linguistic state of affairs in the U.S. The title *celebrates* that state as it describes as well the end result of the Latino artist's intentions to break down Standard English until it adequately conveys Latino culture. This does not mean, however, that these writers accept Castillian Spanish without qualification. The Chicano writer shakes up his English narrative with Mexican Spanish, LA street slang or the mixed dialects of South Texas. The Cuban-American might throw in Cuban Spanish idioms and the Puerto Rican writer may balance between his island Spanish and Nuyorican slang. In fact, Latino writers reject the academy's Spanish in favor of some Latin American form, or even indigenous dialects. The reader detects the tendency to simultaneously veer away from two traditional linguistic codes. Gloria Anzaldúa claims that Pachuco or Caló,[2] for instance, "is the language of rebellion, both against Standard Spanish and Standard English. It is a secret language" (*Borderlands* 56). When Latino writers use the Spanish language, they are no more giving their approval to an authoritative Academy of Spain, than they are endorsing the English Only Movement by writing their books in English. Each Latino writer has a particular attitude toward the Spanish language and all that it carries with it in terms of memories, relationships and experiences, but their affections are most often tied, not to the Spanish of Spain, but to one or more of the varieties of Spanish born in Latin America and the Caribbean. The language of the conquistadors is no more their own than is Standard English.

Essentially, Latino writers are following their British/American modernist precursors in trying to introduce vernacular into their literary work. Eliot recorded British dialects (i.e. the famous bar scene in "The Wasteland"), and Pound sought to blend literary rhetoric with everyday American dialect that he mimicked in phonetic spellings (i.e. "Kulture). Frost attempted to authenticate the colloquialisms of New Englanders by combining "Yankee" speech with measured blank verse. For writers to look outside the academic world toward the folk traditions for material is nothing new. The difference here is that for Latino literature, the vernacular material is often derived from the dialects of two different linguistic codes and forms itself from the mixtures and blendings of both. In this case, the language of the people is a reflection of Spanish and English in confrontation with each other, and the music and rhythms (what Brathwaite called the "very software of language" 311) thereby produced give imaginative writers a material that is new and vital. The creative use of "interlingualism" (or what is more commonly referred to in negative terms as "slang," "spanglish," or "tex-mex") is an integral part of Latino fiction. Rather than lament, like Ilan Stavans, that "Spanish is in a state of degeneration by its daily contact with the English Language" (165), or that English is being dismantled and destroyed by the same process, or that one of the two is more important for success than the other, a more productive view is to see "interlingualism" as a powerful form of communication, a "positively creative innovation in literature" (Aparicio 797). If English and Spanish are "broken here," the literary mosaics that result from the intermingling of both languages can be viewed as something original and dynamic. In Latino fiction, the blending of languages becomes both the source of imaginative, linguistic experiments and the most direct and obvious spectacle of Latino hybridity. Language determines identity. The legitimization of generally considered "inferior" language intrudes upon one's notions of the "truth of language" at the same time it authenticates those peoples (Latinos) who speak such languages in daily life—serves to give them voice, to sanction their self expression, and consequently, their culture. Interlingualism obliges readers to cross linguistic borders and to consider the deficiencies of the particular cultural frameworks through which they view the world. At those points where languages intertwine, the liminality of Latino characters will present itself with a special clarity, just as the novels and stories will open themselves to subtleties of meaning previously unnoticed.

Latino writers nearly always display affection for the Spanish of their Latin American heritage. First of all, it is the language of family and the link to cultural values, to "abuelitas" and "abuelos" [grandparents]. Spanish is the language that communicates precisely the Latino's emotional memory (Cisneros's "Tepeyac"), and the language spoken between mother and infant (Sáenz's "Obliterate the Night"). In a well-known passage of her story "Bien Pretty," Cisneros makes the case that Spanish is the language of passion:

> ¡Ay! To make love in Spanish, in a manner as intricate and devout as la Alhambra. To have a lover sigh mi vidi, mi preciosa, mi chiquitita, and whisper things in that language crooned to babies, that language murmured by grandmothers, those words that smelled like your house, like flour tortilla, and the inside of your daddy's hat, like everyone talking in the kitchen at the same time, or sleeping with the windows open . . . Nothing sounded dirty or hurtful or corny. How could I think of making love in English again? (*Women 153*)

In her novel, Cristina Garcia concurs: Pilar and a Peruvian boyfriend named Rubén "speak in Spanish when [they] make love" because "English seems an impossible language for intimacy" (*Dreaming* 180). Spanish is fluid and easy where English is filled with "starched *r*'s and *g*'s . . . crisp linen syllables. English crunchy as apples, resilient and stiff as sailcloth" ("Bien Pretty" 153). Rosario Morales records the "high rapid fire" of Puerto Rican Spanish with its "softness of dropped syllables and consonants, round and soft and familiar . . . [suggesting] the laughing: high loud laughter out of wide open mouths" (Morales 19), while her daughter notes the "accentless English . . . the sweet cadence of . . . open-voweled words ironed out . . . the edges flattened down, made crisp, the curls and flourishes removed" (24). Junot Díaz writes about "the awful crunch of sounds that was English" (173). Spanish is what bubbles out unconsciously when inhibitions are removed. The Santería preacher of Abella's novel, *The Killing of the Saints*, literally "speaking in tongues," moves from the language of law to sermon:

> Where will it lead us, Your Honor, where will it lead us? I will tell you where it will lead us, to the gates of Hell, Your Honor, to the gates of the infierno, that abre sus puertas y nos espera allí in the darkness amid the gnashing of teeth y el concierto de las almas malditas, allá in the heights, where the empyrean coro de angelitos danza en torno the clouds mientras que un God choleric wreaks his wrath . . . (263)

This tirade stuns the narrator: "I couldn't believe what I was hearing. The non sequiturs in Spanish and English rolled in and out of Ramón's mouth . . . as though some perverse spirit were seizing control of him" (263).

In Latino fiction, Spanish is the language of emotion. English is reserved for the practical, the necessary. Richard Rodriguez, in his famous essays from *Hunger of Memory*, sees Spanish as "private" and English "public," but his rejection of Spanish for this reason is in no way typical of Latino writers. One Hijuelos character in *The Fourteen Sisters of Emilio Montez O'Brien* delivers a lecture to his children concerning the necessity of speaking English in his presence, as Spanish has no "value" to him except as a means of dealing with the children's mother when "she doesn't understand some things in English" (*Fourteen* 82). With this long speech (something uncommon in Hijuelos's writing where dialogues are short and infrequent), the writer may be advancing the Rodriguez side of the argument that Spanish should be kept at home. Yet Nelson O'Brien is not Latino and his attitudes toward Spanish cannot reflect those of his son and fourteen daughters who, one assumes, are the subjects of the novel. Couched as they are in a chapter Hijuelos fills with a nostalgic tone (i.e. "as Scott might have said"(28), "as a crooner might have sung—66), Nelson's opinions can even be judged as the suspect delusions of a solitary man. His spirits "sometimes low" (87), he is perpetually "drinking his medicinal concoctions" (61), and taking "refuge in silence" from the "overwhelming femininity" of his many daughters (89). Bejamin Alire Sáenz's Richard/Ricardo Díaz has purposely forgotten Spanish because it "made him feel like he was all alone and stupid," yet having English as "his only tongue" gets him no closer to what "people said, people thought, people meant" ("Kill the Poor" 73). For the Mambo Kings, Nestor and Cesar, English is necessary, and they study a book called *A Better English Grammar for Foreign Speakers* and learn to say, among other things: "Yes sir, no Sir. Please don't call me Pancho, sir."

Still, "the hard consonants and terse vowels of the English language never fell on their ears like music" (37), never, in short, reached the emotional depth that Spanish could. For the protagonist of Rodriguez's *Spidertown*, his mother's use of English is "always a bad sign. English made her voice sound testy and severe, hinting at an oncoming barrage of churning, scathing Spanish if the answer didn't please her" (205). Affection is restored when he agrees with her demand to speak Spanish: "Yes. I mean si" (207). She considers his use of English as "being contemptuous" of her, and he recognizes her using English as an indication of her anger. The emotion, when it reveals itself, whether anger or affection, does so through Spanish. The central character in *The Ultraviolet Sky* uses Spanish only when she refers to her grandmother's phrase "Los estoy juntando" which Villanueva translates as "I am gathering." The meaning is connected to gathering anger, something "like a threat" (143). In this novel of feminine anger, of a woman's coming to terms with her "wild" side, her inner "wolf" personality (if we borrow the notion from Pinkola Estés's Jungian study), Spanish is related to an emotional depth both vital to the protagonist and perhaps inaccessible through English.

As with most aspects of Latino fiction, attitudes toward Spanish are complex. Latina writers, for example, often connect Spanish with an authoritative male voice. In a story by Helena Viramontes, a father, Apá [Papa], pounding the table, warns his "disrespectful" daughter that if she didn't go to Mass every Sunday, she "had no reason to go out of the house, period. Punto final" ("The Moths" 25). The same father figure shows up in the following story with similar authority: "TU

ERES MUJER, he thundered like a great voice from the heavens, and that was the end of any argument, any question, because he said those words not as truth, but as a verdict" ("Growing" 32). An intolerant husband in "The Broken Web" lapses into Spanish cursing as his anger overcomes him: "You tramp. You righteous bitch. Don't I have the right to be unfaithful? Weren't you? Vete mucho a chingar a tu madre, más cabrona que la chingada . . . " (55).[3] For Viramontes, Spanish is often associated with the voice of Mexican/Chicano machismo and working class, dominating, male figures. Such a character, a man under stress, struggling to cope with daily hardships and the prejudice that surrounds him (like the "hard" father in "The Jumping Bean"), a man in fear of losing control—presents a character type who reacts aggressively against his family's insubordination and stands in the way of women's creativity, independence and voice. "Her father could no longer trust her, because she was a woman" thinks Naomi in "Growing" (38) while the colonized wife of "The Broken Web is "tired and wrinkled and torn by him [her husband Tomás], his God, and his word . . . He owned her, her children owned her, and she needed them all to live" (56). It would be a mistake to claim that only Latina writers focus upon this negative side to Spanish as is clear when one considers the character of Hector Santinio in Hijuelos's first novel, *Our House in the Last World.* Hector rejects the "enemy" Spanish of his authoritative, abusive father to such an extent that in the hospital he becomes "deaf" (103). While Chicana writers are critical of Spanish as conveyor of Mexican machismo, many Latino writers take exception to that aristocratic brand of Spanish with ties to Castillian snobbery and conquistador traditions. Arturo Islas, Ana Castillo and Alfredo Véa confront directly the prejudices of those, especially the Hispanos of New Mexico, who claim superiority over all of mixed Indian/Mexican/Spanish blood. Islas's Mama Chona and her family (i.e. Angels) consider themselves "better than the illiterate riffraff from across the river" (15), and refuse "to associate . . . with anything Mexican or Indian because it was somehow impure" (27). This sort of racism becomes overt in Celia's offensive mother-in-law in *Dreaming in Cuban* who leaves cream on her face overnight in order "to remove any evidence of her mulatto blood" (41). Véa's Josephina from *La Maravilla* often laments the loss of her "most marvelous educated Spanish." To her way of thinking, this "perfect Spanish, a gentleman's Spanish," this "Español de Granada, de Sevillc" hardly compares with the "Mexicano Spanish or Español de Nueva Mexico or that pocho stuff from over in California" (147). Yet, she will eventually come to understand the good in her Yaqui husband's ways, to appreciate what Véa calls "the fugue of . . . mixed bloods" (286). Usually, Latino writers see the valuing of their mestizaje heritages as essential. To glorify the European roots at the expense of the Indian and Mexican cultural ties is counter-productive since it negates the living reality of Latino hybridity that feeds their creative imaginations. Aurora Morales condemns the racism that lies beneath such linguistic snobbishness in *Getting Home Alive:*

> I'd say 'Puerto Rico' and watch the oh-oh sort of look creep up over their faces before they tightened up their *how nice* look . . . They get a kind of flat look in their eyes, not the interested, excited look they'd get if I said 'Spain' or 'Argentina' or something else exotic and faraway and not associated in their ratty little minds with cockroaches or welfare or knives (173).

A character in Ed Vega's story "An Apology to the Moon Furies" justifies Puerto Rican Spanish this way:

> although the language was Spanish, it was ciphered and sifted through the common experience of harried people to protect them from outsiders; the language twisting and turning uncomfortably, the words five, six, seven times removed from their original meaning so that when they were spoken, one could tell immediately whether the person was friend or foe . . . (*Casualty Report* 88)

To Ed Vega, the deviations of Puerto Rican Spanish (from Castillian Spanish) are the result of political circumstances, and the coded language spoken by Nuyoricans serves that marginalized community. Nuyorican writers recognize the validity and power of a language otherwise considered substandard and reflective of uneducated minds. Vega confronts the purists who argue that the Spanish spoken by Puerto Ricans has been destroyed by its contact with English. Yet, since Puerto Rican Spanish stands at the opposite end of the Spanish language continuum from Castillian, and closer to the Latino's English, it offers the Nuyorican writer a wealth of linguistic possibilities in terms of "creating signifiers . . . derived from linguistic 'deviations'" (Aparicio 798). Chicano Spanish is in a similar position: frowned upon by purist Mexicans, it is nevertheless celebrated by

Chicano writers for its deviations and peculiarities. This is why writers like Castillo privilege the vernacular of their characters, highlighting the indigenous over the European, emphasizing the interlingual blendings of their speech. Nuyoricans do the same thing, in an effort to legitimize their hybrid language. For example, we find characters in Castillo's *So Far From God* referring to each other continuously as "parna" meaning partner, while in Rodriguez's *Spidertown* they call each other "pana."[4] Here, Puerto Rican and Chicano are connected across cultural borders by an interlingual word derived from English (partner) but molded into a Spanish form. Such language is an example of how two separate Latino groups have twisted standard English and Spanish in similar ways in order to communicate their own sense of community and fellowship.

Conversational fillers or verbal pauses—the equivalents of North American English's "ya know," "it's like," "I mean," or "like"—crop up within informal Latino dialogues as "ese" (Chicano), "pues," "mi hermano," "bueno" (Latin American), "coño," "chico," "que va," "tu sabe" (Cuban). These interjections may be tangential to official Castillian Spanish but they are integral to Latino identity and sense of community, as much so as any other element of culture like dance, music or food. Furthermore, the argument Luis Leal makes about food can be made about words: some of these expressions are untranslatable since they have no Spanish or English equivalents; they are terms from the spaces between the languages, distinctly associated with Latinos and often have no English or Spanish equivalents (*Three American Literatures* 16). Neither Castillian Spanish nor English can sufficiently cover what Latinos wish to express. Rodriguez's Miguel hears "stiff, formal Spanish" as something "alien, barely used" (*Spidertown* 124-125). In Véa's novel, the mystical connection between Manuel, the elder Yaqui Shaman, and the Arizona desert lies outside either language. "Spanish can't say this," he declares to the initiate Beto who gathers the meaning from a musical interweaving of Yaqui simultaneously translated into English and into Spanish: "The three languages interleaved and beat frequencies; only the summed, third upper harmonic excited a vestigial bandpass in the boy's mind" (216).

Loyalties to one or the other of Spanish or English often reveal emotional relationships between members of different generations. The younger generation Latino may explicitly ridicule his or her parents' ties to a lost past. In a scene, for example, in Virgil Suárez's short story "Full House," a young boy named Danny serves dinner to his father and his father's Cuban friends during a poker game. One man, Coco, calls Danny "ratón" which the omniscient narrator translates immediately: "Ratón means mouse." Interestingly, Danny responds by saying "The only rat here's you," and in so doing makes his linguistic affiliation clear; he has understood the word as an English speaker would, as referring to a rat, not a mouse. From this particularly dialogic use of language, the story will proceed to outline in a much less subtle manner to what extent the younger boy longs to imitate his rebellious older brother Rudy and to reject his father's world of gambling and cigars. The father "can't play like he used to" (*Welcome* 84) and so now enlists his daughter's help in cheating at cards. The linguistic disconnection in the beginning of the story hints at the young man's loyalties outside the family (to English rather than Spanish), beyond the smoky, Cuban atmosphere of the room upstairs where the men play cards and the women abide by chauvinistic rules. Early in Arturo Islas's *The Rain God*, the young Miguel Chico misunderstands Mama Chona's reference to the cemetery. "Campo Santo," she calls it, meaning "Field of Saints," but the boy understands a "place where Saints go camping" (9). As in the Suárez story, the miscommunication because of the false cognate presents the reader with a character bound to be, as Miguel and Danny are, somewhat disengaged from the monolingual, familial sphere. The language here communicates their liminal status, which will become the center of focus as the stories progress.

In Viramontes's story "Neighbors," a poor old man named Macario Fierro de Ortega is visited by the ghost of his dead son. The young boy first appears during Fierro's morning shaving ritual in a scene accented by the father's use of Spanish which solidifies the warmth between father and son. When the age of the boy ghost changes to that of a nineteen year old street tough, so does the form of communication, shifting into a mixture of Spanish and English as the father rejects the son's idiomatic usage of the English phrase "lay off." Finally, in Fierro's memory of their last encounter, on the day the son will be murdered, the language between them has changed into slang vocabulary ("Chavoalos", "tecatos"), and ultimately become pure Caló: "Ay, te watcho, Jefito" says the boy, the distance of his language from Fierro's Spanish paralleling the distance he has gotten from his father. A similar situation arises in Hijuelos's *The Fourteen Sisters of Emilio Montez O'Brien* when Emilio is emotionally separated from his mother because he cannot fully understand her Spanish and she can't express her love for him in English (248-249). Eventually, she will watch him performing on stage and think of him, the actor, as an "absolute American," at which point she will regret her inability to really know her son (297).

We see again the importance of loyalty to a language in Véa's *La Maravilla.* Beto's wayward mother angrily rejects her parents' poverty in favor of the American dream of "sliding aluminum windows with real glass" and toilets and a refrigerator: "You are sickening people. Sickening, old superstitious people. You still live on mud and you shit down holes in the ground and you're telling me how to live my life! I got out of this place . . . " When she switches to English for the benefit of her companion ("unhappy about this time wasted in a foreign language"), her mother, Josephina, is genuinely hurt:

> "Not English," Josephina cried, "not between la familia."
> "It's English from now on," Lola said, turning on her heel and heading for the car. "Get used to it."

Despite the vehemence of her daughter's earlier insults, it is the switch away from the language of "la familia" that constitutes the real betrayal in the mind of the mother: "'Malinche, Malinche,' she sobbed, invoking the name of the traitorous Indian woman who betrayed the entire Aztec nation for the love of Hernán Cortés—the only word strong enough to express the faithlessness of a daughter" (22). As a sort of final insult against her mother, toward the end of the novel, Lola will return to collect her son, accompanied now by a man named Jose Pescado who plans on changing his name to the ludicrous English equivalent, Joe Fish. This is a man who admires the fact that "not one American soldier in the Philippines had ever pronounced his name right or even tried to" (274). It will be left to Beto/Alberto to hear the "soft whispers in Spanish and every Indian language" (278). Beneath the tension here over language exists a series of rifts between parent and child across a wide range of cultural oppositions: family/independence, rural/urban, poverty/material wealth, mysticism/rational practicality, old ways/the new. In short, this conflict over language is simply the overt manifestation of a deeper generational division over how one lives one's life.

In Hijuelos's *House*, Mercedes Santinio is a woman emotionally and intellectually controlled by her Cuban past. English phrases are "painful" for her to learn" (48), and she reads English as "if some words hurt her" (127), yet because of her distorted nostalgia for a lost paradise with her abusive father, Spanish as well is contaminated for her second son, Hector. It is "the language of memory, of violence and sadness. ¡Callate! ¡Callate! ¡No me toques! Mi papá se murió. Yo sufro mucho!" [Shut up! Shut up! Don't touch me! My papa died. I suffer a lot!]. The Spanish he learns comes from his mother's memories of Cuba, and is tainted by her painful childhood experiences. The English he gets from her haphazard and unselective classes is equally limited. English enters him: "from the street, from opened windows, from stores. Fuck you, suck my cock! Good morning! Be quiet down there! How many? English words were long lists of medicines and snippets of books that added up to confusion" (128). Hector becomes deaf, enters a "twilight zone" (190) in part, because of his inability to cope with linguistic schizophrenia. He comes to believe Spanish is "an enemy;" it reminds him of his drunken father (103). Like Pilar Puente who is eventually betrayed by her Spanish speaking lover Rubén, he finds himself in a linguistic limbo common to Latino protagonists.

Retreating from the language of the dominant culture, in this case English, may signal a type of defense mechanism. Hector's mother, for example ("the greatest invalid of all time" 208), withdraws "into her silence" (213) becoming one more in a series of what Cristina Garcia labels the "untransplantable" Cubans. Rechy's Amalia is another example of a victimized Latina, culture shocked into silence. She rejects English. She hates to be called "mom" which makes her feel "fat and vulgar and ugly" (68, 92) whereas "Amá" and "Amita" are linked emotionally to her first son, Manny (37). She despises the gringo pronunciation of Ellay [for L.A.] (4) and the "mocking Anglicized inflection" the boy Lalo gives her son's name: "Were they after John-nee?" (111). She resents her daughter's English cursing and her slang words (92). Her children switch to English when they are mad, she notices, which provokes her increased dislike of the language, just as it signals their linguistic (and cultural) loyalty to peers over family. Yet we discover that what Amalia hates isn't English, but the way this language is used by others to control and dominate her; she hates people defining her which is why she resents Mick's drawling pronunciation of her name: "Am-al-lee-ah" (96). She rebels against the teacher who chides her for pronouncing "sh-sh-sh" and not "ch-ch-ch" (18), ultimately pretending she isn't capable of understanding the difference rather than acquiescing to the teacher's instructions.

The power of language to influence memory is related to linguist's notions of "scripting" where a word or phrase holds a string of information: an event, the context of the event, even the emotional impact of the event.[5] As we saw earlier, while "la bodega" connotes one set of representational information to a Puerto Rican on the island, and where "market" suggests a different script of data to a native New Yorker (or a native Vermonter), the word "la marketa" carries a distinctly separate chain of connotations and emotional meanings that may or may not have anything to do with either "bodega" or "market." Those characters equipped to express themselves through interlingualism, like their creators, define themselves on their own terms. Latinos "struggle for language" (Rebolledo 157), searching, as the mainland Puerto Rican poet Luz María Umpierre puts it, to express themselves "in any voice, / in any tone, in any language that conveys / [their] house within" ("Mishaps").

To explore further the dynamics of the Latino writer's hybrid language, it seems sensible to examine how translations (or the lack there of) influence specific Latino stories or novels. We can focus upon the translation of Spanish since our texts are written in English. It is usually argued that to translate, to begin with, is equivalent to being a traitor,[6] so the writer's methods of translation will frequently point to his or her attitudes and purposes within a text. Untranslated Spanish within Latino fiction instills the English text with the patterns of sounds of Spanish words and the musical rhythms of Spanish syntax. Of equal importance, Spanish transmits elements of Latin American culture tied to it which makes its allusive quality noteworthy.

Bilingual European literature is nothing new. From Tolstoy to Thomas Mann, there are thousands of examples of works that when translated into English contain long passages of a third language, often French. The western European reader is expected to understand French, because, as Anzaldúa sarcastically remarks, it is more "cultured" than Spanish (*Borderlands* 59). One can appreciate then, the importance of Hemingway's treatment of Spanish for Latino writers since he is one of only a few writers of English who compel the reader to adapt a Spanish mode of comprehension. Some part of the Latino writer's agenda is certainly, however unobtrusively, to demand equal respect for Spanish. Latinos are well aware of how the Spanish language is growing increasingly influential, especially in the U.S., and they are directly combating hundreds of years of French influence upon the English language. As "Americans," Latino writers are absorbed in the task of reversing linguistic stereotypes and prejudices that date back to the Norman Invasion. Further, as Gonzalez-Berry, mentions, the use of

Spanish has been, since Colonial times, a way "to affirm cultural identity" and the "Spanish word [is] an amulet against imminent displacement" (*Pasó por Aquí* Intro 5). To put it in post-colonialist terms, Spanish therefore becomes an alternative to English and the "discourses of domination." This is particularly true for Latino populations who recall, as many Chicanos do, the enforcement of rules forbidding the use of Spanish in public schools. It is equally important for Puerto Rican Americans whose families have endured the imposition of English on the Spanish island since the "invasion" of 1898. In fact, Teddy Roosevelt's educational system "demanded that Puerto Ricans teach in a foreign language [English] to students who did not understand the English their teachers could not speak" (Fernandez *Prisoners* 28). Most Latinos share this sense of violation as they battle what Roberto Fernandez calls, the "tongue brigade," a satirical label for the forces demanding "English Only."

William Carlos Williams, an especially important poet for Latino writers,[7] said: "It isn't what [a poet] *says* that counts as a work of art, it's what he makes, with such intensity of perception that it lives with an intrinsic movement of its own to verify its authenticity" (*Essays* 257). In Latino literature, some of that intensity is necessarily lost if Spanish vocabulary is merely translated into English with a superfluous repetition. This is what Earl Shorris rightly objects to in his book *Latinos*, labeling the effect "comic redundancy" (389). Judith Cofer, for example, writes the following: "Someone had said huelga, a strike. They were planning a strike" (*Line* 226), and "Asi es la Vida, hijas: that's the way life is" ("Nada" 58). Alex Abella's second novel *The Great American* begins with a barrage of redundant translations suggesting from the onset that he is willing to conform to an English audience (he even italicizes the Spanish to signal its foreignness) and is less concerned with validating Spanish or "educating" his monolingual readers. His prose, as a result, is often clumsy and distracting:

> Out of the darkness a short man with a spotlight approached Morgan and Laura.
>
> "La luz?"—the light?—he asked.
>
> "La escalera," answered Laura. The stairs.
>
> "Síganme." Follow me . . .
>
> "Por mi Cuba, todo" –everything for my Cuba—he said, and he spun on his heels and trucked upstairs (112)

It is interesting that Shorris chooses to belittle the work of Sandra Cisneros (calling *Mango* a "retreat from the sophistication of [Tomás] Rivera"—*Latinos* 389) when she, perhaps more so than most contemporary Latino writers, displays an aptitude for variety and flexibility of translation techniques. Hugh Kenner quotes Pound's advice for translators: "Don't translate what I wrote, translate what I meant to write" or "Don't bother about the WORDS, translate the MEANING" (Kenner 150). Cisneros seems to have inherited Pound's attitude toward translating, that is, a belief that the sense and the sounds of languages creatively manipulated yields greater meaning than literal substitutions or what Kenner calls "lexicographic lockstep" (554). Take for example, a Spanish word often employed in Latino works: "Sinvergüenza." Owing something to Eliot or Pound, Cisneros blends the translation into her sentence in such a way that a unique rhythm is established that depends upon the use of both languages for sound, yet clarifies the meaning of the word to the English audience at the same time: "That is when she burned the cucumber pushcart and called me a sinvergüenza because I *am* without shame" ("One Holy Night" *Women* 32). Other writers need this word, but almost always rely upon the direct, redundant method of clarification for the monolingual English reader. Castillo leaves it alone: "Ayy, And how that sinvergüenzo could dance" (*So Far From God* 105). Arturo Islas merely explains it: "The word is untranslatable; literally, it means 'without shame' and can be used as a noun" (*Rain God* 57). Even Véa's attempt: "You are shameless! Sin Vergüenza" (21) fails to avoid a repetitious quality though his choice of word order prioritizes the Spanish, and initiates the reader into Spanish rather than reducing the Spanish to translation (148). Here, as is true elsewhere in the novel, the order of the languages mirrors Beto's grandmother's mental progression, following her mind as it glides toward her Spanish memory.

Oddly enough, Shorris speaks glowingly of Hijuelos's work when Hijuelos is often guilty of the awkward, redundant translation: "Abuela, abuelo, estoy muy contento de haber venido aquí, Grandmother, Grandfather, I am very happy to have come . . . Yo te quiero mucho, I love you very much" (*Fourteen* 214). This is writing that no longer requires reader participation in a bicultural atmosphere. Compare, for instance, the seamless contextual translation in Goldman's *Ordinary Seaman*:

> "She told me she has a novio," [Esteban, the protagonist] finally says.
>
> "Who? That little lawyer? Don't worry about him . . . You know what everybody says, Amor de lejos, amor de pendejos."
>
> The worlds most famous love slogan. Even La Marta teased him with it, when he had to go back into the war. And he'd answered, But I'm not going to be that far away . . . " (269).

What Shorris also fails to notice is that the repetition translation can be used creatively as Véa shows in the opening section of his novel. The ghost narrator ends her introduction to the book with a haunting repetition of the line "Hay gente en esta página conmigo. There are people with me on this page" (3). The writer inverts the final word order: "in this page with me, with me on this page" thereby creating a lyrical and haunting, incantatory effect essential to the timelessness of the story to come.

The embedded translation flows naturally where the added repetition in English merely absorbs the Spanish into the English in such a way that negates its power, and subsumes the emotional quality its sound brings to a reader. Adding a translation in English makes the Spanish superfluous, a mere cosmetic extra. In "Remember the Alamo," Cisneros inserts the Spanish but disguises the translation: "That's how it is. Say it. Te quiero. Say you want me. You want me" (*Women* 66). Though the other levels of meaning of the verb querer (to want, to love, to like) are ignored here, the sense of the Spanish word is carried in the syntax, emphasis and repetition and still the language authentically fits the mind of the speaker. In another example, she combines the Spanish numbers with a childhood memory of a staircase in the much-anthologized story, "Tepeyac." In this context, Spanish runs deeper in the child than English does, and connects, like a scent, directly to her emotional memory of her "abuelito" [grandfather]. The counting in Spanish juxtaposes two languages, two worlds and forces the reader to share the power of the Spanish one, to contemplate the narrator's past as fundamentally linked with the legend of the virgin of Guadalupe. The narrator's climbing the stairs parallels the worshipers climbing the hill of Tepeyac where Juan Diego saw the Virgin. The remembered images are tied together in this chain of Spanish numbers which because they continue even after the "twenty-two" steps up to veintisiete (27) suggest the years of the narrator's life and the distance of time. In the same way the story's long opening sentence is a series of images linked by prepositional phrases. The list, like the string of numbers, pulls the reader into the story, the past, and the Mexican flavor of the narrator's memory.

Because Spanish cuts deeper than English, Latino writers let this language set off Bakhtin's "sparks of carnival bonfire" by which he means the language of laughter and bodily pleasure, the unofficial speech of the marketplace and unrestricted freedom of expression (*Rabelais* 17). A look at Latino billingsgate should clearly demonstrate this. Rarely do Latino writers feel obliged to translate profanity. Rather, they exhibit a certain degree of pleasure in the sounds of the words, intentionally allowing their musicality and connotations to reverberate in the minds of bilingual/bicultural readers. Even in earlier fiction, like Anaya's *Bless me, Ultima*, expressions like "this jodido Tenorio" (125) or "chinga tu madre" (124) go unexplained. Similarly, we find expressions of Puerto Rican street slang laced throughout *Spidertown* which are all but indecipherable to the uninitiated: "What a fucken pato" 103) "coño meng"(161) "quemando telo, brodel" (106), or "enough attitude to pull fly chavas" (175). Hijuelos facetiously defines the untranslatable "pendejo" as "ball-busting predatory louse" (*Mango* 38)—a rendering which simultaneously demonstrates the inadequacy and uselessness of translating (the word may or may not have anything to do with this English equivalent), and at the same time pinpoints the writer's delight in the original. Character after character (with their respective creators chuckling in the background) relishes the sound of every syllable of the word "pendejo," or the exclamation, "Coño," a word that exudes a special humor lost in translation. This is why Pilar Puente envies her mother's Spanish curses which make her own English "collapse in a heap" (*Dreaming* 59). The Spanish curse is a frank and free dismissal of official English and the hierarchies associated with it, and it is particularly powerful among Latino characters and writers because it lies outside the mainstream. Cursing together is a form of camaraderie. Even when the actual words aren't used, a writer like Cofer attempts to communicate the flavor of the Spanish curse: "I'm going to kill that son of a great bitch" (60). In the vernaculars of Rechy's LA gang members, Castillo's New Mexican mestizas, Hijuelos's Miami Cuban reactionaries, or Rodriguez's Spanish Harlem drug dealers, one finds a combination of Spanish swearing and epithetical phrases among friends, compadres, and commadres.

The inability to translate effectively may be partly responsible for a writer's maintaining the original Spanish within a work of fiction written primarily in English. Yet more is involved as writers draw from two reservoirs of language. Estella Portillo-Trambley's simply inserts Spanish vocabulary into her novel *Trini,* most often in the form of nouns. Portillo-Trambley's authenticating of Spanish names within an English text is a form of rebellion, however mild, and constitutes a sort of renaming of the world. She gives validity to an outsider's perceptions. Rebolledo and Rivero see this as a narrative strategy of resistance which names the Latina's identity "by detailing the cultural signs embedded in it" (*Infinite Divisions* 17). Ana Castillo frequently neglects to translate Spanish words, in essence, demanding that the reader make the adjustment to a bilingual text. When she speaks of "the favorite chisme" (*So Far From God* 40), her purpose is more than to harass the monolingual reader. The English word "gossip" simply doesn't fit. To begin with, "chisme" refers to the "piece of gossip" and not the person, and carries less of the English word's heavily judgmental (and one could argue, sexist) connotations. Further, the perfectly acceptable practice of talking about others has a greater significance within an orally defined, in this case fairly poor, mostly rural Indian/Latino culture. To cite another example, Castillo makes a conscious decision to describe the "red *ristras* . . . hung on the *vigas* of the *portales* . . . "(170) instead of reworking such a description into a cumbersome sentence about the red strings (of garlic for example), hung on the rafters or beams of the entrance. She is talking about chilis (using the Spanish spelling), and the chili-roasting month in a New Mexican town, and she feels there is no more need to transform (and betray) the original language than there is to translate the word "chile." The assumption being that the reader will simply adjust as he or she is expected to have already adjusted and adapted to "chile," a word whose extensive meanings and connotations fill cookbooks throughout the world. Furthermore, when she states that these "ristras" are hung in the doorways in order to "welcome visitors and ward off enemies," Castillo is partially legitimizing the seemingly superstitious idea held by the townsfolk, an idea that could have sounded somewhat ludicrous in an English translation. The exotic nature of the language serves to tolerate the belief, while the picture created, once understood accurately, portrays a scene outside official U.S. existence.

Untranslated Spanish words within English sentences may also point to the writer's desire to reflect the Latino's linguistic practices of either "borrowing" or "code-switching." According to Rosaura Sánchez, "borrowing" between languages occurs when the vocabulary is transformed to abide by the phonological or morphological rules of the new language. Anzaldúa describes anglicisms used in Tex-Mex speech like "bola from ball, carpeta from carpet, máchina de lavar (instead of lavadora) from washing machine." Borrowing accounts for the Tex-Mex "created by adding a Spanish sound at . . . the end of an English word such as cookiar for cook, watchar for watch, parkiar for park . . . " (*Borderlands* 57). Codeswitching refers to the incorporation of a new word which brings along its grammatical system. Take for example a piece of dialogue between Fausto and his daughter from the first chapter of Arias's *Road*:

> 'You scared me. You weren't asleep, were you?'
> 'No, mijita. I thought I was dead.' Fausto sat up. 'It happens, you know. From one day to the next, poof! Al otro mundo.'
> Well, you come down and eat in this mundo." (20)

Fausto's use of the endearment "mijita" [my little daughter] and the phrase "al otro mundo" [to the other world] and Carmela's sarcastic response are cases of code-switching because the Spanish is incorporated into the English grammatical system and the "two systems are maintained as distinct entities but juxtaposed within the same discourse" (Sánchez 140). In a looser definition, Celia Genishi defines code-switching as "the alteration of languages or dialects to convey social meaning" (133). Regarding the example from Arias, the meanings have to do with generational differences between father and daughter, affection between them ("mijita" and the kindly tolerance of Carmela's sarcasm) as well as each character's state of mind concerning practical versus spiritual realities. Carmela, in fact, seems to undercut her father's emotional drama by forcing the practicality of English upon him.[8]

Later in the novel, Mario, the young Chicano who guides Fausto through his strange journey, says good-bye to the older man with the following remark: "Take care, man, allí te watcho, and if you ever want to get together . . . " (32). While the Spanish phrase is plugged into the English sentence intact, the English word "watch" is transformed into the Spanish grammatical system, becoming in this instance, a Spanish verb and subject to standard verb conjugation. This, then, is an example of borrowing within an example of code-switching. It may be that such distinctions are not always necessary for the purposes of this study, yet it is clear that the mixings and complications resulting from these practices are of vital importance in reaching a sophisticated understanding of linguistic subtleties at work in Latino fiction. Code switching is related to the dynamics of the speech event, as Rosaura Sánchez argues throughout her study *Chicano Discourse*. It is a product of intersecting variables involved in the language situation. The person addressed (the addressee) or the function of the language often determines whether a speaker will change codes. According to Sánchez, for example, talking to peers (as opposed to parents) or the speaker's desire to boast will "trigger the shift" (143). The shifting itself may serve as an "identity marker of membership" to certain bilingual communities which accounts for its prevalence among youthful urban characters in works by Rechy, Rodriguez or Arias (Zentella 130). The speech of an older man in *The Miraculous Day of Amalia Gomez*, littered with code-switches, demonstrates his emotional ties to the gang society of his past:

> She [Amalia] came home from work to hear an old man who lived nearby bragging to a cluster of boys, children, that in his day '*las gangas*' had real '*huevos*'—balls, real courage. '*We* used to *face* the other *vatos*, bring them down with *chingazos*.' His wrinkled face brightened at the memory of the blows he had inflicted . . . 'Nowadays the *vatos* drive by in their cars, shoot, run away, get their courage from *drogas*, not *huevos*' . . . His voice gained authority. 'And we *dressed*, *manos*—pegged pants, classy hats, pocket chains.' He shook his palm, low, from the wrist, a wordless gang expression of grandness. '*Everyone* knew who we were . . . When we were real *chingones*, the toughest' (72).

Recognizing the advantage of taking into account the environment encompassing pieces of dialogue, because, as Zentella mentions, the "linguistic function and social meaning of code-switching vary in each bilingual speech community" (109), the reader must analyze fictional instances of code-switching with a broad understanding of factors surrounding any specific utterance. As Bakhtin argues for the study of all speech acts, one cannot separate language from audience (the influence of the addressee) or context (*Speech Genres* 93-100). It should follow then, that focusing attention upon the "genre" of code-switching would reveal some deeper aspect of Latino fictional dialogue.

The fact that linguists have noted that code-switching often occurs when there is "a shift in the mode of discourse;" that is, it is brought on by emotion, by the need for "expressive speech . . . emphatic speech . . . [or] elaboration in speech" (Huerta-Macias 153) should be helpful to the critic interested in the psychology of a novel's characters. Knowledge of the reasons for code-switches should eventually lead to writers avoiding didactic (and cumbersome) explanations such as the following from Hijuelos: "'Are you all right?' Isabel asked her. '¿Todo esta bien?' repeating the question in Spanish, the language she used when wanting to be more emphatic, or affectionate" (*Fourteen* 23).

Code switching plays a major part in the work of Sandra Cisneros. Take, for instance, a line from her story, "Bien Pretty:" "If you don't like it Lárgate, honey" (161). Her inclusion of the untranslated Spanish provides the emotional power of the advice rendered, the streetwise experience coming exclusively from the Spanish word. In Rechy's *Miraculous Day*, Amalia's gut reaction to a visit from her adulterous husband's girlfriend is forcibly revealed via the same Spanish expression: "Lárgate" (35), an order of vehemence and scorn along of the lines of "Get out of here," but charged with a testiness English can't duplicate except in vulgarity. Cisneros's expression also automatically reveals the relationship between the speaker and her audience; the narrator addressing a peer in a familiar style. The writer uses the shift as one further indication of her narrator's frank, yet informal advice to an audience of women who might share her problems and desires. Embedded in a paragraph condemning the senseless heroines of telenovelas, and exalting the women she has "known everywhere *except* on TV, in books and magazines" [emphasis mine], the Spanish here emphasizes that such women are not media created beauties, but Latinas: "Las girlfreinds. Las comadres. Our mamas and tías . . . Passionate *and* powerful, tender and volatile, brave. And, above all, fierce." The theme of the paragraph, signaled by the code-switching, points us back to the title of the story where the rather flimsy and superficial English word "pretty" is enclosed in a Spanish grammatical structure and the English connotations of the word are redirected into an assertion that Latinas outrank the media created, stereotypical versions of attractive women. This persona, common in Cisneros's work, has no problem with being a Latina and in fact relishes the vitality of her dual linguistic ability. We see this in her unsympathetic attitude toward the monolingual reader's handicaps, when Cisneros even teases the reader, making it clear that the lack of Spanish is a limitation: "Pretty in Spanish. But you'll have to take my word for it. In English it just sounds goofy" (161). Like the word "pretty," here the choice of "goofy" (Disney connotations included) trivializes English, while Spanish throughout the story—the lists of songs, of herbs, of dances, of instruments—conveys what is vital and genuine to the writer.

There are times, for reasons of verisimilitude, when the use of Spanish creates a problem of plausibility for the reader. Why, for example, should the long dinner conversations of the Mambo Kings and their Cuban relatives be in English in the first place? If the Latino writer is compelled to enlighten his English readers, why limit the amount of Spanish at the expense of compromising the authenticity of character dialogue. This is the case in several novels with settings in Latin American countries. For Pineda's fiction, the infrequency of dialogue minimizes the problem, but for Goldman's two novels the reader is always aware of an incongruity among characters. Though he often throws in untranslated Spanish vocabulary to alert the reader to the sounds and flavors of the conversation that *should* be happening, the narrative mechanism only partially suffices. Too often, the tensions between his Central American personalities that should come through dialogue in Spanish are lost in translation.

Also frustrating to the reader accustomed to the subtlety of modernistic prose is an author's didactic attempt to explain the power of particular vocabulary. Alfredo Véa sometimes intrudes upon the characters of *La Maravilla* at times to discuss what "La Chingada" means to Mexicans: " a gashing, pricking word . . . there is no equivalent English word" (43), or to outline the differences between English and Spanish and the Yaqui idiom. Rather than dramatize the conflict of thought such linguistic variety and confusion causes the old man Manuel, Véa chooses to subject the reader to a page or two of instruction which concludes with the interesting, but, I'd argue, misplaced notion that English is the language "that blazed the path to modern loneliness" (32). Fraxedas's novel, *The Lonely Crossing of Juan Cabrera* epitomizes the condescending quality of repetitive translations and didactic explanations. To his needless translations: "Mi padre, my father" (163), "*Vamos*, Let's go" (9), "the *vergüenza,* the shame" (27), or *¡Aquí! ¡Aquí!* Here! Here! (*21*), Fraxedas adds sentences like the following: "We beat the *contra-corriente* . . . The *contra-corriente* is what Cubans call the currents that spin off the Gulf-

Stream, like eddies, and sometimes push you back toward the coast" (17).

Unless an explanation includes some additional information, explaining the meaning of Spanish words is as obtrusive and counterproductive as simply adding a translation. This is true because to do so is to sacrifice the idea that interlingualism is legitimate. Bruce-Novoa has argued that the "interlingual form of expression is the true native language of Chicano communities" and this could be said to be valid for Latinos in general. Interlingualism requires that a writer reject "the supposed need to maintain English and Spanish separate in exclusive codes, but rather [view] them as reservoirs of primary material to be molded together as needed, naturally" (*Retrospace* 50). The editors of the well-known anthology *Cuentos: Stories by Latinas* advocate validating hybrid forms of language as "legitimate and creative response[s] to acculturation" (Intro xi). Gloria Anzaldúa is adamantly in favor of her Chicana "patois, a forked tongue, a variation of two languages" which marks her "ethnic identity." "I am my language," she writes in *Borderlands* (55, 59). Still, not all critics condone the use of interlingualism. Rafael Cancel Ortiz in a 1990 article cites Puerto Rican fiction which links the "imposition of English on PR" with the "degenerative process" (112) of U.S. exploitation, and he describes (and possibly laments) how contemporary Mainland Puerto Rican writers, "exploring new avenues of fiction, present the Puerto Rican as a stuttering, ambivalent individual, incapable of expressing himself/herself coherently in either Spanish or English" (110). It may be true that the critic who focuses exclusively upon the interlingualism of Latino fiction (or poetry for that matter) runs the risk of pigeonholing the creative achievements of Latino writers. Obviously, there are other ways—having nothing to do with bilingual manipulations – that these storytellers exhibit their creativity. There is a danger in that such a critical focus contributes to the simplistic notion that the credible literary contributions of Latinos should always be seen in linguistic terms and that their imagination can only be recognized in terms of some sort of linguistic game playing.

Whatever the critic's viewpoint, it is surely true that characters in Latino fiction sometimes feel the strain of their linguistic uncertainty, as does the protagonist in Abraham Rodriguez's *Spidertown.* Miguel falls in love with Amelia, at least in part because of her words (56), her "crisp clear Spanish"—84), and he feels cramped by his own inability to communicate. Bruce-Novoa would counter with the theory that the "true" language of the Latino individual is neither Spanish nor English, but "whatever form of interlingualism she or he has experienced and internalized" (*Retrospace* 50). The "conflict" (113) between languages and the Latino's "struggle for survival" (Ortiz 113) can be viewed as either creative challenge or negative obstacle.

Some writers feel a need to explicitly describe the differences between Spanish and English and while such explications may point to the importance to the writer of particular vocabulary and give a sense of his or her intended audience, they can also be intrusive. For instance, Cofer explains the word "puta" [whore/bitch] as being "one of the harshest sounds in the Spanish language. Like the expulsion of spit" (78). Other writers exhibit a distinct modernist sensitivity toward the mixing and blending of the two languages. Avoiding translation or instructional commentary, they force the reader to depend upon the context of the speech act in order to decipher subtle meanings behind the interwoven languages. Writers such as Cisneros, conscious of form, exploit the connotations of words from both languages. They revel in the pleasure of the sounds of languages, and play games with the interconnections that spin off of words in juxtaposition. Such poetic constructions come close to what Juan Flores and George Yúdice, borrowing a term from advertising, call "trans-creations," and this type of language, they argue, is a necessary "crossover" that epitomizes "border culture expression" (*Divided Borders* 213-214). It is a form of "translingual play" which Levine sees in the punning of exiles and which is common to Latino literature where language provokes a "binary view" of reality (*Subversive Scribe* 17). Generally, we find examples of such manipulations of language in Latino poetry, especially in poems by Mainland Puerto Rican poets like Victor Hernández Cruz, who speaks of how "national languages melt, sail into each other" (110) or Sandra Maria Esteves, who declares, in her poem "A la Mujer Borinqueña:" "I speak two languages *broken* into each other" (emphasis mine). Latino prose writers are also aware of these linguistic possibilities though examples are harder to find.

The effects of translation techniques, of "trans-creation," code-switching, and borrowing demonstrate a writer's general attitude toward the larger concept of "interlingualism," or whatever name one chooses to encompass these sorts of linguistic mixing. Emily Hicks speaks of "border writing" which "emphasizes the differences in reference codes between two or more cultures." She sees the game playing as depicting "a kind of realism that approaches the experience of border crossers, those who live in a bilingual, bicultural, biconceptual reality" (Intro xxv). In part, we find evidence for this view when writers intentionally distort meanings through faulty, partial translations. When, for example, in Cofer's sketch "American History," a mother tells her daughter she is acting 'moony,' and the narrator explains: "'Enamorada' was what she really said—that is, like a girl stupidly infatuated" (*Latin* 10). The author is here molding the definition of the Spanish word to fit the context of the exchange, and by doing so, emphasizing the distance between the Spanish and the English since the more obvious meaning of the word "enamorado" [to be in love] is ignored. The most common result of such manipulation of translation is parody and satiric caricature.

The process of deliberately mistranslating is often as interesting as the techniques of translating. Pineda deliberately changes the line "Ella me tiene por el culo" into "The muse has me by the collar" (138), depriving the monolingual reader of the humor in the vulgarity. Since the speaker is the ridiculous writer Orgaz y Orgaz, his own deflation of his first sentence is indicative of his general incapacity to render the life around him into words. He insists on shutting himself off from the vitality of his wife's world in a vain attempt to write a novel based upon that world. Judith Cofer translates the word "Piropos" (50) in language more revealing than mere definition. These, she explains, are "those exalted compliments bordering on hysteria that a beautiful woman elicits." Later her definition of the same word becomes: "the poems invented on the spot and thrown at passing women like bouquets from open windows, doorways, street corners, anywhere where Latin men loitered" (186). Embedded in her extended definition is the less than sympathetic view of loitering (read sexist) Latino men.

Writers, at times, intentionally distort meanings through mistranslations. A character in Alex Abella's *The Killing of the Saints* gives the following advice: "Face up to your fears and make your work your *vacation*. Yes. Not everyone can do so, but if you personally do not succeed, I am afraid it *could be drapes for you*" (174-175). This is the sort of talk that Pilar recognizes in her mother's "immigrant English" with its "touch of otherness that makes it unintentionally precise" (*Dreaming* 176-177). It is also comical, especially for a writer like Roberto Fernández. Mary Vásquez points out Fernández's use of "calques" by which she means "over-literal" translations and she sees them as "markers of cultural alienation and conflicting cultural values" ("Parody" 100). She cites the example of one character's remark: "I don't responsibilize myself with what happens to you" (*Raining* 77) as one of the writer's many parodic quips. The literal translations of a seafood menu are indicative: "Shrimp at the little garlic; pulp in its own ink" (35). Fernández's play with false cognates produces a similarly sarcastic critique of the Cuban exile: "I knew," explains Abuela, "that afternoon he was going to pass by to see her because he had been *enamoring* her for almost a year" (147). "I am no opening for no one," she later declares (187). The mistranslations reflect Abuela's rigid attitudes toward traditional propriety and they mimic her misreadings of the people around her. In another segment of dialogue, Fernández plays with the false cognate "ordinario" which means rude in Spanish:

> ' . . . but I left him because he loved to say bad words and I no like ordinary people. We both worked for the Libby factory, it still makes peaches in heavy syrup. He was the foreman, but he disillusioned me because everyday at five o'clock when the whistle sound he used to tell me, 'Nelia, cojón, no more work, enough for today, cojón.' That is why I left him and we never became nothing. I never like ordinary people that say bad words.
>
> 'Abuela, he probably was saying 'go Home,' not cojón.

Not all mistranslations are intended to be humorous, or to sarcastically deflate characters. Instead, Sandra Cisneros often relies on the false cognate to stretch her meaning. When the narrator of "Eyes of Zapata" states that she "could support the grief" (97), the literal translation adheres to the exact meaning of the Spanish word "soportar." Cisneros refuses to dilute that meaning with the English "stand" or "bear." When one considers the larger implications of words like "soportar," and "aguantar" [to endure] and their relationship to the lives of Mexican women—as stereotypically passive—it becomes clear why Cisneros holds on to the Spanish meaning. Her translation is literal rather than accurate because the Spanish word's implications direct the reader toward the strength of Emiliano Zapata's mistress.

A character's grammatical expertise in English signals his or her level of assimilation into the dominant English environment. Agrammatical syntax may suggest a street level Spanish vernacular separating urban youth from mainstream society. We find examples of this in Rechy's LA or in Rodriguez's South Bronx: "I want we should always talk" (*Spidertown* 216). The Spanish word order is maintained in the English sentence. Distortion of the English language symbolizes a refusal to enter mainstream systems. This is the case with most of the women who populate the books of Ana Castillo, a writer who (in the tradition of Gertrude Stein), intentionally refuses to conform to standards of English or Spanish, using double negatives in English, phonetic Spanish spellings "medio austao" (*So Far From God* 45), agrammatical code-switches "my mi'jito" (90), and unusual borrowings like "ñervos" for "nervios" [nerves]. Whether or not Castillo's novels are her attempts to do what Luisa Valenzuela advocates—that is "decode the perverse discourse of those in power,"[9] her characters are free to exist uncritically in their own liminal, linguistic environment. The vernacular variety of their language in no way reflects any sort of intellectual deficiency, rather the opposite: individuality, creativity and strength in the face of oppressive powers.

Yet there are also characters who cannot adjust linguistically to English and who therefore remain powerless outsiders. These people often fall away from language itself, becoming silent. Their submergence into the non-verbal impedes their survival. It points to their "cultural, linguistic, theoretical, psychological exile" (Debra Castillo 81). Rechy's Amalia is an example. Her fear and her dislike of English keep her silent, as when, confronted with the truth that her children "know nothing" of the sacrifices she has made for them, she finds it "impossible to speak" (188). Moreover, her silence is indicative of Chicano silence in general which contributes to the invisibility of Latinos amid the dominant U.S. society. "They just don't see us," Amalia explains at one point (67), "to become invisible, too, corazón . . . that's not hard when they've never really seen us" (177).

The inner voice of the Latino may therefore rise up through linguistic distortions of accepted language, but Latino writers also guide readers beyond language toward the non-verbal. In Alfredo Véa's *La Maravilla,* a black man named Toop speaks of magic words that sit "in the spaces between the regular words" and "whole lives" that "come and go with no words attached." "Shit, there's a universe between all the words we got" (84). This is why so many characters, especially women, communicate by mystical, intuitive means. There is a bond between the narrator of Cisneros's "Eyes of Zapata" and the absent revolutionary hero that she feels through "a silence between us like a language" (99). Between Pilar and Celia, in *Dreaming in Cuban*, the relationship is psychic and magical like "steady electricity, humming and true" (222). Pilar worries over the fading connection (138), something her abuela felt even when Pilar was an infant who "seemed to understand her very thoughts" (119). The young girl narrator of "The Moths" and her "speechless" abuelita share a similar bond, and are united like Pilar and her grandmother in a similar type of ritualistic bathing—both stories stressing a communion through images of weightlessness, of floating or swimming and abandoning the hard practicality of rational and logical thought.[10]

Kristeva's terms can be applied here to these characters choosing silence as rebellion against the symbolic order associated with the father and as affirmation of a semiotic, pre-oedipal relationship with the mother. Certainly the dreamy, trance-like, nonrationality of silent women (and some men) throughout Latino fiction could be viewed through this psychological, critical perspective, especially in works where elements of the semiotic are replicated in the musical concatenation of the prose. Debra Castillo argues as much in her perceptive analysis of Helena Viramontes's "The Cariboo Cafe" (76-95),[11] highlighting instances which reveal "some dilemma involving a woman's silencing" (77). Viramontes's story "Birthday"—concerning a young woman in an abortion clinic—with its gaps, ellipses and Joycean narrative turns clearly suggests this sort of powerlessness. Kloepfer maintains in her work on Jean Rhys,[12] that the birth scene (or the memory of it), somehow psychologically "reactivates" a woman's pre-oedipal, subverbal turbulence, and here Viramontes's Alice is thrown into the topsy-turvy dreamworld of her confused emotions. Speechless, in her negative "wonderland," her mind bounces between past conversations and the present of the makeshift office, while recollected voices and "watercolored" university students "float like balloons" through her semiotic trance, beyond, what Kloepfer labels, "all reference" (*The Unspeakable Mother* 86).

It is certainly clear that the social constraints of the Latino's world tend to push such linguistically liminal beings toward the periphery whenever they can't or won't conform to the standards of the center. Thus abiding by non-verbal criteria relegates a character to the margins—either victim of prejudice or rebel against injustice. This might account for the frequent allusions in Latino fiction to "The Yellow Wallpaper," a story about the ways society forces the nonconformist to the brink of psychological chaos. Cristina Garcia traces a sequence of psychological declines through several characters that recalls Gilman's famous story. Celia, as a young bride, is confined to the oppressive household of Palmas Street, and abusively ridiculed by her in-laws until, during the final stages of her pregnancy, she breaks down and is sent off to an asylum for cure. Institutionalized, she begins to write her poetic letters, and meets one Felicia Guitiérrez, a woman "unrepentant" for having burned her husband to death (51). When Celia later names her second daughter after this rebellious woman, and Felicia attempts to destroy her own husband Hugo by burning him with boiling oil, the multiple allusions to Gilman's narrator, a fiery, (laughing), Medusa figure, and the trapped Bertha Mason type (from both Brontë and Rhys) begin to mesh together. Garcia explicitly mentions that Felicia "laughs when she recalls her husband's screams" (82), and that her "hair springs from her head like electric wires . . . as if her chaos had a rhythm" (85). Her son, Ivanito, trapped by his mother's behavior, incapable of speaking his "sisters' language" imagines that "the wallpaper comes alive in the moonlight," and, dancing to songs like "Rebel Heart" and "Treat Me As I Am," he can feel his mother's heart "jumping" to the rhythms of Samba drums "like it wants to come out of its cage" (85-86). Here, the mad woman in the attic is one La Muñeca [the doll], Pilar's paternal great-grandmother, a Costa Rican, "Indian as they come" and "locked upstairs," according to Celia (herself ostracized as a result of her racial heritage) because she tried to maintain her Indian customs of childrearing.

Felicia is unable to communicate in English (Garcia humorously mentions that she can't read the text of American weightlifting magazines—152 which may or may not be a detriment) or Spanish when her emotional breakdown renders "something . . . wrong with her tongue. It forms broken trails of words, words sealed and resistant as stones" (83). Without language, she occupies "the fringe of life" which she feels is "free of everyday malice" (184). She grows more distant as the novel progresses, removing herself from reality the and role of mother—she becomes for her daughters: "not mamá:"

> [Her] mind floods with thoughts, thoughts from the past, from the future, other people's thoughts . . . Every idea seems to her connected to thousands of others by a tangle of pulsing nerves. She jumps from one to another like a nervous circus horse. It is worse when she closes her eyes (76).

To varying degrees, other characters in Latino fiction exhibit similar denials of outward reality. Often, factors of spiritual orientation come into play, such as beliefs in unorthodox forms of religion like Santería,

Voodoo or Spiritualism to be discussed later. Our concern here is with how this type of escapism is related to language or lack of it. Felicia and Amalia are pushed to extremes in part because they are incoherent to others, but also because they are refused the natural outlet of speech that the privileged enjoy. Like many Latino protagonists, they are silenced.

For some characters, entrance into the non-verbal sphere is the result of a psychological incapacity to cope with their lives for whatever reason. For others, like Mercedes and her son Hector, the key to their frustration lies in their inability to linguistically orient themselves. Felicia moves away from language into her trance for a number of reasons, but a conflict between languages, or the traumas of multilingual society do not necessarily impact upon her. Her loss of voice ("Her own voice is mute to her"—81) results from a combination of her husband's abuse, her friend Herminia's influence and her family history. Amalia, on the other hand, as a "Mexican-American" (as she calls herself, disliking the word "Chicano"—4) struggles with two languages. She retreats toward Spanish and rejects English as the pressures of U.S. society force her into fearful silence. Her retreat is mirrored by Rechy's narrative technique where gaps and dashes indicate her loss of words, her growing silence and her agitated thought patterns.

> Gabriel was discharged, and he moved in permanently with Amalia. Sex with him was like with the others, something expected of her; and like the others, Gabriel didn't even notice that. . . . Amalia loved this: Throughout the night, he held her tenderly (35).

The gap here points to Amalia's inability to reveal her own sexual desires to her lover Gabriel as well as her quickness at censoring herself, and redirecting her attention toward a less emotional, yet still positive aspect of the relationship. Later in the book, the gaps in this momentary interior monologue suggest a further incapacity to face her past:

> Or because he had sighed, that way, that long? Gabriel. Yes. She remembered that, how often Gabriel had sighed. And Salvador . . . Yes. No, never! But her father . . . ? (60).

She pushes away "those odd thoughts" from her past as the disjointed prose jumps from thought to thought. The frequency of dashes increases as she finds out about her son Manny's crimes:

> In that courtroom she came to despise—and she went alone, did not *want* anyone with her—she learned—certain finally—that her son—who listened fascinated as if people there were talking about someone he did not know—dominated one of the toughest gangs in the city . . . (79).

Rechy's stylistic duplication of Amalia's mental disarray continues throughout the book, becoming more pronounced as Amalia's illusions are stripped away. Logical thought gives way to broken fragments of language. In one scene, her random thoughts disintegrate into part of some modern day "Trojan Women" chorus, part of the "terrible lament" coming from women (themselves growing "drabber, poorer, more desperate" by the minute) waiting in line to see their sons in prison:

> "—drugs—" . . . "—resisting arrest—" . . . "What will we do now?" . . . "—las gangas—" . . . "—drogas—" . . . "—no job—" . . . "—What will we do now?" . . . "—the police said he—" . . . "I don't know why, mujer!" . . . "—the gangs—" . . . "drunk but he—" . . . "What will we do now?" (83).

A similar type of stream of consciousness occurs in Rodriguez's *Spidertown.* Early on, Miguel considers disclosing his involvement in arson and drug dealing to his new love, Cristalena. As Miguel ponders his confession, Rodriguez's narrative becomes a jumbled, explosion of agrammatical fragments, a dramatic monologue of the bits and pieces of thoughts bubbling in the protagonist's tortured brain (10-11). The position of the words on the page—centered or oddly spaced—in these instances mirrors a character's strangled inability to communicate. Or, to cite another example, consider the dramatic monologue of Jack Agüero's "Molly Bloom" figure in the story "Malig; Malig & Sal; Sal." Preparing to end her relationship with Sal, Malig reasons to herself in front of a mirror, her thoughts running on for several pages, pushed together and gathering momentum with each consecutive "and." When the confrontation comes in the second and third sections of the story, repetitions (often triples) communicate her frustration and anger at the intellectual Sal: He was "too much, too strong, too opinionated, too,

too, too crazy . . . " (85). When he beats her up, the wild prose feeds the pace of his escape: "smashed smashed smashed . . . fell down the first flight [of stairs], stumbled, fell, tripped, flew down the next and the next and the next and the next and the next, voices in the yellowed cinder blocks of the stairwell echoing 'What is it?' 'Que pasa,' 'Are you alright?'" (90). Toward the end of Goldman's *Ordinary Seaman* a similar telegraphic style speeds up the narrative, but in most of this work—a novel virtually without substantial storyline where situations are described over and over and events few and far between—the prose produces lists of information rather than insights into character.

As a stylistic device, when viewed at the level of discourse, this sort of sentence distortion suggests the Latino writer's use of Bakhtin's "carnival idiom" where the breakdown of language signals an intention to subvert or disturb standard modes of expression, to turn rational and logical communication inside out. The Cuban-American novelist Roberto Fernández is particularly adept at playing with multi-voiced narrative and disturbing all linear, chronological systems. *Raining Backwards* is a mosaic of Cuban-American voices fractured into nearly every form of discourse available to a writer. As Rolando Hinojosa with his *Klail City Death Trip* series had done for the Chicano world, Fernández creates a complex portrait of a Miami community by shifting voices and juggling types of prose. The oral culture of Miami is given full vent, just as Hinojosa had done for the borderland culture of south Texas, yet here Fernández's tone is decidedly sarcastic as his own "mosaic of anecdotes" (Zimmerman 85) gives way to language that mimics travel brochures (123-141), news broadcasts (61), etiquette columns (25, 36), government letters (65), applications (94-96), recipes (70), news releases (31, 90), and even poetry (20, 57, 124). Both writers have an interest in forcing the written word to conform to what Kanellos calls "the orality" of Latino culture.

Latino characters share a general distrust of words, particularly the written word. Herminia, for example, is decidedly distrustful of writing, specifically, the inaccurate histories of her African ancestors (*Dreaming* 185) while Pilar is in constant search for what Lourdes (who speaks "another idiom entirely"—221) cannot reach: the "old sentences beneath the mattress" (237). Under English labels exist Latino truths: In Rechy, "Elmer's Bar and Grill" becomes "El Bar and Grill." The name Elmer transforms into "El" and the actual "grill" disappears (140). We are left with the truth of an unpainted, desolate bar that sells Tomales. In Viramontes, as Debra Castillo points out, Cariboo Café becomes the zero, zero place, and the "Carib" (Caribbean, Caribe Indians) gets lost, while the double negative remains (81). In the Cisneros story, "Barbie-Q," under the toy maker's advertising labels for Barbie Dolls, "Sweet Dreams," "Career Girl," and "Bendable Legs Barbie," we find two poor, Chicano children in a Flee Market with few dreams, and a collection of "water-soaked," dolls that smell like soot, their bendable legs "melted a little" (*Women* 14-16). The title of the story implies that women need to destroy the artificial stereotypes associated with Barbie dolls if they are to be seen on anything but a superficial level. Like Herminia's, the history of Latinos has been recorded erroneously, and thus the quest for voice pushes the Latino against the mainstream, away from the officialdom of the English language. Franklin, a Central-American refugee in Sáenz's "Alligator Park" typifies the Latino existing outside the world of books and words. The lawyer's taking notes disturbs him:

> "It's strange, it's like all my words, everything I say, is being put to a sheet of paper. It doesn't seem right. Words are supposed to be said, I mean, words on a piece of paper aren't real like what comes out of the mouth . . . I've never trusted words that were written down. I like words better when I can hear them instead of see them." (93).

Another Sáenz protagonist resents those who do have a voice in society, who "parade" their opinions with slogans and signs. Richard/Ricardo Díaz from "Kill the Poor" is an embittered Chicano with misgivings toward written language. He hates to read and yet works in a library. He tries to quit smoking in, of all places, a bowling alley. Having intentionally erased his Spanish, he feels no comfort from English, and he lives in a state beyond language, a "drought" of words (79). These are the voices of people, if not silenced, to some extent powerless; they are those, in Debra Castillo's words, who are "illiterate, who dare not speak, for whom the supposedly universal right to free speech has no more significance than any other phrase of oratory" (80).

Throughout Latino fiction, the characters search for a form of self expression, a language that will "bear the burden" of their hybrid, cultural identity. Some falter into silence under the weight of English (and the dominant society it reflects), while others are left stranded midway between the two languages, trapped in a halfway house, like Gilb's YMCA, where everyone wants to communicate, everybody waits for the mail, but the mail never comes and everybody lies.

Elsewhere, the Latino is given voice by the validation of his linguistic world when writers choose the freedom of interlingual creativity, or as Tato Laviera puts it by "speaking new words in Spanglish tenements" ("AmeRícan"). Once comfortable with the creative potential of working between languages, Latino fiction writers acquire an imaginative strength from the games of blending and mixing and they code-switch themselves into storytellers like no others. The discourse available to them entangles the nuances and flavors of English and Spanish, molding and shaping each language to accommodate a cultural borderland neither separated from, nor entirely distinct from either side.

NOTES

1. See Gina Valdés's poem "English con Salsa" in *America's Review* Vol. 21 (Spring 1993) 49-50.

2. Sanchez defines Caló as an "urban code . . . spoken by Chicanos in the Southwest" incorporating "standard Spanish, popular varieties, loan-words from English and even code-switching." She links it primarily to young males (*Chicano Discourse* 128).

3. In *La Maravilla*, Alfredo Véa spends a paragraph defining "La Chingada" as, among many other things, "anyone who is fooled, prodded, ripped open by the *chingón*, the ripper. Every Mexican is a son of *La Chingada*. There is no equivalent English word" (43).

4. Rodriguez perhaps suggests the falsity of this linguistic peer camaraderie since the word is frequently used between the protagonist and the central drug dealer he will eventually betray.

5. For a discussion of "scripting" consult Nelson, K. (1986). *Event Knowledge: Structure and Function in Development.* New York: Academic. and Griffiths, P. (1986) "Early Vocabulary" in P. Fletcher and M. Garman (eds) *Language Acquisition* (2nd. ed. pp. 279-306. New York: Cambridge U. Press

6. Citing Freud, Suzanne Jill Levine mentions the "well-worn" pun: "taduttore, traditore, meaning 'translator, traitor,' the most oft-used cliché in translation debates, betrayed of course in translation" (*The Subversive Scribe: Translating Latin American Fiction*. Saint Paul: Graywolf Press, 1991.

7. The importance of Williams's Puerto Rican background is explored in Julio Marzán book, *The Spanish-American Roots of William Carlos Williams.* For writers like Judith Cofer, who writes of urban New Jersey (specifically Patterson), Williams is certainly influential.

8. In an interview with Bruce-Novoa, Arias made it clear that English was his family's "practical language" and that his parents downplayed Spanish

for practical reasons (Bruce-Novoa *Chicano Authors* 242); He stated that the "living language around us has become English" (Interview 247), and thus Fausto is here linguistically revealing his impractical nature which the text will certainly confirm.

9. Valenzuela remarked on her reasons for writing fiction in the Presidential Forum of *Profession 91*, December 1990 in Buenos Aires.

10. See Chapter Six for further discussion of the mystical element.

11. Of the stories in the collection, *The Moths*, critics have chosen to discuss this story most frequently. Besides Castillo's chapter in *Talking Back*, see also Roberta Fernández (1989) and Franklet (1989).

12. Rhys's work is important to Latino fiction for a number of reasons. Her modernist prose style (specifically the use of stream of consciousness) serves as an example for novels such as Lucha Corpi's *Delia's Song*, or Gina Valdés's story "Rhythms," but Rhys was also an innovator in blending languages (in her case French and English) and exploring the non-verbal worlds of woman on the outskirts of accepted society. One thinks of Sasha in *Good Morning, Midnight* or Selina in "Let Them Call it Jazz."

CHAPTER FOUR

Dreams and Betrayals: Latinos between Worlds

The phrase "between worlds" recurs so frequently in Latino fiction and in post-colonial and Latino criticism as to nearly smack of cliché. If we turn from the linguistic implications of this borderland condition (such as the "interlingual" patterns of language discussed above), and look instead at thematic issues, we find ourselves immediately at the heart of Latino hybridity, confronted with notions of cultural marginality, prejudice, and the betrayal of illusory dreams and expectations. We need to consider the American Dream through the minds and hearts of Latino protagonists – often immigrants, outsiders, or aliens, and always in some way detached from the center of U.S. society and yet perhaps belonging nowhere else.

The transition between a space of safety and order into one of difficulty and pain (oppositions Northrop Frye, after Blake, labeled worlds of innocence and experience) is particularly apt in Latino fiction since so much of this literature concerns the movement from one cultural world to another and the spaces between the two. Mircea Eliade refers to the original Edenic setting as a "land of innocence . . . a privileged land where time stands still" (*Myths* 34) and "a pure region," "earth's navel," a "primordial Paradise, " and "man's ultimate problem" (*Myth* 16-17). Everything else after the "fall" constitutes, as Stephen Dedalus tells us, the "reality of experience" to be "encountered." The parallels between the pre-European Southwest, the pre-Castro island of Cuba and the distant island greenery and peace of Puerto Rico in the imagery of these writings indicate the centrality of the overall motif: the archetypal, spiritual journey away from a lost paradise, the initiation into a North American world, and the desire to return. The figurative language that portrays this pattern, though obviously not unique to any one group of literary works, is perhaps central to the underlying questions Latino fiction raises. This is true because Latinos write of crossing cultural and spiritual boundaries and about the problems of self-image and fragmented identity that such journeys and displacements create. Examining the various dimensions of this particular trope should lead us toward understanding Latino hybridity as characters throughout the fiction confront the metaphorical oppositions of past/present, ordered peace/the trials of the unknown, and innocence/experience.

In her book *Borderlands: La Frontera,* the Chicana writer Gloria Anzaldúa has succinctly explained the importance of Aztlán as the central "Edenic place of origin of the Azteca," home to the first inhabitants of what is now the U.S. Southwest. Ever since the Aztecs ("the Nahuatl word for people of Aztlán"), one of several Toltec tribes, completed their migration south to Mexico in the twelfth century, events have led to the continued exodus of "Spanish, Indian, and mestizo ancestors." The U.S. government took control with the Hidalgo treaty of 1848 at which point the "truncated, disemboweled, dispossessed" Mexican Americans began dreaming of a return to the "homeland" (4-10). Chicanos were subsequently harassed (even lynched) by Texas Rangers, driven from their land by agricultural corporations, and exploited by the injustices of sharecropping in patterns similar to those suffered by black Americans following the civil war.

The return to a mythic homeland in the U.S. Southwest is evident throughout Chicano fiction in one shape or another. In Estelle Portillo-Trambley's novel *Trini*, the motif is a central structuring element as the novel's heroine, Trini, struggles against obstacles that bar the path home to her "rainbow cave" (and Native American mysticism) until she finally reaches her "Valverde" (green valley) where she "belongs." In fact, Portillo-Trambley's stories are somewhat one-dimensional because the plots of her fiction (and its detailed imagery) so adamantly conform to her belief in what the critic Tomás Vallejos defines as "ancient mythical structures [that serve] as models of an ideal balance in the cosmos" (54). Her "vision of cosmic wholeness" (54) and her optimistic conviction in an "unending cyclical regeneration of the universe" (55) which Vallejos traces in Portillo Trambley's early story collection entitled *Rain of Scorpions and Other Writings* underlies her novel as well. Like the characters in the early stories, Trini, the mestizo heroine, is on a clearly archetypal journey "toward oneness" (56) from the city of falsehood to the rural region of truth, from classist society and discrimination by rich, white men to nature, the earth and native American culture. In the urban world, like those mistresses locked by their rich men in "blue casitas" (143), she is physically imprisoned by her carousing husband, Tonio (29). Women must rely upon either the escape of marriage like Licha's to Don Alejandro Sosa (145), or the comfort of religious doctrine as does Trini's aunt Pancha (38). Trini, however, moves "through a dark hole to a "church on the other side (204-207) and is "reborn" to a natural earthly paradise, reconnected to dance, wind, music and laughter—all qualities linked specifically to her—and allied to Tonantzín, earth/fertility goddess, female deity of the mountains. Portillo-Trambley's portrayal of the Latina's need for indigenous spirituality can be faulted for its oversimplification, and, if we agree with Cherríe Moraga's article "The Obedient Daughter," for its romantic idealization of the male savior/hero (i.e. Sabochi, Trini's protector, lover and spiritual guru). The novel, however, clearly sets up a pattern of oppositions frequently found in Latino fiction, a pattern that becomes increasingly more complicated and problematic as Latino writers, especially women authors, manipulate the motif.

Principally for political reasons, many Cuban-American writers look toward Cuba as the lost island paradise. The pre-Castro garden of peace and pleasure for middle and upper class Cubans who fled after the 1959 revolution remains an integral part of the Cuban-American writer's psyche while the (generally poorer), second generation of immigrants who "escaped" in the early 1980's (the Marielitos) have perhaps a different, less nostalgic perspective, and the "balsero" exiles of the 1990's even less still. Paralleling the political arguments going on in Washington, debates between characters from both generations over Cuban issues dominate much of the fiction's thematic content.

Eliana Ortega discusses the notion of Puerto Rico as island paradise, the legend of "Anacaona, the pre-Hispanic origin, a mother origin, an Afro-Antillean origin" with respect to Puerto Rican poetry ("Poetic Discourse" 122-123), and the metaphorical motif of the paradisal island of Puerto Rico is common as well to Puerto Rican literature written on the island itself. René Marqués's classic play of disillusionment, *"La Carreta,"* follows the tragic story of a family's migration from rural paradise to urban (first San Juan and later New

York) disaster. Yet Nuyorican fiction writers have perhaps intentionally shunned the motif in their efforts to assert themselves as Latino writers, uninterested in a mythical land that is less real to them than the urban social ills of New York. Avoiding the myth of a lost paradise becomes a means of establishing a mainland U.S. Latino identity separate from the island's ideals. Occasionally, as in certain stories of Nicholasa Mohr, there are characters who long for the glory of a lost past, a pre-Columbian "Borinquen," and whose lives are twisted or complicated by an "impractical" desire for the impossible. The theme occurs, nevertheless, in Judith Cofer's *The Line of the Sun*, where Guzmán flees into the tropical forest of the island and there understands how the original inhabitants, the Taino Indians "had led an easy life in an earthly paradise" (134). Piri Thomas's famous autobiographical novel of urban struggle, *Down These Mean Streets,* opens with the family's attempt to create the warmth of their "Puerto Rican Paradise" with games and music in a freezing Harlem apartment (8-14). Generally, however, perhaps because of the intensity of the inner city conflicts of poverty and crime with which mainland Puerto Rican fiction is so often concerned, the problematic, psychological dilemma of longing for the perfect world back in the mountains of the island becomes somewhat secondary. There is also the fact that access to Puerto Rico is very different from access to Cuba and that while Cuban-Americans are essentially in exile, a Puerto Rican "enjoys" a dual citizenship. Still, without dwelling on the motif as often as other Latino writers, mainland Puerto Ricans are conscious of the distinction between original home and present reality. They are constantly juxtaposing the often sordid practical reality of New York with a green and peaceful island simplicity, the cruelty of U.S. poverty and isolation versus the sharing of the burden on the island.

Nicholasa Mohr, one of only a few Nuyorican fiction writers – and often at odds with her island counterparts—usually presents the dream of returning to a perfect past as a delusion which afflicts most of the first generation Puerto Rican immigrants of her stories. A father in "A Very Special Pet" from her story collection, *El Bronx, Remembered*, plans on returning to an idyllic farm: "We gonna get everything and we gonna leave El Bronx" (3); a mother in "Tell the Truth . . . " speaks of "making a killing on the 'bolita'" [the lottery] and moving home to the island; an uncle in "Uncle Claudio" longs for his home (specifically fruit and food) in Puerto Rico. Where, in the minds of these characters, the cold weather kills a young boy in one story (19), the island's climate cures (20). These unhappy immigrants relish memories of their "beautiful island where tall green palm trees swayed . . . "(12), their "Island of Paradise" (28), where all is "magical" and "wonderful" ("Lucia" 95). Younger generation Puerto Ricans in Mohr's stories harbor different feelings. They revolt against the prejudices of the U.S. as well as the nostalgic fantasies of their relatives. They make fun of recently arrived Islanders ("greenhorns," "jíbaros:" farmers). They see the palm reading of the elderly island woman as "hocus-pocus" (19); they don't speak Spanish (166) and they resent the daydreaming adults as much as they do the religion of the "Aleyluya" people (*Bronx* 194). In "Uncle Claudio," the children cannot understand why Claudio is offended by a young man in the subway, until it is explained to them that he "lives in another time and that he is dreaming instead of facing life" (25), that he is tied to classist island society and cannot cope with Nuyorican deviations from old world traditions. One young girl listens to her grandmother's stories with enthusiasm, but recognizes also that they are "too impossible to be true" ("A Thanksgiving Celebration" 85). Like the young, women often refute the delusions that sustain their husbands, as does the wife in "A Time with a Future."

Chicano writer, John Rechy, reflecting a similar urban skepticism concerning overly mystical connections to a past perfection, illustrates the progressive deflation of the dream of Aztlán in *The Miraculous Day of Amalia Gómez*. In the first LA wall mural, Amalia Gómez sees a proud Aztec figure, "amber-gold-faced, in lordly feathers" as she hears from an old man the dream of "muslin-clad" revolutionaries and a future "promised land of justice" (45). The next mural, however, startles her with its image of a tall, plumed Aztec carrying a dying city child (56), and finally the myth is rewritten, in the "red bleeding paint" of gang graffiti as "Aztlán es una fábula" [Aztlán is a fable] (70). To the inner city, crime-ridden world of Amalia's family, one's ancient heritage is useless, or, in the words of her daughter's biker boyfriend: "bullshit." "Where's all that pride bullshit got you?" He tells Amalia. "What are you? Just another fuckin' Mexican maid" (181).

Balancing a (usually impractical) desire for the lost Eden of one's youth with the need for success in the modern U.S. world preoccupies characters throughout Latino fiction. William O. Deaver, Jr. writes in an essay on Roberto Fernández that the Cuban-American is spiritually absorbed with aspects of Cuban life like Santería or the Calle Ocho parades (and one might add dominos, cigars, coffee and a legion of other elements of Cuban culture), but materially connected to credit cards and consumerism. It is Deaver's thesis that *Raining Backwards* is about the disintegration or "death of Cuban exile culture" (112), and that members of the older generation are drowned "in a process where assimilation and reintegration actually destroy their uniqueness without fully incorporating them" (117).[1] The generational division is comically demonstrated when one Grandpa, for instance, in *Raining Backwards* is "blind" to anything except the memory of Cuba while his granddaughter thinks "Cuba" is a restaurant (213).

Name changes, usually from the original Spanish to an anglicized version, signal a symbolic transition from one culture into another. As a shift in clothes or outward appearance can reflect an inner change,[2] a name change often suggests some form of identity modification. Deaver cites four young Cubans in *Raining Backwards* who, on route to "The American Dream," anglicize their names: "Jacinto becomes Keith, Consuelo becomes Connie, Joaquín becomes Quinn, and Miguel becomes Michael" (Deaver "Raining" 115). The street youths of Abraham Rodriguez's *Spidertown* are equally oblivious to the organic essence of a mythical island paradise. They, like the characters in Rechy, Fernández and Mohr identify themselves ethnically only as a recognition of community, a sense of belonging to a certain group marginal to the labyrinthine urban society. Subverting the police, members of drug gangs change their names to simplistic symbols of their underground reputations: "Firefly" (a pyromaniac) and "Spider" (a drug dealer who climbs walls). Surrounded by people named Toasty (119), Domino (118), Boom (126), and Flyboy, the protagonist, Miguel, has little connection to his Puerto Rican heritage. Though these Latinos seek support from group identity, they see the rituals connected with the island as extraneous. The youth of Alberto Rios's stories similarly nickname themselves after animals: "Sapito" ("The Iguana Killer"), "Pato" (His Own Key"). In one story, a boy from Guatemala calls himself Usmail and another boy is named Usnavy—identity becoming dependent more upon U.S. institutions than upon family, culture and individuality. This is how Faulkner debunked his Snopes: Montgomery Ward Snopes and Wallstreet Panic Snopes in *The Town*, and, by inference, lamented the decline of southern society into materialistic capitalism. A black Mississippi mother in *La Maravilla*, in search of a name for her daughter, is "not overly fond of the new urban black predilection for naming the child after the first thing the new mother sees in her hospital room after delivering the child. 'Visine Robinson' did nothing for her, nor did 'Aspirina,' 'Chlorina' or

'Sylvania" (91). Ultimately, she chooses the name Boydeen, after a Harlem waitress, a beautiful Liberian girl named after her great grandfathers, both former slaves. Véa, like Faulkner, suggests the necessity of linking one's name and, consequently one's identity to something of greater value than material objects. For Rodriguez's protagonist, distance from adults like his own absent, negligent father, his older sister who abuses her daughter (126), his on again/off again mother or Amelia's traditionally moral, old world father (188) constitutes a separation from island myth. Though gang members refer to themselves as "Boricua," there is no intentional reminiscing, or longing, or belief that anything in Puerto Rico holds value for them. In fact, Miguel's ability to escape the underground world of gangs and drugs is to some extent dependent upon his being outside the clique of Puerto Rican allegiance. He relinquishes his "Boricua" self by refusing some "empanadas"(238); he doesn't like "Gloria fucken Estefan" (279) and unlike his political friend, he has little use for island philosophers like Betances or independence minded revolutionary heroes like Albizu Campos. In these respects, he resembles the older son of Alejo Santinio in *Our House in the Last World,* Horacio, who rejects Cuban cuisine as "too greasy" and "boring" (83). Most importantly, in a novel almost entirely dialogue, Miguel reads books and thinks about becoming a writer. Like his more famous Latino predecessor Richard Rubio from Villareal's *Pocho,* he is caught in the basic tensions of immigrant life; in José David Saldívar's words, he must "either assert an Americanized individuality, or succumb to the burden . . . imposed upon him by his father and his community" (*Dialectics* 110). This is essentially the problem for the narrator of Rodriguez's story "The Boy Without a Flag" around whom the mythic revolutionary figures of twentieth century, Puerto Rican political history have metamorphosed into a group of accommodating weaklings. From Jose Martí, we now have Miss Marti, a militaristic assistant principal with "a battlefield for a face and constant odor of chicklets" (13), with the "mouth of a lizard" (19) and "reptile legs" (25). "You're nothing," she tells the narrator, "You're not worth a damn" (19). From Filiberto Ojeda Ríos, one of the founders of the Puerto Rican revolutionary group "Los Macheteros,"[3] we get Mr. Rios, a man with "rodent features" having an adulterous affair with a woman named Miss Colon (read Columbus). "You're just a puny kid," (24) he declares to the young man. Even the boy's father fails to live up to the revolutionary ideals of Pedro Albizu Campos,[4] the very same ideals he has struggled to instill in his son. When the boy refuses to pledge allegiance to an American flag and not become what his father calls, a "Yankee flag-waver," there is no one around to support his small rebellion. The glorious political rebels of Puerto Rico's past fade into irrelevancy and it is up to this Nuyorican teenager to compromise, to make "peace with The Enemy" (29). Somewhat didactically, Rodriguez ends the story with the boy accepting the U.S. flag in recognition that through his "Americanized individuality" and not through his father's political rhetoric ("once so rich and vibrant"—28) he will find his "own peace, away from the bondage of obedience" (30). He winds up "without a flag," between worlds.

An allegiance to an Edenic vision of "Borinquen" (the indigenous name for the island of Puerto Rico) is not, for Nicholasa Mohr, a healthy reality, but rather a restrictive force against Nuyorican achievement. Mohr has spoken against the "mythic vision" of PR as a paradise, claiming that such ideas have "little or nothing to do with Puerto Rico, its inhabitants, and the reality of that culture" ("Puerto Rican Writers" 114), and her younger generation Puerto Rican characters seem to reflect that view by their frequent intolerance of their parents' nostalgia. Constancia, in Garcia's second novel, *The Agúero Sisters*, shuns the Miami Cuban's version of this "habit of fierce nostalgia, their trafficking in the past like exaggerating peddlers" (46). Judith Cofer's characters suggest a similar mistrust of the nostalgic paradise of the island. In *Line of the Sun*, the recent immigrants gather in "EL Building"—that "bizarre facsimile of an Island Barrio" (220)—to reminisce about Puerto Rico. Feeling "safety in numbers," they grow "misty and lyrical in describing their illusory Eden" (174), yet their peaceful nostalgia will be shattered by a fire (the "horrible disaster" 279) which destroys their fragile sanctuary. Nuyorican Miguel Algarín, in his poem "A Mongo Affair," bluntly sums up the younger generation Puerto Rican's anti-nostalgic attitude: "don't fill me full of vain / disturbing love for an island / filled with Burger Kings."

If aspects of some works of fiction seem to concur with the much debated argument put forth by Richard Rodriguez in *Hunger of Memory,*[5] other works suggest a synthesis of two views, a blending of the value (often metaphoric) of an indigenous myth and non-European history (often oral) with an understanding of the deficiencies of old world life and the complexities and ambiguities of a hybrid U.S. existence. At odds with the view that practicality dictates abandoning the myth of island purity and perfection, is Ortega's argument that it is precisely "the oral, matriarchal tradition that gestates [Latina's] discourse *a priori*" (123) and that it is the figure of a pre-Hispanic, indigenous woman—Anacaona—(like the Aztec figure of Coatlicue) that authenticates a lost oral tradition and is used by recent poets as a model for their "subversive poetic discourse" (122).

In the stories of Benjamin Alire Sáenz, various characters struggle with such divided allegiances as is reflected in their names. One angry young library worker battles between the "Richard he had created" and the "Ricardo" of his family. His renaming himself mirrors his futile attempt to escape the Spanish language ("The language of suffering") and his family's poverty. "Ricardo" reminds him of "desert, of drought, of too many years of praying for rain" (65), and of his nephew's death. As Richard, he flees words, until a final cathartic explosion of language ("a downpour after many years of drought"—79) allows him to open up and vent "the scream" which up to this point has been "stayed inside him" (66). In another story, a young man corrects an English nun, insisting on Miguel, instead of Michael, though the sister pretends not to hear him ("In London There is no Summer" 106). While Ricardo's dismissal of Spanish shows a debilitating incapacity to confront his own ethnic past, the Miguel of the later story (living in London) asserts his past affiliation and struggles to confirm his heritage. He declares at one point that peanuts are a "New World food" though no one in his boarding house kitchen understands what he means. Miguel grows to envy the anger of his friend Lizzie as he learns to recognize "the stench of London history" (123). Crossing the channel from France, he feels the majestic images of the poem "Dover Beach" (whose author he can't remember) give way to the real cliffs: "gray and thick with old age like medieval prison walls" and he watches the seagulls (read English imperialists) "flying down like mad dogs racing to pick off a piece of trash from the waters, fighting each other in flight, making [as does Arnold] the violence seem like something graceful" (123).

The process of transition from one world to another involves psychological and social acculturation (adapting) and assimilation (changing). Transition is therefore an instigator of change in characters' lives which, when focused upon, can reveal the nature of the conflicts and oppositions people encounter as they cross borders, both real and metaphorical. Here too, the reader can discover the qualities of a liminal space inhabited by characters who traverse borders continuously, who never fully cross from one side to another, and who remain caught in what Eliana Rivero calls a "permanent, unresolved dualism" ("Rewriting Sugarcane Memories" 170). In the traditional ritual progression from innocence to experience, the archetypal seducer robs the innocent of virginity, takes advantage of naiveté or destroys the innocent's optimism and forces entrance into cruel reality (death and sin), and into confrontation with the facts beneath the illusory appearance. The result of seduction is growth and maturity (often filled with disillusionment and pessimism) at the expense of childishness and ignorance. Yet the transition in Latino writing is often blurred and confused, the result a hazy blending of growth and loss that defies the practical notion that the initiation is a maturing process.

Beyond the level of betrayal in terms of individual characters' psychological growth, the motif is often suggestive of the larger, political betrayal of the U.S. in that the dream it presents is illusory to the immigrant. Though nothing earth shattering in itself, the subtlety with which such suggestions are made metaphorically in various texts allows the reader to simultaneously trace the development of character and detect elements of commentary upon U.S. life that might otherwise go unnoticed. Alphonso de Sintierra (whose name translates into "without land), the phony genealogical expert in Candelaria's *Memories of the Alhambra* is a case in point. Characterized by his cousin, a Señor Gomez, as one of those having the "devil in their tongue and money in their pockets," Sintierra's underhandedness makes him "a good Norteamericano" (33). That Sintierra has made his living threatening Mexican migrants into purchasing printed copies of the Declaration of Independence (19) only emphasizes Candelaria's point that U.S. luxury and freedom come tainted, that the national anthem can "turn sour . . . like spoiled milk" (160).

Oscar Hijuelos intertwines the themes of sexual and cultural initiation by mixing the seduction of lovers and their betrayals with immigration and introduction into the U.S. Over and over, the beginnings of a character's sexual activity metaphorically parallel that character's crossing over into the deceptive allure of U.S. culture and life. In *Mambo,* the thirteen year old Delores Fuentes encounters her sleeping father in "a state of extreme sexual arousal" and, feeling "her soul blacken as if she had just committed a terrible sin and condemned herself to the darkest room in hell," she expects "to turn around and find the devil himself standing beside her, a smile on his sooty face, saying, 'Welcome to America'" (65). The devil himself appears just pages later in the form of an "American fellow" whose ears turn "a livid red from the wine" (74). Claiming to work for Pepsodent toothpaste, this seemingly wealthy smooth talker tries to recruit her for a beauty pageant and then, on a deserted beach on Long Island, attempts to rape her. His "clean" smile and "wavy blond" (71) hair and his job in cosmetics suggest the larger image of the false attraction of superficial U.S. advertising. His hair "whipped like a sea flag in the wind" (73) and he throws up his arms "as if to say 'I'm not armed . . . '" On an allegorical level, Hijuelos could be alluding to the U.S. flag, patriotism and U.S. intervention into Latin America in general, the governmental pretense of peaceful assistance followed by brutal attack and violation.[6] Delores's two early clashes with "the devil" are connected further in her mind as the Pepsodent man's attack becomes a frustrated attempt at masturbation and she is reminded of her earlier initiative experience with her father's frustrated attempt to relieve himself. In *The Fourteen Sisters of Emilio Montez O'Brien*, there is a similar mixture of U.S. capitalistic seduction and sexual initiation. Margarita's first romance leads to disappointment when the object of her attraction, Curtis the aviator, proves to have a "sweet," blonde, farm girl fiancé in another town (71). The romance of her flight with this Douglas Fairbanks look alike (137)—in his daredevil, sopwith camel, trailing a "brightly colored banner" advertising an airshow—is deflated by her nausea, and the glow of the air show, like Delores's beauty pageant turns hollow and empty. Margarita's husband, Lester Thompson, is even more disillusioning despite his possessing all the "qualities and attributes that all young American men should aspire to" (*Fourteen* 137). It turns out he sexually degrades her in his desire to recreate "the happiest time of his life" (158)—a certain Parisian, carnival past with a French whore named Jeanette. Actually a lousy businessman, he is perversely "obsessed with her [Margarita's] bodily parts and secretions and scents" (182). Though he is photographed as the epitome of U.S. success, manager of Thompson's Electrical Appliance Department Store, with a house "on one of the better streets of Cobbleton . . . impeccable in a worsted English suit and hand-made shoes . . . perfectly tailored and elegant" (137), in actuality, he has bought her ("winning over the family" with gifts—187), and married, not for love, but out of a desire to disturb his wealthy and "proper" parents. She eventually recognizes being "demoted from wife to parent-rankling device" (184), throws away *Ivanhoe,* and, like the elderly grandmother Celia in *Dreaming in Cuban* (equally trapped in a marriage arrangement devoid of romance), begins reading *Madame Bovary.* Roberto Fernández mocks the same sort of romantic delusions in *Raining Backwards.* At one point, Connie tells her gringo lover Bill: "Bill, hold me, Kiss me. Thrill me. Make me your baby, forever. But hurry up. I've got to be back home before five to help Mima fry plantains" (97).

In contrast to past traditions, rarely in Latino literature is the seducer a woman, though there is some hint that the dyed platinum blond of gringolandia, the figure with the "fly-catcher tongue" seen kissing Pilar's father in *Dreaming in Cuban* could be the adulterous betrayer of "innocent" husbands.[7] Usually, the male figure (whether symbolic of larger facets of the American Dream or not) betrays a woman. Moreover, when the infamous mistress does appear, especially in Latina fiction, she instills in the reader a certain respect rather than disdain. This kind of privileging of the stereotypically negative female figure (for Helene Cixous: to see the "beauty" in the Medusa's laugh) allows writers like Sandra Cisneros to reverse the traditional image of the mistress. We sympathize with Clemencia, the narrator of "Never Marry a Mexican" and her gummy bear rebellion, not solely because we get the story from her perspective, but because we sense her frustration beneath her wit. We feel her vulnerability at the same time she lashes out (protesting too much) at those around her. She doesn't want to be "owned" by a man, especially one who will "plant" his toothbrush "in the toothbrush holder like a flag on the North Pole," yet her desire for independence (to escape being territorialized) means she sleeps alone in a "bed so big because he never stayed the whole night" (69). Similarly, we understand the nostalgic reverie of the adulterous couple in the car and their feasting in "Bread," mainly because the woman narrator offers a fleeting glimpse into the poverty of her childhood, pointing our sympathy toward the hardships of her life—so different from his—and away from the betrayal of the man's wife and family. Helena Viramontes's story, "The Broken Web," leads the reader into deeper and deeper understanding of the complexities of a family love triangle. By the end, we have come to sympathize, not only with Tomás's abused wife (who is never given any name), but also with her sister, Olivia, the mistress. Piecing together narrative threads, we learn of Olivia's trials growing up in the shadows of her more attractive younger sister, and her genuine love for her sister's husband: as, for instance, in the saloon, when she pets and comforts the drunken Tomás, in a futile attempt to share his pain (54). Olivia's revelation to her niece that she, Martha, the young girl whose confession opens the story, is not the daughter of Tomás, but the result of a clandestine relationship between Tomás's wife and another man, further strengthens the reader's empathy for the mistress/sister.

Both Cisneros and Viramontes clearly identify with the compound image of La Malinche and La Llorona in their willingness to disrupt the traditional roles of Latinas. As Sandra Messiner Cypress makes clear in her study *La Malinche in Mexican Literature: From History to Myth*, depending upon one's perspective, it is possible to see the legendary figure of La Malinche in both positive and negative terms. The traditional view, expounded by Octavio Paz in *The Labyrinth of Solitude*, depicts her as the betrayer of her Indian heritage and responsible for "malinchismo" or "the preference for foreign over native." As mistress of Cortés (Malintzin; Doña Marina, "La Lengua" or "the tongue), she worked as Cortés's confidante, translating between Montezuma and the conquistador, and thereby aiding the destruction of her own people. Through the years, her image then becomes symbolic of betrayal, violation (La Chingada) and due to blendings in Mexican folklore with the other negative female figure, La Llorona, abandonment.[8]

The contrasting view, that of most Chicana writers, argues that her liaison was justified by virtue of her being a slave and having no choice in the matter; she is therefore, "victim and not an instigator" (Rebolledo and Rivero 193). Called Malinal at birth (La Malinche is the hispanisized "syncretic mestizo" form of her name—Cypress 7) in 1501 or 1502 in Jaltipán or Olutla, she was the daughter of an Aztec family and sold into slavery as a young girl (by a jealous mother if we concur with Rosario Castellanos's poem "Malinche"—96-97). Along with others, she was given as a gift to Cortés. Modern writers reconstruct her symbolic image by pointing out the unpopularity of despotic Aztec rule, the betrayal by her own mother, and her individualistic integrity in breaking down the stereotypical domestic barriers for women of her time and place. She was "a woman who had and made choices rather than . . . the woman so often portrayed as the passive victim of rape and conquest" (Rebolledo and Rivero 193). She returns, in the Castellanos poem, to "scratch up the earth / in the place / where the midwife buried her umbilicus" (96). According to Anzaldúa, an ancient Indian tradition dictates that a baby girl's umbilical cord is buried beneath the house in order that "she will never stray from it and her domestic role" (*Borderlands* 36). She becomes the central image in the trio of Chicana "mothers" (Anzaldúa 31) celebrated in Chicano fiction and poetry: La Virgin de Guadalupe, La Llorona (who, betrayed, has killed her own children and now ghostlike threatens children from the riverbeds), and La Malinche. In some sense, La Malinche engendered the Mestizo/Chicano race by giving birth to Martín Cortés, and she remains a symbol of a certain pride in the capabilities and intelligence of the Indian woman, the feistiness of the threatening rebel. So too, because La Llorona's cries echo the wailing "feeble protests" of Aztec women who's sons were sent off to the ritual "flower wars," the mythical blend of both figures has come to represent an alternative to the negative, passive roles for women in Latino life. For this reason, their combined prestige, like that of their mythic counterparts, Medusa or Medea is a source of strength for Latina heroines.

Sandra Cisneros's sympathy for the La Gritona/La Llorona figure shows the writer's understanding of the reasons, or the "quiet" (51) things that could drive a woman to "the darkness under the trees" (51). The battered wife with the unromantic name of Cleófilas in "Woman Hollering Creek" is first betrayed by her family: as her father leaves her he says: 'I am your father, I will never abandon you.'" Then her romantic notions of love and marriage give way to a cruel reality of abuse and poverty. So, on the way to her new home in Sequin, she laughs *at* the creek named La Gritona, but when she escapes the trap of her domestic torture, with an independent woman named Felice (happy) in a pickup, Cleófilas laughs *with* the creek. Cisneros transforms the haunting folkloric image of a women's mournful crying into the sound of a "gurgling . . . ribbon of laughter"(56). The question of whether La Gritona had cried from pain (the pain of not having been able to be the dutiful mother) or from anger (the anger of having been forced into a domestic role despite a husband or lover's betrayal) haunts Cleófilas throughout the story. Changing an eerie cry, associated in childhood stories with loneliness and despair and grief to an assertive "Tarzan" bellow of laughter and freedom for women is a significant alteration of the folk tradition.

Deflation of romantic notions, especially those implanted in young women by novelas (soap operas) and romantic novels is prevalent in Latina fiction. Cisneros traces how Cleófilas grows away from a self-deception ingrained in her by her parents and her Mexican culture. In the cinema, there is a hair "quivering annoyingly on the screen" which is later tied to "a doubt. Slender as a hair" (51) regarding her husband's fidelity. When her husband throws her romance novel at her (literally "throwing the book at her"—Cisneros turning metaphor into life) and gives her a "crack in the face," (53) her romantic delusions begin to disappear. The power of various "mass-produced fantasies" (to use critic Tania Modleski's phrase) begins to crumble as Cleófilas (a name she resents at first because it is not sufficiently romantic) sees the reality of her abusive husband. The telenovela of her childhood "Tu o Nadie" (You or No one) is transformed into a soap opera her neighbor watches called "Maria de Nadie" (Maria of No One) which follows the archetypal plot of a Harlequin romance outlined by Modleski (36). In her domestic trap, the heroine is sandwiched between the mysterious widow Soledad (Solitude, loneliness) and a faithful, religious widow La Señora Dolores (Pains). The "crack" between her neighbors' houses, between pain and loneliness is the arroyo called La Gritona, the space of freedom and laughter.

Cleófilas resembles Ed Vega's narrator Mendoza in "La Novela" who falls "under the spell of the soap opera" and sees his life "in those terms" (Vega *Mendoza's Dreams* 158). Cecile Pineda overtly mocks these romance traditions as, in her third novel, the heroine, Ana Magdalena Figueroa da Cunha, about to be abandoned by her first heroic idol, seems well aware of the implausibility of typical romantic scenarios gleaned from her secret reading in the convent. Each imagined script "breaks down," as she gets closer and closer to the river where Ballado keeps his boat. The first scenario that "the wind would carry her call to him like a flight of evening doves. He would wave in recognition . . . she . . . would run toward him breathlessly, her long dark ringlets flying in the wind . . . " is rejected because they don't really know each other. The second and third possible unfoldings are disrupted when her high heels break off (*The Love Queen of the Amazon* 50-51). Whereas in the Vega story, as in the earlier novel *Aunt Julia and the Scriptwriter* by Vargas Llosa, the complications of people living in delusive worlds of novelas result in absurdist comedy, both Cisneros and Pineda treat the results of mass-media romantic instruction on young women somewhat more seriously. Cisneros's Cleófilas is not altogether escaping, after all, rather returning to "chores that never ended" and her "six good-for-nothing brothers, and one old man's complaints." What is more, her father has always known that she would long to return. Her life bears similarities to the fantasies of TV, not in its romance and "happily ever after" marriage, but in the typical "soap opera" trauma of abuse and pain (55). Betrayed on both sides of the border, she can only admire a woman, like Felice, who laughs at everything and does what she wants. Pineda parodies the dreamy prose of romance at the same time her heroine is allowed to deconstruct that sort of language as it occurs to her:

> "Sergio Ballado?" she would intone with the unblushing assurance of knowing what she was about to do.
>
> "That's me," he would reply.
>
> (*Idiot*, she would think, *of course, I know it's you*—but instead she would smile in a mysterious but engaging way.) (50)

Returning for a moment to Hijuelos's novel, *Fourteen*, we find again a form of romantic betrayal. Margarita's sister Jacqueline, seventy five, "after a lifetime of virginity" suddenly falls for a twenty-five year old "Spaniard from Málaga" who takes her on a picnic to Bear Mountain on the Hudson river, only to be caught later "on a street corner, necking furiously with a brunette." Hijuelos allusion to the Bob Dylan song "Talking Bear Mountain Picnic Massacre Blues" (about an eventful picnic at Bear Mountain where a boat capsized) foreshadows this disappointment. The fact that the unfaithful young lover is a Spaniard suggests that the Latino's belief in glorious European roots (a symptom of Paz's "Malinchismo") is just as dubious as are the allurements of the U.S. In *House,* Hector Santinio is betrayed by Cuba in much the same way. He longs for a Cuban drink for years until he learns the object of his fantasy is actually Hershey's chocolate syrup (179). When the family gathers at a farm, the "big event of the day," a Cuban pig roast, is tainted somewhat by the black tarantulas that "rain down" from a nearby tree like "hundreds of black flowers . . . creeping like fire in all directions" (82-83). Moreover, while in Cuba, he picks up certain "microbios" which damage his liver and he comes to associate the shape of that organ with the shape of the island itself (104). Cuba, for Hector, "had become a mysterious and cruel phantasm standing behind the door" (106).

Emilio O'Brien is romantically betrayed first by an actress, appropriately named May Springweather (Jacqueline's affair also occurs in early summer) with a voice like music, who leaves him as quickly as the season she's named after. As "glamorous as Ginger Rogers" (240), she's about as reliable as the Douglas Fairbanks aviator. Two years later, during World War II, Emilio is enchanted by an Italian woman he sees framed in a window: "beautiful and serene . . . hair falling down over her shoulders, a baby in her arms, the child reaching up and touching her face" (252). This Madonna figure brings him into dinner with the family and then abruptly stops him when he attempts to kiss her. It is her voice as well that haunts him, and her "expression of pure affection" (252) which attracts him so. That she is inaccessible only points to Emilio's irretrievable infancy of love and peace to which he (like Nestor in *Mambo*) is obsessively devoted, to the extent that his desire to "suckle" the breasts of women seems nearly perverse. Even when his wife Jessica dies in a fire, he looks down at her corpse and thinks of "the pleasure of his tongue on her breasts" (374). Like many of Hijuelos's protagonists, Emilio is trapped by an infantile desire for his mother's protection and his lost state of innocence.

Nelson O'Brien, the Irish patriarch of *Fourteen*, has stock in a flag company (61) and he has clearly bought into the American dream in all its manifestations. The same is true for the practical Lourdes Puente in Garcia's *Dreaming in Cuban* with her "Yankee Doodle Bakery" with "tricolor cupcakes and Uncle Sam marzipan" (136). She wears a bicentennial "red, white, and blue two-piece suit" and to her daughter, she is "a thrashing avalanche of patriotism and motherhood" (144). Yet, in *Fourteen*, the glory of the U.S. at the time of Nelson's photography job in Cuba will fade by the end of the century so much so that Margarita will find Nelson's pictures of the Spanish American War unsaleable. Hijuelos purposely juxtaposes Nelson O'Brien's proud saluting of the marching U.S. soldiers (their "brilliance, their heroism, their manly virtues") with Margarita's disastrous marriage. Both the fourth of July celebration and the wedding occur on the same church steps. The American male image (soldier, salesman, manager, pilot) takes a beating here as time after time, the shallow nature of U.S. advertisement and deception is undermined by event. Near the end of the book, in many ways a journey from dreamy, hazy nostalgia to pragmatic understanding and coping, Hijuelos further hints that immigration to the U.S. may have drawbacks. Cobbleton for instance, first presents itself as "desolate . . . but it was America!" (381). The porch of their new home is filled with "cocoons and spiderwebs" and "America *looming* in the distance" (382). Impressions change as people grow and this house, opened first with a skeleton key, will become the image of paradisal heaven for the fourteen children, and, especially for Emilio, come to represent that lost past "when everyone in the world seemed good," "clean and sparkling and sinless"(339), a Jungian womb of nurturing and perfection, forever gone, always desired.

The dream of easy life, the tempting qualities of North America are usually countered in Latino fiction by stark reality. To the perceptive

Pilar Puente of *Dreaming*, there is a discrepancy that needs addressing in the fact that "families of guajiros slept in the city's parks under flashing Coca-Cola signs" (206). This is why the products of U.S. capitalism often symbolize the deception that North American governments and companies have visited upon immigrant populations. "All Anglos think about is money" says "Nana" the earthmother, grandmother figure in Candelaria's *Memories of the Alhambra* (71). Judith Cofer's jíbaros will learn that "La tierra de nieve" only *sounds* like paradise; it isn't (*Line of the Sun* 152). The narrator of Cisneros's *House on Mango Street* buys a replica of the Statue of Liberty at a junkshop for a dime (20).

As early as Tomás Rivera's classic . . . *Y no se lo tragó la tierra,* the migrant workers, scorching and suffocating in the sun, are warned against drinking ice cold Coke because its sweetness will make them sick. This notion of U.S. product as "forbidden fruit" is common. The easy materialism of the U.S. suggests a "magnetic world" of "treasures" that sucks up Jose Rafa (in *Memories of the Alhambra*) "from the beanfields of Los Rafas like iron filings from dirt" (35), and eventually lures him away from the natural familial world of his Indian/Mexican ancestry. An Arlene figure from the Viramontes story, "Miss Clairol" represents the totally lost soul, the bleached blonde incapable of recognizing what is truly valuable, and metaphorically changing her true "roots" by administering the cosmetic falsity of cheap product. In *Mambo,* Cesar Castillo and Vanna Vane, in *Fourteen,* Nestor and a "bleached blonde," in Garcia's *Dreaming*, an adulterous father and his "puffy blonde with a "flicking, disgusting . . . flycatcher tongue" (25)—these are characters indicative of the hollow superficiality of U.S. life where people live on easy U.S. credit, and are incapable of resisting the temptations of the cheap and valueless in the United States. The Latino who falls for the blonde-haired gringa is cleverly satirized in Goldman's *The Ordinary Seaman* when one sailor, on his way to paint solvent induced insanity, finds a blonde hair (delivered by the wind) stuck to his chest and proceeds to sleep with it and run it through his fingers and mouth in utter devotion. He calls it "La Gringita (336). Thus, the symbolic dyeing of the hair to cover the true Latin American heritage refers to bleaching out the culture—erasing racial and ethnic markers—and concealing the authentic self in favor of the trivial, yet cosmetically acceptable. This is what Pilar rejects in *Dreaming* as she "goes south" toward her grandmother and Cuba in the opening of Garcia's novel.

The motif of betrayal by the U.S. mirrors the reality for Latinos in a world where, as Bruce-Novoa has pointed out, serving your country in the military service or educating yourself in U.S. schools or reaping the benefits of the Bill of Rights itself have proven unworthy and disillusioning, that in fact, though tempting in its democratic preaching, the U.S. has "duped and exploited" the Latino believers more often than not (Bruce-Novoa 120). Anzaldúa remarks that the border patrol, la migra, "hides behind the local McDonalds" (*Borderlands* 11). Betrayal in the fiction reflects economic and political betrayal by a country whose immigration barriers fluctuate around the volatile rates of U.S. unemployment (illegals are overlooked in good times, condemned in bad ones) or the U.S. government's need for soldiers to, in Algarín's phrase, "clean the battlefields" in foreign wars (i.e. the Korean war saw a drastic increase in Mexican—American casualties[9]). It should be remembered that Wilson's famous Jones Act of 1917 which gave Puerto Ricans U.S. citizenship cannot be divorced from the wartime U.S. government's need for military recruits. Recognition of the duality of U.S. promises, the deception and seductive elements of U.S. culture constitutes maturity. "In this country all you really need to know is how to count" declares Nina in Arturo Islas's *The Rain God* (42). In Judith Cofer's *The Line of the Sun*, a character's back is badly burned when, as part of the American's "economical new system" canisters of pesticide are strapped onto his shoulders (11). Later, Truman's lottery system (in which desperate Jíbaros—rural Puerto Rican peasants—were rewarded with degrading migrant labor contracts) comes under the control of "enterprising con-men" (150). The generally omniscient narrator of the first half of Cofer's novel steps away from her objectivity to describe in judgmental terms, more than once, one character's useless military death: "three months later he was blasted into a thousand pieces over the soil of Korea" (53). The double standards of U.S. Corporations come under fire frequently in Latino fiction: Goldman describes a military base in fairy tale terms: "a few blocks down from the embassy . . . like a Disneyland castle with its bright gray castellated walls, turreted towers, drawbridgelike entrance and antique cannons" (72). In Cofer's novel, the boss of the Nabisco cookie factory betrays Rosa (30); in Castillo's *So Far From God*, a high-tech weapons company, Acme International, poisons its diligent workers with toxic chemicals (180). In *La Maravilla*, "*pobre* Maria [is] sprayed with pesticides in a field near Glendale" (8) and later the "Liquid-Ox plant" uses migrants to "clean up and bury the chemical spillage," handing out "impressive, new white cotton gloves and paper masks to attract their workers" (Véa 25). The "chemical faces" in the sideshows of the local carnivals (88) fascinate Young boys. The U.S. betrays Miguel Grande, the protagonist's father in Islas's novel when the land of opportunity shows that it is ruled by prejudice and he is denied his promotion (61)—a result, correctly noted by Rosaura Sánchez, of the scandal surrounding his homosexual brother's murder (Sánchez 124). Hector Calderón even reads Anaya's *Bless Me, Ultima,* as commentary on the devastating effects of the nuclear tests at Los Alamos.[10]

Roberto G. Fernández's *Raining Backwards* mocks the American dream in an even more obvious fashion. Jacinto Enrique Rodriguez, alias Keith, eldest son of one of the novel's two central Miami Cuban families, tries to go to school, but is beaten up for being a "SPIC" [in capital letters] and subsequently finds the "land of opportunity"(73) in drug dealing which allows him to buy his father a doughnut shop and his mother jewelry. His encounter with public education reminds the reader of Antonio, the protagonist of *Bless Me, Ultima* and his journey into the belly of the "cavernous" school building where he will feel like a lonely "outcast," experiencing for the first time, a grown-up's "tristesa de la vida" (54-55). In Rodriguez's novel *Spidertown,* a young Puerto Rican street "runner" searches for success and respect in the cramped environment of New York City's South Bronx. The drug dealer Spider mocks the "American dream" and Miguel's admiration for Spider as father, as "every image of family and sharing and teamwork, of power, success, and fame" actually "negates" it. Miguel's attitudes are confused. At the same time he rejects Spider's opinion that the two of them are "livin" the American Dream, "climbin' the ladder," and feels that his own goals, of "making it to the top honestly and cleanly" are the real American Dream, he also thinks the whole thing is a lie, that "no spick kid was going to make it that way" (185). The critic Alberto Sandoval rightly questions whether ideologemes like "Number One," "All-American Boy" or "American Way of Life" are ever "guaranteed to all immigrants" and whether buying into the hegemonic "America" means losing forever one's previous cultural background (201-202). It is the inability of characters to satisfactorily answer such questions that feeds their complexes and anxieties, and impairs their relationships with others.

That there is danger in those figures who exemplify the larger U.S. is clear throughout Latino fiction. In Arias's *Road,* for instance, Fausto and Mario meet up with a bare-chested, smiling Mr. American with his pink frisbee and his doberman. This character is the male counterpart to Cisneros's Megan from "Never Marry a Mexican," a "redheaded Barbie doll in a fur coat. One of those scary Dallas types, hair yanked into a ponytail, big shiny face like the women behind the cosmetic counters at Neiman's" (79). Or, as Véa puts it during Josephina's surreal dream on the bus, an example of impossible "*gringo americano* code requirements" which dictate that woman have "no distinguishing facial features, no pores, no hairs on the upper lip. The nose itself simply must not exist" (189). Sandra Benítez has an interesting story in her story-novel *A Place Where the Sea Remembers* in which the stereotypical American tourist's fear of the dangerous Mexican is turned upside down. Here a Mexican photographer grows increasingly paranoid about a "gringo" in a Ford station wagon (incidentally wearing a "thick, blond ponytail") who gives him a ride home to his coastal village of Santiago. Suspecting he is about to be robbed and murdered by the gringo, the photographer is overcome by a "fear as misshappened as the trees" (Benítez 35) which radically distorts his understanding of an innocent situation. The gringo, in turn, catching the paranoid Mexican rummaging through his belongings, also misreads the events and abruptly leaves his passenger stranded on a deserted beach in the night. What the story reveals is what Cisneros hints at with her description of the Texan menace: that stereotypical fears of North Americans are just as powerful for Latinos (and perhaps more justified, given the political history)[11] as those fears of Latinos are for the average North American. A simple reversal of perspective and the enemy is friend, the friend, enemy. An episode early in Francisco Goldman's *The Long Night of White Chickens* demonstrates the problem. The narrator, half Guatemalan but raised in Massachusetts, betrays his Guatemalan friend by breaking their pact to jump simultaneously into a walled off yard protected by a ferocious German shepherd. Though perhaps a typical adolescent prank, the narrator becomes a "Gringo de mierda" (36) and the betrayal becomes allegorically important; it is the U.S. side of Roger Graetz's personality that is at fault, and it destroys, at least in the eyes of the Guatemalan native, the "amistad" that led to the pact to be begin. What is suggested here is that there is something unreliable and devious, something superficial and selfish about the U.S. For the inmates of Miguel Piñero's now classic drama *Short Eyes*, the most despicable character—amid murderers and thieves and drug addicts—is the "gringo" child molester, Clark Davis. His deranged personality, however normal he at first appears to the audience, is eventually seen as a twisted product of contaminated societal values that the microcosm of the prison world exposes. In Judith Cofer's *The Line of the Sun,* a young Puerto Rican girl is scared of the basement. The lost heroine, Flor, in Goldman's novel is similarly petrified of her finished basement room in a New England home (47-48). Until the reader understands that rooms beneath the earth do not exist in Latin American homes and therefore carry the connotations of graves, the fear appears unjustified, even a sign of neurosis. Flor's suffocating sense of isolation leads her upstairs to the kitchen where the narrator, Roger Graetz finds her with "eyes glowing like a frightened forest animal's devouring, as if it were a candy bar, a whole bar of butter.

The short story "Sometimes, If You Listen Closely, You Can Hear Crying in the Zoo" in Ed Vega's collection *Mendoza's Dreams* interestingly reflects on U.S. materialism and its enticing allure to the vulnerable. Gregory Sandoval's upper westside apartment is a veritable museum of material products and Gregory's marital problems revolve around his struggle to escape their influence. He treads upon his wife's "yellow rubber daisies" glued to the bottom of the tub (95). He resents his son's fascination with a cereal that tastes like sugar coated "dust" (102). He dislikes working for an advertising company that sells "cans and boxes of junk . . . harmful not so much to the body but to the psyche" (103). His profession, his bathroom rituals and his marital frustrations remind the reader of Leopold Bloom. Most of all, he resents his blonde wife, Gayle, with her "angelic pose," and "porcelain-like" arms who smells like "Camay and Johnson & Johnson baby powder (105), and is "almost commercial perfect" (104).[12] She stands in her kitchen "poised at the bronze colored stove with its matching grease and smoke removing unit, preparing to dish up his eggs onto a bright orange enameled dish" (105). Gregory (like Lester Thompson in *Fourteen*) desires to escape the sterility of his domestic life (his wife's vitamins, his daughter's righteousness, his son's athletic prowess) and delve into bohemian fantasies of art, wine, sex, Greenwich Village, Tribeca and Paris. He longs to exchange "the heaviness of an American breakfast" for the "magic ingredient" of the croissant made by the "magicians of love:" French Bakers. Obsessed with the seedy side of Italian Mafia, he sees his wife as a stewardess, cut from a uniform "mold" with a "deceptive sweetness." In fact, he reasons, it was his own "greed" and "need to possess America" that attracted him to her

(105), as she had been attracted to him because of his adamant desire to reduce his accent through "clear enunciation" (90). Yet her "All-American" cheery self has left her so sterile that Sandoval is "convinced she timed her flatulations to the crash of the cymbals" in the Dvorak symphony she plays while in the shower. By contrast, in the shower Gregory sings Spanish gibberish with reckless abandon, the "only time of the day when he felt totally uninhibited" (94). His ultimate bizarre act of dressing up as a gorilla and attacking her is the culmination of pent-up instinctual desire, pure Dionysian sexual frustration (like Victor in another Vega story, "Collazo's Diet"). He commits, to use Gayle Sandoval's euphemism, "a USA," an "unnatural sexual act" (100) and while he smashes up the "mushroomlike, molded plastic, white kitchen table" he roars in bestial, if illogical pleasure. By destroying the sterile products, rejecting the U.S. influence that has convinced his fifteen year old daughter that parenting is "outmoded" and turned his son into a mindless sportsman, and by attacking the rigid superficiality of his wife, Sandoval asserts his conviction that the real value of the U.S. lies not in advertised products, but in "action . . . movement . . . leaping headlong into danger . . . shooting from the hip, no holds barred" (109). He impetuously rebels against the "closed minded" vacancy that his "All American" ("near Nazi"—108) wife has come to represent, and doing so he overcomes his lifelong fear of not conforming to U.S. popular culture. He has tried to look Italian when Italians threatened him, then claimed allegiance with Puerto Rican gangs to protect himself from others. He has attempted to reduce his accent and become a part of advertising. Finally, his imitation of the sad gorilla in the Central Park Zoo costs him his marriage, but he has asserted his individuality. Like his namesake Gregor Samsa, he is awakened from his passionless and sterile existence through metamorphosis which allows him to disregard the "sweetness" and "sugar coated" kind of stale and vacant life he has been living and which by inference suggests life in the U.S. commsumerist society.

A short story writer like Benjamin Alire Sáenz uses the triviality of U.S. products, the cheap plastics, for example, to subtly critique through juxtaposition a character or a belief, as well as to symbolically debunk capitalistic paltriness in this country. After Olivia, in "Obliterate the Night," reads her husband's farewell letter in which he claims he is leaving her, "playing the heavy," for both their sakes, she sticks the letter on the refrigerator with a "watermelon magnet" where it hangs "like an unread grocery list" (Sáenz 46). This symbolic trivialization of the man's words is integral to a story about the inability of words to communicate what is vital and the deceptions of language, but it also insinuates the larger idea that somehow practicality and colorful gimmickry replace written language. Similarly, there is Roberto G. Fernandez's Mirta, a woman who wipes off her Bella Aurora conditioning cream with Burger King napkins, then recreates the beaches of Cuba by spreading cat litter over her bathroom floor, and simulates the ocean waves by pointing an electric fan over the water and dropping in Alka Seltzer tablets. When the drug dealer Jacinto (Keith) is captured by a policeman named Jim Carter and dragged out of his parent's home, he laments the lack of "sense of family" in the U.S.: "It was humiliating being treated like dirt right in front of my mom" (73). On the one hand, Fernández points to the superficiality of the American dream, to how often it is distorted into capitalistic greed, and on the other, he pokes fun at the importance of "family" to the Cuban—American, achieving a sort of satirical bicultural parody.

Interspersing products across cultures juxtaposes cultural traditions in sometimes unflattering ways. In Arturo Islas's *The Rain God*, for instance, a Mexican/Indian seance is somewhat hampered by one character's nose "itching from the Aqua Velva they [had] sprinkled into the air to induce serenity (*Rain* 34). This is the method of Joyce in the parallels between Ulysses and Bloom, the lofty mythic deflated by the banal everyday. As Vásquez has shown, in *Raining Backwards,* Roberto Fernández's allusions to classic titles (i.e. "Keithlied," "La Chanson de la Cousine") present a situation where "the dubious present-day heroes . . . are parodically measured against their medieval ancestors-in-myth" (Vásquez "Parody" 99). For a writer like Helena Viramontes, the opposition of cultural items and products enhances the sense of displacement felt by people making do with what they have despite (sometimes oblivious) to ironic incongruities. Thus in "The Moths" the herbalist abuela prepares to grow her plants in Hills Brothers Coffee cans (24) and prepares a "balm out of dried bats wings and Vicks" (23) while the daughter/narrator uses Vaseline for shoe polish (25). Taken together, images like these can be read in interesting ways: the organic (bat's wings, the herbalist) confronts the conglomerate manufacturer and the synthesized chemical product; the all-purpose slimy substance serves to gloss over reality. Juxtapositions like these deserve attention because they reveal the writer's attitude toward the cultural connotations they invoke.

Other writers use similarly disrupting techniques that pit U.S. culture against a past ideal. The hyperbole, typical of Roberto G. Fernández's *Raining Backwards,* satirizes, not the U.S. or Cuba as countries, the gringo or the immigrant as people, but the "enabling fictions" or pipedreams of individuals who can't see the illusionary nature of both old world and new, who do not understand the uselessness of either exaggerating a golden past or believing in an ideal future. The motif of a lost paradise, common to writers in general, is particularly important to Latino writers. The attempt to recover a world which does not exist, to regain the mythic perfection of a lost homeland (Aztlán) or an island paradise, be it Puerto Rico, Cuba or the Dominican Republic, is futile and consequently a source of parodic humor to the Latino fiction writer. Moreover, the lost paradise (the illusory center) changes as characters move and grow, as the disillusioning present becomes the ordered, controlled and unalterable glory of the past. Paradise exists in the future as well. For the Montez O'Brien family, the idea refers to Ireland, Cuba, Cobbleton, PA, and even Mars depending upon the character and his or her own sense of memory and nostalgia. Shifting notions of Edenic perfection are central to Elena Castedo's novel *Paradise.* A refugee from the Spanish Civil war, the young protagonist, Soledad or Solita,[13] is brought to a rich South American estate called "El Topaz." To Solita and her mother, paradise means their lost Spanish town, Galmeda. To the children of the estate, their home is their paradise. Though her mother believes that "the best way to get where you want to be is to please those who own the road" (281, 304), Solita grows to recognize the illusory, false paradise of the wealthy, and to believe with her practical father that "paradise was a hoax invented by priests to seduce nitwits (3). She resolves never "to go to Paradise, nor do what the Romans did . . . [but] do what the Gypsy said: cross the oceans and find love" (327).

Sustained by enabling fictions, various characters move through their disrupted lives in a sort of daze, often infatuated with memories and dreams connected with the orderly perfection of the lives they have forever lost. In the works of Garcia, Fernández and Hijuelos, there are several melancholy Miami Cubans "succumbing to a cloying nostalgia" (*Dreaming* 113) for their "martyred island" (Fernández *Raining* 221), because, like Rufino Puente, Pilar's father, they just "can't be transplanted" (129). Hijuelos frequently describes his characters as "floating" away from reality. In *Mambo*, Delores metaphorically "floats away" and recalls Havana during her first sexual encounter with Nestor (90). Nestor, playing the trumpet is thrown into "a heaven of floating space . . . lost in melody" (113). Delores's father, at a bar, is "for one moment . . . lifted out of himself, [and] float[s] upward to a place of eternal relief and comfort" (71). For Hijuelos, Eliade's "magic flight" becomes a "magic float." In his earlier novel, Mercedes, "the greatest invalid of all times" (208) is likewise a floater. During her honeymoon, she seems "to drift away, floating off the bed" (29), and she repeats this act during routine sex with her husband Alejo (65) and during Hector's birth. Cecile Pineda, in her novel *Love Queen*, relies on magical realism to parody this dreamy release from life when the elderly Clemencia, with her tendency toward repeating "one nostalgic reminiscence after another" finally, literally floats away.

Overall, Latino writers, especially Cuban-Americans, take nostalgia seriously. Cubans gather in Miami bars to play dominos and critique Castro in purely negative terms. In New York as well, these men (and they are usually men) see the world from a Cuban perspective. Locations, like Pablo's apartment in *Mambo*, are measured in terms of Cuba: "two minutes from the 125th Street El, an overnight train ride and forty-five-minute flight from Havana, and five minutes from Harlem" (34). Cesar's girl friend, Vanna Vane, is as "prestigious as a passport" (19), the document most coveted by the exiles. A similar drunken and displaced Cuban in Abraham Rodriguez Jr.'s *Spidertown*, with eyes like "black marbles in tomato soup" pays homage to Castro ("Homenaje a Castro") with his flatulence: "a long raspberry that inspired some applause" (76). Such incidents occur in films as well, as in Leon Ichaso's "El Super" which sympathetically depicts a Cuban who can't adjust to New York City winters. Mercedes Sorrea Santinio of *Our House in the Last World*, to provide another example, is never able to quite come to terms with the "cultural schizophrenia" of being Cuban and living in New York. She slips into illusions that center around her childhood house in Cuba where she sits in a garden surrounded by "the smells of food cooking," and her beloved dead father's affection (215). She remembers "only the good and not the bad," and although Hijuelos has intentionally left out the "bad" from the opening chapters of the novel (in order, presumably to narratively infer his character's repression and denial), we are told later of the beatings and the suffering she endured in her mythic childhood home (49). Her husband Alejo and his friends "soften up and bend like vines, glorying in the lost joys of childhood" because "political talk about

Cuba always led to nostalgic talk" (*House* 167). Others fantasize about the revolution to come and the illusion keeps them going. Slipping in and out of his characters' minds, Hijuelos as narrator ironically deflates certain island fantasies, especially the machista opinions of Alejo Santinio. In Cuba, "they know how to raise children so a man doesn't get involved . . . a man could truly have his way" (67), and there "you could always find some poor unhappy person who could clean a house" (113). In Cuba, "the world was different [and] people believed in God and children died at early ages of the fever and tuberculosis" (12). These melancholy people are not limited to Cuba, however. One of Nicholasa Mohr's heroines, Lucia, in a delusional state, drowns herself in a river of "quiet bliss," recalling the "beautiful riverbed in her mountain village," her lost island innocence ("Happy Birthday" 95, 102). There is too, the character of Zoraida in "Aunt Rosa's Rocker" who rocks herself into a nostalgic trance because of her sexual frustrations in life. Her chair is directly connected to her world in PR (25) and becomes "the one place where she felt she could be herself, where she could really be free" (29) and where she could "remember" (30): rocking, regressing, returning. *The Mambo Kings Play Songs of Love*, one reviewer has stated, is not so much about Cuban immigrants searching for the American dream, but about Cuban Americans dreaming (Jefferson 24). The dream of returning to an Edenic paradise recurs in the novel with the same pounding insistence of Cesar's many-faceted drums (*Mambo* 252), or the cyclical repetition of "Beautiful Maria of My Soul," the 78rpm record playing and replaying throughout Cesar's last days in "The Hotel Splendour."

Not all characters, however, succumb to an overwhelming nostalgia for the past. Delores Fuentes (before she marries Nestor Castillo) comes to terms with her illusions as a result of her sexual initiation with the "Pepsodent man." She is no longer a child repudiating the world like the heroine of the poem she has memorized: Poe's "Annabel Lee" (72). Her initiation experience brings with it a maturity of character such that she can no longer escape into an imaginary "kingdom by the sea," nor evade practical reality by reading romance novels or detective stories which previously have succeeded in taking "her mind off the terrors of the world and the sadnesses that ran madly through her heart" (62). Like Alejo Santinio's cousins in Hijuelos's *House*, Delores tries not to "allow the old world, the past, to hinder [her life]" (182). Where the earlier novel's heroine, Mercedes Santinio, entombs herself in her illusory past (as Annabel Lee is "shut up" in a "sepulchre there by the sea"), Delores enters the liminal space of hybridity. One of the problems with Gustavo Perez Firmat's reading of Hijuelos's novels is his denial of this mid-way state which is why he views Mercedes in purely negative terms, as a "manic-depressive." Characters must either remain Cuban or become American as "life on the hyphen" is a mere transitional state, doomed to disappear when Perez Firmat's own "1.5" generation of Cubans is replaced by younger Cuban-Americans. Hijuelos, he argues, is writing his "anglocentric" novels "toward America" (*Life* 137). Yet the America we find in the books indicates the author's mixed feelings. Further, Perez Firmat's analysis, in many ways insightful, is based entirely upon the male protagonists, their cultural adjustments to the U.S. and their oedipal struggles with father/uncle figures. Nowhere does he allow for the complexities of the women who, like Delores, walk the line between cultures, and like the characters in other Cuban-American novels journey in both directions.

Achieving one's heart's desire is often tied to a plan to get back what was lost upon leaving the old world. Cesar and Nestor long for a club that mirrors the pre-Revolutionary success of the Cuban night life scene of the 1950's. Later, Cesar plans to open a small store: the "bodega" dream of numerous characters. In Nicholasa Mohr's "A Very Special Pet," the Fernández family dreams of their island village and owning their own farm where the children's pet chicken named Joncrofo (after Joan Crawford) might "run loose" (*El Bronx* 4). By the story's end, however, while Mrs. Fernandez continues to sing her "familiar" song about "a beautiful island where the tall green palm trees swayed under a golden sky and the flowers were always in bloom" (12), her attempt to butcher the chicken for an island style meal of "arroz con pollo" is unsuccessful. The desire for fricassee made from cabra (goat) sends an Ed Vega character (in a story aptly called "The Pursuit of Happiness") into an illegal business scheme of raising goats for slaughter, the result of which is typical Vega style, slapstick comedy. The writer pokes fun at, among other things, the storeowner's inability to replicate PR within East Harlem. Rufino Puente in *Dreaming in Cuban* has a similar scheme to supply "all of Brooklyn" with honey by developing apiculture in an abandoned warehouse, but his idea is quashed by his ever practical wife who secretly releases the bees, getting stung in the process so badly "she could hardly open her eyes" (30). Another Vega hero in the story "The Barbosa Express" is more successful when he ingeniously steals a New York subway car and then transforms it into a replica of everything he misses from the island of Puerto Rico. The success here, though it provides a momentary illusion of the old world, has less to do with the possibility of regaining the Edenic island as it does with Barbosa's knack for subverting the system—literally in this case, as he works underground to force the trains to change directions, and free him from the channels and regulations that the Independent Subway System or IND dictates. The story is about the power of Barbosa, a Puerto Rican "Jerómino Anónimo," a small fry, who, having been through his share of "immigrant nonsense" (114), exerts his own independence (on the fourth of July) to the ultimate degree and creates a Puerto Rican paradise beneath the city: brightly colored living rooms, kitchen, nursery, dance floors etc. Vega again celebrates the little man in his story "Mercury Gomez" in which a small black Puerto Rican relies on his invisibility—the result of his being "black and small" (145) and on his understanding of U.S. principles for speed and uniformity: "They want everything in a hurry and they want everybody to kinda be the same. You know, carbon copies. Polaroid and Xerox" (147). Working with other "invisible" friends, he develops a procedure for delivering mail throughout Manhattan and rises above a position of servitude (in which he is derogatorily known as "Speedy Gonzalez") into one of power and prestige as the head of Mercury Communications. Jack Agüeros tells a tale of two similarly efficient clockworkers who manage to do quite well amid the hectic "Bim Bam Boom" ("Horologist" 48) of New York life, maintaining their own island sense of time and craftsmanship. In another of his stories, a resourceful hotel laundry washer teams up with a woman to start a food business in Central Park.

The Puerto Rican's underground success is suggestive of ambivalence toward U.S. business ventures in general. As Mary Vásquez points out about Roberto Fernández's, Vega's humor also depends upon the reader's understanding of a U.S. "consumer paradise" and its materialistic allure for Latinos.[14] The Cubans in his stories (where Cubans own the majority of small stores, bodegas, etc.) are not particularly admirable, just as Mima's plantain business for Fernández, or Lourdes Puente's "Yankee Doodle Bakery" for Garcia are also signs of an assimilation and denial of cultural heritage that the novels do not support. Vásquez notes the skill with which Mima embodies "the classic American ideal of the self-made (wo) man" as "negotiator with the encompassing majority culture" ("Gender in Exile" 81), and the same could be said for Lourdes Puente. Both women celebrate their patriotism in grandiose fashion: Lourdes dresses in a "red, white, and blue two-piece suit for her bicentennial grand opening of her second store (144) and Mima is interviewed by TV cameras in her home while a chorus sings "God Bless America." Yet both these exiled women, despite their skills in the "navigation of majority waters" (Vásquez 82) pay the price of estrangement from their children, especially their daughters. Pilar mocks the statue of liberty; Connie rejects her mother's lessons. Both mothers rigidly adhere to conservative sexual codes for their daughters (i.e. Pilar is admonished for bathing too long) and both daughters reject such restrictions as hypocrisies and antiquated customs. Pilar agrees with her "abuela" that Lourdes's behavior is the result of her "frustration at things she can't change" (*Dreaming* 63). The vehemence of parental control serves only to drive Pilar toward her grandmother, her boyfriends, and her Cuban heritage, and it pushes Connie toward her own demise. Mima's son Jacinto, on the other hand, adapts the capitalistic enthusiasm of his mother, but uses it to subvert the system by becoming a drug dealer. Jacinto is one of those Latino characters who resolve their cultural tensions through marginal lifestyles: in the urban setting, through crime. Rodriguez's *Spidertown* depicts a band of urban youth in Harlem manipulating an underground world of drugs and arson and murder. Like the characters in Spider's favorite book, *Oliver Twist*, these Puerto Rican "lowercase people," "tiny pins on a map, [who] hardly registered at all" (288) survive on the margins of society. The alternative course, often the means of escape, is often the creation of art and the therapy of words. Thus there are many portraits of the Latino artist as young people: Rodriguez's Miguel, Cisnero's Esperanza, Casteda's Solita, Garcia's Pilar, Rivera's young boy, to name just a few.

Betrayal in Latino fiction is usually two-sided. Deception just as often comes from the other side, the Mexican side, the island side. The illusions to be shattered exist on both sides of the border. When modern Latino writers depict the futility of a reunion with a paradisal lost world, they are rejecting mythical structures as the basis for organizing the modern world. Unlike in the early magical realism of Carpentier, this is a practical worldview in which belief in the ideal equals romantic self-deception. The connections to one's past are not the only solutions to life's difficulties, but often pipedreams that ultimately result in painful disillusionment. In *Raining Backwards*, Eloy, the laundry women's young nephew, is seduced by Mirta Vergara's nostalgia because she holds the stories of his Cuban past. As the dear Abbey figure of the novel sees, in a moment of uncommon astuteness, he wants to "possess history" (*Raining Backwards* 75), but Mirta lives in a fantasy world of self-indulgence. Eloy dreams of a heritage, desires a connection to Cuban; he is "thirsty for information"(11), has a "need to talk"(12), to hear the stories that will reconnect him, but her words that have a "narcotic effect" on him (13) are the ravings a deluded woman. When he asks what Ireland is, she tells him: "It's a deodorant soap." The stories she tells as she coaxes him into soaping her back are no more real than the tall-tales of the domino players who claim that pre-Castro chicken eggs "were so big that the layers had to have C-sections" (203). They are dreamy fantasies that he thinks will give him a heritage and which she uses to seduce him. The situation is paralleled in the Cisneros story "One Holy Night," where a poor girl is betrayed by the allure of a mythical Mexican history. The sexual initiation, reminiscent of Esperanza's in *House*, is both cruel since she winds up pregnant and ostracized from her family, and dangerous since her mythical "boy baby," her Chaq Uxmal Paloquín, descendant of "an ancient line of Mayan Kings" turns out to be Chato (or fat face), and a serial killer. In reality, her seducer was born "on a street with no name in a town called Miseria," the son of a knife sharpener and a mother who "stacks apricots into pyramids and sells them on a cloth in the market" (*Women* 33). Such treachery from a man who claims he will love her "like a revolution, like a religion" (*Women* 27) suggests Cisneros' belief in the uselessness of tying oneself to fantasies like the mythic ideas of Indian purity and Mexican origin. Ron Arias demolishes a young boy's pride in his hometown Tomazunchale when the stage director of the dramatic scene in *The Road to Tomazunchale* declares that any name would have sufficed as the name is a mere invention to replace the word "hell" (82). Similarly, one of Anna Castillo's heroines falls in love with a college student named Rubén who changes his name to Cuauhtemoc "during the height of his Chicano cosmic consciousness" only to "dump her" later "for a middle class gabacha [white woman] with a Corvette" (*So Far From God* 25-26). Garcia's Pilar is similarly disappointed by a Peruvian named Rubén Florín, her compañero, with whom she shares the intimacy of her Spanish language, and who she discovers in bed with a Dutch exchange student with "enormous pink nipples" (180).

Commentary on the deceptions of causes, revolutionary or religious, is part of the Latino writer's subversive tract. Tomás Rivera rejects Protestantism and Yankee Coca-Cola with the same power that he questions forms of organized religion and the blind, whole-hearted endorsement of ancient Mexican values. In the pivotal chapter mentioned above Protestant priests arrive to teach the migrant farmers carpentry and don't even come out of their trailers (Rivera 107). Even more vehement in regard to the seductive falsity of spiritual salvation is Rechy's treatment of Amalia in *The Miraculous Day of Amalia Gómez.* Here is a woman who is raped by a man named Salvador (savior), abandoned by a soldier/husband (from Fort Bliss) named Gabriel and betrayed by a phony Nicaraguan "coyote" named Angel. In *Dreaming,* Pilar's mother Lourdes, having been raped by Cuban revolutionaries, winds up abandoning her mother and later her daughter for the false glitter of U.S. practicality and capitalism incarnated in her "Yankee Doodle Bakery." What complicates the matter further and what gives Lourdes a multi-dimensional personality is that she is the one who recalls the symbolic association between U.S. intervention and the contamination of an island world: "She remembers a story she read once about Guam, about how brown snakes were introduced by the Americans. The snakes strangled the native birds one by one. They ate the eggs from the nests until the jungle had no voice" (227).

Though the deflating of the paradise on both sides of the border is sometimes humorous, the motif, symbolically, forces upon both reader and protagonist some recognition of the liminal position with which Latinos must come to terms, an understanding that the construction of an ideal pre-westerner existence is as false and, ultimately, as disappointing as the commercial images of perfection and beauty put forward by the U.S. media. What remains is a dynamic, Latino, borderland identity, constantly in a state of renegociation and change that must always bounce between two cultures, and two worlds. The notion that success depends upon accommodation and assimilation into the central culture (generally that of the U.S.) is often problematized as is the alternative extreme of a return to a mythic homeland or golden island paradise which will somehow survive outside the dominant metropolitan atmosphere of prejudice and discrimination. Throughout Latino works, there is a split that results in characters, to use Anzaldúa's phrase, being "plagued by psychic restlessness" (*Borderlands* 78) and that requires Latino writers and individuals to maintain "a tolerance for ambiguity" (79). The critic Eliana S Rivero claims that "the nostalgia ever present in the Cuban-American's parent's generation has given way to a split, hybrid cultural consciousness in the sons and daughters of exile" ("Re-writing" 180). Bruce-Novoa, referring to Rudolfo Anaya's *Bless Me, Ultima*, says the book called not "for returning to a static past, but for recuperating a traditional way of living the dynamic oppositions of the present" (170). These "dynamic oppositions" produce the "psychic restlessness" which in turn becomes the subject of Latino fiction. A clear example is Garcia's *Dreaming in Cuban* where the notion of a Cuban paradise is questioned from the outset. Pilar longs for the "green" of Cuba, and symbolically in the novel, "green" is good and healthy, unlike "blue" (the color of her grandfather's eyes), which is not (33). Yet Hugo Villaverde (green village) who beats up Felicia (47, 80) is also a part of Cuba. This side of Cuban sexism, metonymically glimpsed in Hugo, dampens the Edenic scene substantially. Hugo, after his wife burns him, winds up a pitiful, suckling thing, reduced to orgasm with a masked whore, and rejected by his twin daughters (125). Playing further on the man's name, Garcia is certainly questioning the validity of the familiar Cuban-American exile desire: You go (Hugo) to the green village, or country house (Villaverde). Going home to Cuba is not, in the end, enough for Pilar. She belongs in New York, a Cuban-American.

As Latino writers scrutinize the dual aspects of their own and their characters' identities, they shift their status from ethnic writers attached to particular cultures to mainstream "American" storytellers. The complexities of their hybrid protagonists become fused and confused with all other cultural intricacies of "American" life. It seems only a matter of time before writers like Gilb, Pineda, Hijuelos or Cristina Garcia will turn their sights away from Latino culture exclusively and toward the complex mixtures of peoples surrounding them within the U.S. The first step is often an analytical attack on the notion of a lost world that must be regained. Writers concerned with borderlines must necessarily recognize that outright borders are artificial, that no one lives entirely on one side. Therefore, Cisneros, Sáenz, Viramontes and Véa, among others, purposely dwell upon those lives lived along the continuum between the old and new, the past and present, the Latin American and the Gringo, the Spanish and the English. In their portrayal of blended dualities, they help break down "us" versus "them" oppositions by challenging the notion of static identities. Midstream (or mid Rio Grande), their characters have insights into both sides, into both worlds simultaneously.

NOTES

1. Mary Vásquez, a critic who has written several articles on Roberto Fernandez would probably disagree with Deaver, since she has referred to Fernandez's works as being "satirical, yet *loving* depiction[s] of life in Dade County" ("Gender in Exile" *Literature of Emigration and Exile.* Ed James Whitlock and Wendell Ayrock. Texas Tech. U. Press, 1992 Studies in Comparative Literature #23). According to Gabriella Ibieta, the title of the novel refers to "a sign of death, a return to a beginning, the end of a cycle" ("Transcending the Culture of Exile: *Raining Backwards*" *Literature and Exile*, ed. David Bevin. Rodopi, 1990, 72) and that the Fernandez's novel, while sympathetic to the Miami Cuban world, suggests that at least a part of that world is disintegrating, probably for the better.

2. For example, Fausto's dream of pulling off his own skin in the opening of Arias' *Road.*

3. For more on Puerto Rican political history see the works of Ronald Fernandez, specifically: *Prisoners of Colonialism: The Struggle for Justice in Puerto Rico.*

4. Revolutionary leader of the Nationalist party in Puerto Rico between 1924 and 1950 (when he was imprisoned in the US) and the central political voice calling for independence. See Ronald Fernandez's *Prisoners of Colonialism: The Struggle for Justice in Puerto Rico.*

5. The lengthy discussion concerning the extent to which the Latino must assimilate, accommodate or abrogate US culture and education is outside the scope of this study. See, for an Intro to the debate, Earl Shorris's discussion in his work *Latinos: A Biography of the People*, New York: Norton, 1992.

6. Other Latino writers compare people to flags as well. Viramontes describes, one suspects derogatorily, the "Saturday tourists" in Tijuana waving "like national flags along the sidewalks" ("The Broken Web" 52).

7. Jane Rogers' mythical reading of the La Llorona legend in Anaya's *Bless Me, Ultima* points to one clear case in which the siren/mermaid/seducer presents a classic moral dilemma for the novel's hero ("The Function of the La Llorona Motif in Anaya's *Bless Me, Ultima" in* Lattin, Vernon E., ed. *Contemporary Chicano Fiction: A Critical Survey.* Binghamton, NY: Bilingual Press / Editorial Bilingüe, 1986.

8. The intricate connections and complicated relationships of such mythic figures are discussed in numerous studies. See Rebolledo's *Women Singing in the Snow*; Anzaldúa's *Borderlands/La Frontera.*

9. The Peruvian writer, Julio Ramón Ribeyro, has an interesting short story which evokes both U.S. military exploitation of Latinos as well the

desperation with which the Latin American poor succumb to the enticements of Gringolandia. In "Alienation: An Instructive Story with a Footnote," Ribeyro's hero begins by "killing the Peruvian in himself and extracting something from every Gringo he met" (Ribeyro 57), illegally entering the U.S., changing his name from Roberto, to Bobby, to Bob and enlisting to avoid deportation. In Korea, "the first blast blew his helmet off and his head rolled into a trench, all of its dyed, tangled hair hanging down" (66). Even more disillusioned is Roberto's original object of infatuation, Queca, who winds up in Kentucky, married to an Irish Puritan who beats her and calls her a "shitty half-breed" (67).

10. See his article "Rudolfo Anaya's *Bless Me, Ultima*: A Chicano Romance of the Southwest." *Critica* I, no. 3: 21-47.

11. This is the sort of inversion which cannot help to alter all sorts of unjustified opinions once the opposite view has been comprehended. A clear example would be that for Cuban's the fear of nuclear threat during the early sixties had to have been more profound than for North Americans given that the U.S., openly trying to topple the Cuban government by every means conceivable, is the only country to have ever dropped the bomb.

12. Compare Sal's opinion in the Jack Agüeros story "Malig: Malig & Sal; Sal:" "Americans have no expressions, no emotions, they are like the porcelain enamel, passive – you know, I don't think they ever have orgasms (84).

13. The word "soledad" carries the connotations of both "solitude" and "loneliness." Thus the word holds special value for Latin American and Latino writers: *Cien años de soledad, El laberinto de la soledad* etc. The Portuguese word "saudade" stretches the meanings across an even wider range to include solitude, loneliness, melancholy, sadness, even solidarity, and it is the word's flexibility that Castedo relies upon to communicate not only her heroine's solitude and loneliness, but also her pride, independence, strength and her loyalty to her refugee community.

14. Though the allure is different for Cubans and Puerto Ricans in many stories. In *Mambo*, Puerto Ricans are often servants: a salesgirl at Bloomingdale's (402), a butler named Garcia, and in Cristina Garcia a Puerto Rican steals from Lourdes Puente. The Puerto Rican heroes of Vega, Agüeros, Mohr and Rodriguez, by contrast, often operate beneath the legitimate business world, subverting the system or denying its power over them.

CHAPTER FIVE

Carnival and the "department store called america"[1]

It would be a mistake to assume that Latino fiction confines itself to the pressures and tensions of immigration and acculturation. After all, generations of Chicano writers have lived within U.S. borders for a longer time than any writers of Western European ancestry, and the people who fill their novels and stories, while still often socially, politically, and economically marginal—still excluded from the mainstream—are in no sense "foreign" to life in the U.S. Puerto Ricans have been citizens since 1917. The stereotypical view, spread in part by the prevalence of Latino autobiographical works – stories of personal success as the outsider Latino makes good, adjusts and adapts in every way (gets his or her picture in *Hispanic* magazine) – suggests that a thin line divides the newcomer from the assimilated "American." Cross over the bridge (border, ocean) and things change. Nothing could be farther from the truth. Most Latinos inhabit some sort of large and obscure borderland territory and from it derive their strengths. There is no concrete frontera. The job of Latino writers becomes in part an attempt to portray the complexities of that hybrid world which means that the prevailing, mainstream structures of Anglo society (the laws, institutions and systems) need to be scrutinized, and critiqued so that flaws and prejudices can be exposed and so that the dualities of life in the middle be made credible.

Towards the end of Alfredo Véa's novel *La Maravilla*, two Cushion-Aire boxcars go off the track spilling bonded whiskey and car parts through a shantytown outside Phoenix. To the poor people (the outcasts who populate the book[2]), this occurrence disrupts the solemnity of the moment—it happens on the day of the funeral for the Yaqui shaman Manuel—and turns the atmosphere into one of festival and celebration. "It was the mired who moved as a train was sacrificed in honor of the dead." Here, the rational gives way to the spirituality of party and freedom. The grieving "shake off their grief;" the silent yell: "Qué milagro! Ay, qué milagro" (243-244)! In *The Labyrinth of Solitude,* Octavio Paz has described the Mexican festival as a group enterprise where "the individual is at once dissolved and redeemed" (48), where during this celebration, he can "leap over the wall of solitude that confines him during the rest of the year" and therefore "escape from himself" (49). Whether occurring within Elysian mystery rite, roman saturnalia or modern holiday, the release of oneself from hierarchical, institutional order is a dissolving of the individual into a larger fellowship, a communion with a group and ultimately a joining with all other humans. Times of festival therefore carry with them ingredients of pleasure and laughter, of food, music, drink, sex and humor—all part of a timeless atmosphere of what Clark and Holquist call "communality" where "the individual feels he is an indissoluble part of the collectivity, a member of the people's mass body" (*Mikhail Bakhtin* 302). The festival nullifies chronological sequence and becomes, as the narrator of *La Maravilla*, explains, "a time machine . . . a mechanism that re-creates all times at once and allows all who participate to breathe the past; to touch every bundle of time; to taste the ages" (98). The elements of carnival communicate a sense of change (because they alter people—distorting their sense of time, changing their emotions, disturbing their rational thoughts) which is central to the festival liberation from convention and the carnivalesque violation of societal boundaries.

When the boxcars overturn, the people run "to eviscerate the beached, haughty leviathans that had always rhythmically clicked their cold-shouldered distance from all those pinned by poverty to the same spot on the map. Distance. Distance. Distance" (243-244). This time, the "boxcars went nowhere" and the distance between the cold "iron voice boxes" and the people of Buckeye Road disappears. Shocks and springs and ball joints from the boxcars' "innards" will be reborn in "every battered motor vehicle from Yuma to the Four Corners Reservation" while the whiskey will unite a community in drunken revelry. As one man says: "It was like Miss America went blind and thought I was her husband." The episode becomes the stuff of legends, of memory, of mythic nostalgia (uniting generations to come), not just because everyone has a good time, but because the rules have been broken. The cold isolation the people always feel as trainloads of unattainable goods pass them by, day after day, disappears for once with this accidental and miraculous gift. The inverted train cars, with their wheels spinning in the air, suggest an inverted, ruptured system. The wheels of "capitalism" have been rendered useless for a moment, and the privileges of the upper class transferred to the poor.

Véa employs the carnivalesque because *La Maravilla* is a novel that refuses simple truths. The reader is thrust into the world of people discarded by society—bums and alcoholics, prostitutes and poor Indian spiritualists—but the book is linked as well to the recognizable themes of a young boy coming of age, of family loyalty and love between this boy and his grandparents, and of the conflict between conventional (Catholic) and non-western (Yaqui mysticism) spirituality. Yet the polyphonic inconclusiveness of it all allows no easy answers. As readers, we explore this world exposed and highlighted by the carnivalesque and inhabited by "people of the gaps," knowing that "the gaps are where life really is" (221).

In another moment of carnival magic, Ed Vega's Sinfo (like a Juan Perón figure) speaks to an adoring crowd ("Qué Viva Don Sinfo . . . Qué Viva Puerto Rico") and when he raises his hand in salute, lightning and thunder and "a tremendous downpour" send the crowd for shelter. The rain cleanses the people of their "pent-up anger" and washes away their resentments. Momentarily released, they commence a celebration, "a ribald fantasy" where the "Bermuda socialite does a topless dance, and the solemn Frances ends up in the cellar with one Don Cipriano, minus his accordion ("The Pursuit of Happiness" 230-232). It is a moment when "young and old, cop and militant" are joined in laughter. Washed clean of his capitalistic schemes, the protagonist finds the love of Elissa. Even the "tantalizing" music itself, a Puerto Rican "plena," displays a political reversal, because the song "tells of the demise of a U.S. strike-breaking lawyer whose disappearance was attributed to a female shark" (232). The workers, the marginal outsiders, the Puerto Ricans in general, gain the upper hand for a festive moment. The moment is significant because a carnival atmosphere once established in a novel permeates the entire text, and the reader, having glimpsed the other side—that which negates the practical struggles of life—can never again completely accept the status quo. Neither Vega, nor Véa wish the reader to return to the norm. Rather, the carnivalesque instills in the work a necessity for the reader to perpetually question the laws and restrictions of society.

The celebration of carnival in Latino fiction is either humorously and positively subversive or destructively deviant, depending upon the situation, the author, and the characters. Thus, Latino carnivalesque is ambiguous; rather than set up a new "truth," it serves to "consecrate inventive freedom . . . to liberate from the prevailing point of view . . . from conventions and established truths" (*Rabelais* 34). A dual perspective often forces the reader to see, among other things, images of the carnivalesque as representing either happy release, melancholy self deception, or a combination of both. In any case, the reader recognizes that the overall function of carnival is to free the human consciousness from restricting, unconditional values in order to allow the imagination to contemplate new potentialities, to "escape the false 'truth of this world'" (*Rabelais* 49). The desire on the part of these writers, both male and female, to exhibit what Debra Castillo has labeled a "willed undecidability" (*Talking Back* 69), and their refusal to accept absolutes manifests itself in the narrative use and the language of the carnivalesque. Because the carnival is always in flux, combining opposites, inverting hierarchies, and abandoning etiquette, no one truth holds, and the reader is left with ambiguity and potential. It is to see things upside down, like Vernetta in *La Maravilla*, who, looking at an abandoned house feels strange, "as though she were suddenly privy to a contrary world of houses where the people burned down instead" (254). These sorts of inverted perspectives and humorous distortions fill Latino fiction with a polyphonic uncertainty where altering views of life compete endlessly.

The carnivalesque, in its overt form, has been recognized by Latino critics in the early Spanish novels of the Cuban writer Roberto G. Fernández.[3] Setting aside Fernández's elaborate use of language and styles of discourse (an essential part of his carnivalesque idiom) discussed above, one festive scene early in the novel will throw light upon various thematic complexities. The comic reversals and twists of the Christmas dinner scenario help instill in the novel as a whole a "topsy-turvy" atmosphere of transformations and inversions in such a way as to complicate the simplistic view of party as mere release and freedom. The scene begins with Mima's kitchen preparation which, contrary to general opinion, she hates: "Every year, the same old people, the same old shit" (39), she grumbles. Beneath the superficial level of the festivities lies a multitude of disparate voices reflecting the actual feelings (usually negative) of these Miami Cuban exiles at their Christmas eve dinner. There is gossip, anger, fighting, and resentment under the gaiety of the dancing, the wine, and the food. The whole scene is watched carefully by a dead pig on the grill whose perspective may be the only one of objectivity and balance. A neighbor brings .99 cent wine disguised with fancy labels; a son involved in drugs lies about his Colombian "business trip;" Barbarita refuses to talk to the hostess because she's convinced Mima is making her husband Jacinto a cuckold; someone complains about the "American custom" of leaving the TV on all the time; the pig is too big for the grill; it rains; a child dressed as Balthasar explains mid-recital that no one in his family is really black—in short the harmony of festival is actually a chaotic jumble of conflicting lives, and people's fears, prejudices, lies, distortions and sexism ("roll her in the flour and go for the wet spot ha ha ha" (39-52). Fernández's description turns into a series of snatches of dialogue, a list of angry emotions and outbursts that undermine any communal quality to the holiday party. Despite the music, the dancing, the food, there is no humor shared by the characters, perhaps because the social codes and family roles are not, in fact, reversed. Fernández displays his characters ranting and complaining as the party unhinges their inhibitions, but nothing is drastically inverted for them and their attitudes remain selfish and antagonistic.

More often than not, the carnivalesque signals a release from authoritative rigidity. Judith Cofer's town of Salud is transformed during carnival week from a "dusty hamlet" into a colorful festival "eclipsing the countryside and even the church, a massive white structure sitting on its hill like a reproving matron, dim and dowdy" (*Line of the Sun* 66). It is only fitting that the carnival provides Guzmán with the opportunity to meet the object of his fantasies, Rosa, for the second time. Disguised as a gypsy, she reads his palm, and they embark on a passionate affair that leaves the "Ladies Civic Council and Holy Rosary Society" scandalized. The servants of El Topaz estate in Castedo's novel *Paradise* use their "peasant" festival to counter the repressive laws of their wealthy employers (217-219). Solita joins the "soul-raising event," because she relishes the freedom of those people, who, like her fellow refugees were noisy, "didn't do prearranged things," who were "cheerful" and "comfortable" (59), and who sang the songs, like the songs of Spain ("pieces of Spain"—39) with unrestricted emotion. A similar scene occurs in Pineda's *The Love Queen of the Amazon* when the convent girls go down to the river for their bath.

Having arrived, they pass through an "astonishing transformation" during which "pandemonium" breaks out," and there is "no longer any way of civilizing them" (8). Their recess becomes a release from the "stringent oppressions" through "all the canonical hours" (11). The effect of the scene is consequently to juxtapose their laughter and freedom with the hollow threats of a disciplinary nun beating on her frying pan. The frying pan may itself suggest Pineda's commentary on the renowned women protesters who carried pots and pans up and down the streets of Santiago during the Allende government. Though decorum will be restored, the interval provides one of the novel's many reversals of perspective. Later, at Ana Magdalena's wedding reception, the father of the bride commits adultery, local prisoners do the cooking and then escape, kidnapping the bride, while the drunken armed guards sleep. The sequence of bizarre party events will lead the reader down a twisting path of inversions in which his or her fairy tale expectations will be rearranged. This Cinderella (Ana Magdalena) wants no part of marriage—the contract for her own marriage is in fact too long to fit on any table and must be laid out on the piano (43). After the kidnapping, Ana Magdalena winds up in a brothel (and leaves her slippers there the following morning—slippers which magically appear at several times in the narrative—101). Life in the whorehouse becomes the not unpleasant result of Ana's marriage which rather than a conventional, romantic happy ending turns out to be a happy beginning to her life as a madam. Inside the brothel (and Pineda makes it clear we are seeing the brothel from an insider's perspective), converted from a Capuchin convent, in the middle of the "vast ground-floor room," Ana finds a "circular settee . . . where people could lounge while admiring the surrounding splendor from various angles (102). This "most curious" piece of furniture is suggestive of the lack of such perspectives in the outside world, and how limited are the angles of vision permitted women by societal controls. The brothel, "La Nymphaea," is run by her great aunt, her "protecting angel" Ofelia (171) and she and her "rainbow girls" supply Ana with "tears and laughter and companionship" which neither her "mummified in . . . flannel nightgown" mother, Andreina, nor her "exotic talking mummy from another world" mother-in law (172) can provide. In her more serious first novel, *Face*, there is no capacity for women to unite in any way. Not only held back by men, they must bear the burden of their male companions' frustrations: Helio doesn't share Lula's ambition for him to get a barbershop of his own (19), and when she refuses to make love to the disfigured protagonist, he beats and rapes her (77).

Both Pineda and Fernández, like Ron Arias before them, structure their novels around hyperbole and stretch the limits of plausibility for the sake of parodic humor. Ron Arias once mentioned in a interview that the "best, most incisive most humanly appealing humor I've heard is from women—but this is always in kitchens, classrooms, bailes [dances] or in stores. Not much in writing—so far" (Bruce-Novoa *Chicano Authors* 248). This prophetic remark made during the winter of 1978-1979 is now countered by the writings of Pineda, Vega, Hijuelos, Cisneros, Garcia, and Roberto Fernández—writers who consciously distort perspective for the sake of inverting stereotypical ideas. Pineda's tone and irreverence recall the narrative voice of Woolf's *Orlando,* a novel which paved the way for much of the sardonic humor found in *The Love Queen of the Amazon.* Pineda's narrator's discourse, as Judy Little says of Woolf's, "often slides easily from the rhetoric of affirmation into comic doubt" (181). There is a similar twinge of the magically real in Ana Magdalena's mythic birth which echoes Woolf's elements of the bizarre such as the "Great Frost" where "birds froze in mid air" (*Orlando* (33). As we have already noted, Pineda's scene in Federico Orgaz y Orgaz's literary salon owes a debt to Woolf's famous portrayal of eighteenth-century British literary life. Surely the discussion concerning the value of literary gaps and "lacunae" amid Latin American writers alludes to the humorous gaps and omissions in Woolf's novel, (i.e. Pope's witty remarks are excised) and both pompous conversations leave both protagonists similarly unimpressed.

Pineda's novel deflates authority and the official in the tradition of Bakhtin's carnivalesque altering of hierarchical standards. She switches around those categories within what Guillermo E. Hernández outlines as the "Hegemonic Spectrum" of fiction. She purposely confuses the whore with the wife, the husband with the fool; greed is associated with formal institutions like the church and the bank, and lust and sin with the heroine. Breaking down the oppositions of the spectrum is an integral part of Pineda's deconstruction of her patriarchal fiction world. On the physical level, we find City Hall "embellished by revolutions and pigeon droppings" (76). Federico's massive "Casa Orgaz" (whose many rooms recall Bluebeard's castle—97, though Ana is no helpless young bride) is architecturally sterile and Ana Magdalena struggles to "soften the uncompromising granite columns of the courtyard" (178) much the way Isabel Allende's Clara from *The House of Spirits* struggles to alter the rigidity of El Patrón Trueba's solid mansion. The "gleaming white mansions" to which the convent girls aspire will, according to the narrator, become "their mausoleums" (10). The structures of power rather than offering security and safety in wealth and privilege are seen as traps and prisons. Often, male political authority is the target of Pineda's ridicule. Toward the end of her novel, in one farcical scene, she satirizes a wide range of the Presidents of both Americas. George Washington, in a "crazy-looking boat" arrives at Ana's brothel with his son, George Junior, "as transparent as a fetus." Teddy Roosevelt shows up boasting of his son, Ron, who has just "bagged his first mestizo." Juxtaposing historical personalities, Pineda has the "not-yet-born" George and Ron (Bush and Reagan) playing with "instruments of torture," while Ana is unable to stop them because neither speaks Spanish and both are in favor of "a program of '*English only' in utero*" (227- 230). The international monetary fund is debunked as the "International Fiduciary Fund" which is overly willing to loan money to a brothel, under the condition that it also be allowed to supply "Yankee" muzak which promotes haphazard indiscriminate buying (234), but turns out to be detrimental to the sex business (210-213). When Ana raises doubts about deceiving her new husband, Ofelia advises her that "respectable family men, the bankers, the lawyers, the doctors, [and] especially the politicians" are the most frequent customers (105).

The institution of marriage suffers extensive ridicule in this novel from the beginning. When her friend Aurora gets married (her "reception more in the style of a wake"—31), she explains to Ana the benefits of marriage, not for domestic reasons, but because having already given up virginity, like a nineteenth-century British widow, you are free to "do anything you want" (15). Visiting Ana's fiancé for the first time, Ana and her mother dress in mourning and Ana is told by Andreina to pretend there has been a death in the family. In short, the heroine can "hardly think of a single reason" for getting married and her life as a prostitute and madam frees her from domestic slavery where she'd "measure her life in rounds of baking, cleaning, and preparing sad little suppers" (172).

Perhaps organized religion is attacked with the most vehemence, for, at one point, the small town of Malyerba (Mala hierba, or weed) is accosted by a "pestilential tide of prophets" and preachers (181) so numerous they rush to the door anytime a citizen attempts to leave the house. During this "storm," Horatio Alger arrives and Ana receives him only because he carries a letter from her unreliable (and greedy) lover Sergio Ballado. One thinks of Alger's *Ragged Dick Series* and their sermons on how battling poverty and avoiding temptation would lead to riches. How useless such advice is for women (most especially prostitutes) who must find economic security outside the male dominated system. Finally, there are Ofelia's expressions, "God's little kneecaps"(154) and "God's little booties"(149) which belittle the notion of an all-powerful God. Just as she diminishes Presidents into "transparent," squabbling "boys" (230), Pineda is adept at taking swipes at all higher authorities. Her earlier novel, *Face,* similarly debunked the necessity of God, in the character of Teofilho Godoy. The plastic surgeon's name, Bruce-Novoa has noted, is an "interlingual play in which God is doubly named and adored" ("Deconstruction" 78), and because Helio will reconstruct his face without the aid or financial support of the doctors, the reader assumes Pineda is advocating symbolically some sort of liberation theology. What Helio can do for himself, because he can simultaneously redo his identity and come to terms with his past, makes the authority figure of the doctor (read God) immaterial.

Like Pineda, Fernández, in *Raining Backwards,* aims his sarcasm at both sides of the border. Cuban customs are as susceptible to criticism as is U.S. materialism. As Febles has made clear about Fernández's first novel, *La vida es un special* (1981), nothing escapes the writer's humor because everything (from lofty values to trivialities) is upset and twisted by an atmosphere of carnival. A parody of the customary celebration of a young girl's quiceñera or "Golden Fifteen" party (31) during which the guests dress as lobsters and clams is mingled with hyperbolic attacks on the supporters of "English only" laws where members of the feared "tongue brigade" consider Spanish "a form of disglosia, a degenerative disease of speech centered in the brain" (153). Organized religion is debunked along with Santería; Barbarita's gossip (65) is critiqued along with news programs (155). Whether or not the collage of parodic discourse Fernández assembles in the novel ultimately endorses Cuban "reintegration" as Vásquez argues ("Fantastic" 75-76) or its opposite, the "death of Cuban exile culture" as Deaver claims ("*Raining*" 112), the work is an explosion of humorous debunking of Miami life, Cuban or otherwise. It is the open-endedness Fernández insists upon that makes for a dual interpretation of the character of Mirta Vergara and which consequently fuels this critical debate. Either Mirta is obsessed with her own nostalgia and physical pleasure and therefore degenerate, or she truly believes herself to be the sole transmitter of Cuban heritage which she deems so necessary for the young boy Eloy (representative of a younger generation), to inherit. Given the extent and range of the novel's "mixture of affirmation and subversion, of praise and blame" (Vásquez "Parody" 94), a reader can only conclude that both possibilities are true, that Fernández celebrates the inconsistencies of his multivoiced world, and that, as is true to the carnivalesque in general, the novel confirms a spirit of change, of undecidability, and showing life in "twofold contradictory process" (Bakhtin *Rabelais* 26).

Overt examples of the carnivalesque (parties, fesitvals, masquerades etc.) invert the status quo, but images of specific ingredients or elements associated with carnival also carry a symbolic weight because they are related to the overall atmosphere of the carnivalesque, particularly when the opposition between the official and the unofficial worlds centers around ethnicity. In Latino fiction, those aspects celebrated during the festival are frequently germane to Latin American culture. Food, for example, is the central ingredient of the marketplace and, according to Bakhtin, the marketplace is the center of the carnivalesque, the unofficial. Food symbolizes the ever-changing, growing, transitory nature of life. This is why feasts occurred at important transition times in natural cycles, emphasizing the "never static," eternally "unfinished" image of the carnivalesque (*Rabelais* 52). The carnival images revolve around continual "becoming," growing, and incompleteness" (Clark 310). Thus food becomes an outlet, a release from a painful world. This is especially true in Latino life in the U.S. where each ethnic parade, concert, festival, and holiday exhibits a longing for the traditions of a world left behind, each celebration providing an outlet, an oasis from the pressures of "Gringolandia." Culture shock is understood in terms of food and drink: "Migration scrambles the appetite" concludes Garcia's Pilar Puente (173). "This country changes people. I think it is the water. It makes them crazy" says Fernández's Barbarita (85). Yet the meaning of the celebration of that outlet by a writer depends upon the characters involved and the authors' sense of something larger. For if the festival—and by extension all elements of Bakhtin's carnival, that is food, music, sex, dance, and song—is connected to a cultural heritage, then its depiction in the fiction will resonate with attitudes held toward that culture and indicate through suggestion the depth of emotional value which author or character feel toward that heritage. From images of carnival, moreover, the reader infers an implicit critique of U.S. culture as it is suggested by what Latino characters, during holiday, reject. Examining how food, for instance, is used should lead us then to understanding how close a writer is to that culture, and how much distance he or she feels is necessary for Latinos as they confront the problems of acculturation and assimilation.

On one level, food connects the immigrant with the past, or the individual with the family. Indulgence in eating is therefore a ritualistic attempt at tying oneself to past pleasure. This is why so many characters smell like food. Cisneros's rebellious Lucy (in the opening story of *Women*) smells like corn, like tortillas, like bread and the scent itself seems to connect the narrator with her true desires, to all the frowned upon pleasures of a mischievous child (3). In "Obliterate the Night" by Benjamin Alire Sáenz, a young woman hovering in nostalgic depression decides her mother smelled like bread and the power of the memory provokes the childishly pathetic plea: "Mama what am I going to do?" (55). Another Sáenz character relates to his migrant grandfather, the cebollero (onion picker) and reaches his Mexican/Chicano heritage through the onions in the supermarket (Sáenz 15-16). Mainland Puerto Rican writer, Aurora Morales, in *Getting Home Alive*, laments the loss of her warm Puerto Rican "pan de agua" (24). Ed Vega has a story called "The Angel Juan Moncho" in which a party of men on Christmas eve ("it was the night before Christmas and all through El Barrio everybody was stirring . . . " -75) gather together "hooked in the same circuit" (76) to talk of food, their words carrying the aroma of foods from the island. A long list (in untranslated Spanish) of favorite dishes completes the paragraph (76). While the food of the immigrant's homeland ties a character to the positive, stereotypical foods of the U.S. are cause for ridicule and disgust. In Ana Castillo's *So Far From God*, rural Chicanas working for the high-tech weapons company, Acme International, eat "balogna and Kraft cheese subs from vending machines while toxic chemicals eat off their finger nails (180). Rolando Hinojosa's migrants are forced for lack of money into surviving on salteens, coldcuts, Coca-Cola and worst of all, Velveeta cheese (*Klail City* 59,66). Junk food and fast food restaurants (cf. Rechy's Amalia Gómez in a Macdonald's) for obvious reasons contrast with the richness and freshness and abundance of home cooked Mexican, Cuban, Puerto Rican meals. An elderly character in Véa's *La Maravilla* laments the Chicano youth's distaste for traditional food: "They wouldn't even take burritos to school, we had to make fucking sandwiches. Can you believe that, sandwiches! Bread like air and meat that was never alive" (49). Elsewhere in the same novel, Véa makes the contrast explicit: "Mexicans embrace one another with their meals, sumptuous, ample embraces" (104) whereas feeding a person "white food" takes "the red out his marrow, kill[s] his spirit (136). Describing window drapes, one character remarks: "They're just so . . . they're just so . . . Velveeta" and then laughs "happily at locating the perfect word," a synonym evidently for tacky, cheap and tasteless (168).

Because food is so intricately connected to one's notions of culture and value, to spurn the staples of U.S. diet constitutes a rejection of some part of what many people in this country treasure. You can't be "American" (the ethnocentric nationalist declares), if you don't like MacDonalds and burgers and chips and hot-dogs and peanut butter and jelly, etc. You can't call yourself truly a part of the U.S. if you eat your large meal for breakfast and skip dinner. We are what we eat, and the war of diets closely parallels larger cultural skirmishes where the weapons of war are often food and drink, music[4] and sports (i.e. football or fútbol). Further, when a Latino refuses to acknowledge the importance of hamburger, he or she is rebelling against more than the particular manner the meat is prepared. Behind the patty of meat lie major systems of food production (relying on chemicals), companies within a huge capitalist network (counting on profits) as well as attitudes toward meals and the time it might take to eat one. What we eat, and when and how and where reveals who we are and discloses much of our cultural baggage.[5] This idea accounts for the pleasure Latino writers take in listing the aromas and tastes that tie them emotionally to their families and heritages.

On another level, the savoring of food becomes extreme and depending on the situation can suggest over compensation, self-indulgence and nostalgic delusion. Whether connection to valued heritage or the means of decadent pleasure seeking and indulgence, food is often highlighted. Laura Esquival's novel *Como agua para chocolate* (*Like Water For Chocolate*) ties food to fiction through recipes and has been heralded for demonstrating the matriarchal connections between women across generations established through the kitchen. Aurora Morales speaks of cooking as "a magic, a power, a ritual of love and work" which unites her to "the river of my place on earth, the green and musty river of my grandmothers" (*Getting Home*

Alive 39). Ana Castillo seems to have borrowed this idea for her novel *So Far From God* in which La Loca has surpassed the cooking expertise of her mother Sofia and her grandmother. The narrative even breaks for several pages into "Three of La Loca's Favorite Recipes Just to Whet (sic) Your Appetite." A part of a larger feminist project privileging the interior over the exterior, the house over the journey, this kind of work emphasizes food in order to celebrate the role of the cook, the maid, the servant—in Latin American tradition, female occupations. Recipes, as one of few types of feminine written records are naturally of concern to female authors, yet the kitchen artist/creator figure, while usually a woman, can also be male. Alfredo Véa includes recipes in his novel *La Maravilla,* and recognizes as well as Chicana writers that "A recipe is history . . . The *tomal* is history you can eat" (107-109). The transmission of recipes through the ages, first orally and then in written form, parallels the passage of the oral folktales, myths and legends that have become the basis for literature in the western tradition. In Arturo Islas's *The Rain God,* Miguel Chico's domestic rituals include cooking a spaghetti sauce "perfected over the years" (25) and where his uncle Felix (in a "trance" and with his son JoEl looking on "drunk with pleasure" -135) annually prepares a bread pudding called "capirotada" (134). Islas reverses the stereotypical Hispanic male image by allowing his male characters to enter captivatingly pleasant kitchen worlds of fragrance and peace. Crossing gender barriers, Felix and Miguel and JoEL ("yo"/"el" or "I" and "He") are aligning themselves with the female culinary role. We assume therefore that like Nina, their own "poetic nature" can "express itself in the subtle mixture of spices" (40) and in fact young JoEl is a poet with an "unearthly sheen" to his eyes (123).

Roberto G. Fernandez's *Raining Backwards* which mocks nearly everything includes a recipe for "Barbarita's Refugee Meat Spread, 1961," and instructions to use only "authentic U.S. Department of Agriculture Surplus" tunafish. The recipe pokes fun at the gossipy right-winger Barbarita at the same time it both deflates the importance of traditional cooking handed down through generations of Latin women, and takes a swipe at processed North American conveniences like "Spam." In *The House on Mango Street,* Rafaela, an attractive ("too beautiful to look at") young wife indulges in coconut and papaya juices, savoring their sweetness. They are "sweet sweet like the island." The drink momentarily frees her from the "empty room" of her apartment where she is kept locked, like Rapunzel, by her jealous husband out playing dominos (*Mango* 76). Characters like Lourdes in *Dreaming in Cuban*, or Alejo Santinio and his son Hector in *House*, or Cesar and Nestor in *Mambo*, or Emilio in *Fourteen* take this kind of escape through food several steps further to the point of self-destructive over-indulgence. For each of them, as for the narrator of Cisneros's "Bread," the eating is related to sex and the short-lived, ephemeral pleasure of release from pain in life. Garcia's Lourdes Puente stuffs herself ("eats, eats, eats, like a Hindu goddess with eight arms, eats, eats, eats, as if famine were imminent" 174) and wears her husband out in bed. Cisneros's narrator and her adulterous lover drive through the city kissing between bites of "fat-ass" sourdough bread in their literal "feast of the ass" (Bakhtin 5). While the lovers revel in the tastes and sounds of their traveling party, the reader is aware of a twinge of a problem as the man remembers a "charming city" and the narrator recalls a baby dying from swallowing rat poison in one of the buildings. This contrast between his memories and her own less nostalgic ones coupled with her desire to be free of the "pain . . . passed between" them gives the vignette a serious, ironic tone. Cisneros is blurring the distinctions between genuine festive celebration and melancholic self-indulgence.

For many of Hijuelos's male characters, eating and sex constitute full-time obsessions. An entire page is devoted to Alejo Santinio's stuffing of himself, his "absorbing endlessly as if life could be stored," he and his friends "eating and drinking voraciously, like babies suckling breasts, men fucking women" (*House* 145). The exuberance of Hijuelos's description reveals an authentic glee in feasting and the reader cannot help but be appreciative even as she or he judges from a distance. Emilio Montez O'Brien is orally fixated upon suckling and he too succumbs to periods of sexual debauchery. One of Emilio's fourteen sisters, Irene, and a Greek "fellow" have a romance which Hijuelos describes as "moving through the thickest field of sensations, with hungry bites and long appraisals of tasty morsels, with the promise of a happy future and many satisfying meals" (77). In these cases, the celebration of eating and sex combine to form a carnivalesque release from the difficulties of Latino life, here specifically the pain of the Cuban exile.

It is difficult to entirely separate images of food from those of drink (alcohol) or from music. The lovers in "Bread" turn the tango on the radio up "loud loud loud" (*Creek* 84) as if the music were "inside" them, and Rafaela leans out her window to hear the music from the dance hall/bar down the street (*House* 76) as she laments her inability to demonstrate her youthful sex appeal. Food, like alcohol, sex and music in all three Hijuelos novels is tied to regression. Orfalindo Buitureyra from Hinojosa's *Klail City* "glides away" during a tango and goes on "three-four day drunks" ("parrandas serias"), drinking, singing and dancing (132-135). Vega's Mayonesa Peralta in love with a woman whom he thinks is having an affair with Ernest Hemingway puts himself through his own form of drunken mystery rites twice a year. At one point in *Mambo*, the landlady, Mrs. Shannon (a frequently unwanted visitor) brings over a spice cake and Cesar compares it to "kissing a woman for the first time," Nestor to "rum drenched pineapple" and Delores to "eating flan with Poppy"(153). One food sparking various cherished memories (kissing, rum, a father) as each character to varying degrees, regresses to an oral stage of peaceful infancy. In Cisneros, eating the bread takes them back to "when he wasn't married, like before the kids, like if all the pain hadn't passed between [them]" in much the same way that Lourdes goes into the "early-morning refuge" of her bakery, "wanting to work with bread" because "what sorrow could there be in that" (*Dreaming* 18). In fact, she uses her pastries as weapons, sending pictures of eclairs to her mother in Cuba in an effort to convince Celia that Castro's Cuba denies the pleasure of such things (117). Like Hector and Alejo, the "flesh amassed rapidly" and she gains 118 pounds (20).

The meshing of dance, song, music, sex, and food is typical to the atmosphere of festival Bakhtin discusses. Music and dance send characters into reminiscent daydreams from which they sometimes never recover. Though whether such a state is negative or positive depends on the individual work, the idea of any one or several aspects of the carnivalesque transporting someone beyond the practical reality around them is common to Latino fiction. For Cuban men, the song and drink and dance remove them from the frustration and burden of everyday working life. Indulging in musical memories, Cesar Castillo, repeatedly journeys "back to the plazas of small towns in Cuba, to Havana, to past moments of courtship and love, passion, and a way of life that was fading from existence" (39). This is the reason for the seemingly endless lists of Mambo songs and singers and dancers and musicians—Hijuelos's Whitmanesque catalogues of a bygone era.[6] The famous records bring Cesar back to an idealized past success so vivid that he romanticizes how people used to walk down Broadway and look up at the "silhouettes" of the brothers framed in a window, composing their music (27), though how he could have known this is uncertain. The music frees him to dance with feet "darting in and out like agitated compass needles "(79), a metaphor Hijuelos uses twice as if to suggest it too is the invention of his character's memory. The power of his memories is enhanced by the near epic similes such as one describing the real "Rey de Mambo" Perez Prado "off in another world and bending his body in a hundred shapes" (22). Nestor too is "lost" in the melody of his trumpet (113), his "specialty" mournful solos, the 22 versions of a song "about torment beyond all sorrow" (40).

Hijuelos's central male characters all exhibit an excessive desire to escape "the troubles of the world" (*Mambo* 8): Alejo Santinio through food and drink; his son Hector through food; his wife Mercedes through nostalgic dreaming; The Mambo Kings through music, sex and food; Nelson through his medicinal concoctions (*Fourteen* 61); his son Emilio through sex and alcohol (228) and the list goes on. Where the men are often caught in a permanent, sometimes debilitating, state of nostalgic pain, alleviated momentarily by food, music or sex, the women often escape via reading romances or detective novels or through music as is the case with one of the sisters, Maria, who falls in love when Antoine Rameau sings his aria. Margarita finds some relief in exploration of her own body and later in familial love and Mariella, the mother, like Mercedes in *House*, gets tangled up in a longing for a Cuban past. This is often the fate of those women, unlike Delores, who can't adjust. In Garcia's *Dreaming*, we see Felicia enraptured by a sexist Beny Moré record that she plays (as Cesar Castillo does) over and over while she dances in the dark (165). Felicia lives "on the fringe of life" (184) in a Faulknerian oblivion (a la Emily Grierson). She forces her son to dance because "everything makes sense when they dance," but when the music stops, she recalls her husband's physical abuse (78). In practical ways, she is a "Not-mamá" to her daughters (121) and she will step over the boundary society has described for her between sanity and insanity. Cofer's character, Franco Loco, having been attacked by a jealous man with a machete and now completely oblivious to reality, dances a "last dance, hour by hour, day after day," forever frozen ("time had stopped like a dropped clock") in the last pleasurable moment he can recall (*Line of the Sun* 111). Often it is music or dance that allows temporary escape from the kinds of borders set up by society to restrain and control one's spiritual or instinctual expression. For Teresa in Castillo's *The Mixquiahuala Letters*, the ability to dance is at least partially a means of expressing her (homosexual and therefore illicit) love for her friend Alicia. Teresa's lyrics portray how Alicia danced "with such carefree abandon . . . enveloped . . . in sweet delusion like a hit of pure cocaine" (77). Later she describes Alicia dancing with Egberto, her hair giving off an "illusion of innocence" (125). Despite recognizing that the dance is not reality, Teresa still longs for Alicia "to come out and dance with [her], rid [herself] of one night of memories and heartaches" (125). In *Dreaming in Cuban*, as with Rachel's dance of "invented steps" in Woolf's *Voyage Out* (166), Felicia invents her own music which allows her release from an unbearable domestic relationship. Before this, her mother Celia, trapped in a similar domestic nightmare with Jorge Del Pino and his family in the house on Palmas street, had dreamed of dancing flamenco in Spain: "she would drink whiskey with tourists . . . [and] stride through the darkness with nothing but a tambourine" (42). When Felicia dies, Celia dances on the broken shells at a Santería ritual in a "mad flamenco" of grief. Connecting her somehow to an instinctual deliverance, the dance encaptivates her as Nestor's trumpet does or Cesar's sentimental record. Ultimately, for Cuban-American male characters, submersion in the carnivalesque is usually a rejection of life in the U.S. When Nestor Castillo dies, he is completing his overall failure to join a generation of Cuban immigrants progressing in America. He carries around a right wing pamphlet entitled "Forward America" because it contrasts so vividly with the book in his head that takes him back to Cuba. For Celia in the Garcia novel, the dance is part of her abandoning the material world, but this is not seen as delusional or negative. Pilar is an awkward dancer; she dances "like an American" (224) and this deficiency is a barrier between her U.S. self and the rhythms of Cuba. Thus, toward the end of the novel, when she buys a string base and begins to struggle with rhythm and beat, she is, in essence, reconnecting herself to her African-Cuban heritage, reestablishing an instinctual bond with her country via music.

A short story by Helena Viramontes centers on a similar problem. Aura Rodriguez, a solitary, nearly agoraphobic woman (who, like Felicia, resembles Faulkner's Emily) is moved by the dancing and music of her vagabond neighbors. She lives in fear of street thugs, hates their music, and never ventures outside "her perimeters." When she sees her neighbors dance with "barefoot freedom," she recalls how at a dance as a 13 year old, her role was to fill the broken toilet with water, and how the dance went on without her (*Moths* 110). In this extreme case, Aura's incapacity to "loosen her inhibitions" (110) will, the story suggests, lead to her murdering an innocent person. In general, for women, music and dance imply freedom from convention, the trap of domesticity, the confinement of marriage or from depression. This is why Celia in *Dreaming in Cuban* and Josephina in *La Maravilla* both have white pianos made in Spain, the country to which their romantic pasts are bound. In a friend's restaurant called "La Casa" (26), the protagonist of Villanueva's novel senses that a "naked feminine soul was fiercely and finally revealed" by the "uncontrolled ecstasy" (69) of the flamenco (28), creating a "restful . . . lull from reality" (31). "Dancing always seemed to solve the riddle" (137), Villanueva writes, referring no doubt to the riddle of male/female relations. The dance is often opposed to "proper" society which accounts for Cecile Pineda's sarcasm when, in *Love Queen*, she speaks of the Tango: "the shocking new steps that made good society act like pimps and whores, and perfectly good whores act like society" (*Love Queen 17)*. According to the heroine's mother, it is clearly, "the dance of Satan" and therefore highly popular among rebels of the church (41). But for Ana Magdalena who can "glide sinuously to the captivating strains of the tango" (132) dancing brings her the power "to make everything in the world come to her" (135). Cisneros writes of a young woman named Marin in *The House on Mango Street* "under the streetlight, dancing by herself," (28) longing to escape her aunt's rigidity. Later, Esperanza, the narrator, will be released momentarily from the embarrassment she suffers over her old saddle shoes (representative of her parents' poverty) and dance with her uncle "like in the movies" (46).

For Eliud Martínez's complicated hero, Miguel Velásquez, the combination of drink and music is required for the would-be writer. Like his mentor, the mysterious "borracho magnifico" (possibly a fictionalized Poe), the artist must drink and follow William Blake's prescription to "never disobey the vital impulses of [his/her] recalcitrant spirit" (98). Like Nabokov's Humbert Humbert in *Lolita*,[7] the artist is also a "madman, a creature of infinite melancholy, with a bubble of hot poison in [his/her] loins and a super-voluptuous flame permanently aglow in [his/her] subtle spine" (*Lolita* 17). Sex and creativity are linked: "the procreative drive and creativity both have their source in the genitals" (*Voice* 169). Drinking, for Miguel, is a "wild dance, a dangerous one to be sure, but one from which he learned many things about himself, about life and memory, about women and love" (101). He admires the hard-drinking writers: O'Neill, Faulkner, Fitzgerald, Thomas Wolfe, and Rulfo" all who "benefited from booze" (173).

Voice-haunted Journey demonstrates the inability of the novelist main character to complete his work because of his obsession with maintaining control of his life. Hyper-conscious of his life as material for his art, he cannot get it all down in words. It changes and moves too frequently and can't be captured in its entirety. The metafictional novel itself mirrors that inability as Martínez weaves the lives and dreams and memories of the book's characters into the lives of the fictional work within the novel as it is created, piece by piece, by the main character. Though constantly in search of Dionysian escape through the elements of the carnivalesque, Miguel fails as father to his daughters, as husband to his wife, as novelist, as college professor (sex abuse charges forestall his tenure), and most importantly, he is rendered incapable of coming to terms with his own past and cultural heritage. He fails at writing of "his family and the people they knew, [and] about their hardships in that vast land called Texas" (252) and consequently cannot turn his own story into an ordered completeness. The explosion of allusions throughout the novel reflects Miguel's fanatical desire to include everything he has ever read, to rationally categorize and make sense of all the literature he knows. He is out to prove that his father was wrong when he warned him: "Hijo, es peligroso leer tanto. Uno se puede volver loco" [Son, it's dangerous to read so much. One could go crazy] (217).

Miguel Velásquez (if we ignore metafictional qualities of the novel for the moment) is "haunted" by memories in ways similar to Cesar Castillo in Hijuelos's *The Mambo Kings Play Songs of Love.* Both men rework the past in certain phrases and sensations. Miguel on his airplane, Cesar in the Hotel Splendour—both men are provoked by music into memories: for Cesar, his dead brother's famous hit song "Beautiful Maria of My Soul" which he plays on a record player over and over; for Miguel, an "Ave Maria" sung at his brother's funeral. Both men seek some kind of mindless oblivion in orgasm: "the moment of magic and eternity . . . at the edge of the sexual abyss" (*Voice* 127). Both mourn a dead brother.

From the "insanity of family meals" in Hijuelos's *Fourteen Sisters* (174) to the Halloween festival in Alex Abella's *The Killing of the Saints*, the carnivalesque represents in Abella's words: "a burgeoning cry for release, a shifting onto a public sphere of all the fears, desires and malfunctions of private life" (227).

Some writers view with cynicism the Latino's futile attempt to recreate the physical pleasures of a lost way of life. Judith Cofer's novel *The Line of the Sun* concludes that the efforts of her Patterson, New Jersey neighbors ("in cold rooms stories above the frozen ground") produce no more than vague parodies of the "smells and sounds" of Puerto Rican "routines" (223). Some writers, like Cofer or Nicholas Mohr, view the elements of carnival as indications of a character's embracing a delusive enabling fiction, as a psychological problem best overcome. Others like Fernández display the images satirically, or like Hijuelos with humorous detachment. Still others show an unresolved sympathy toward characters (victims or heroes) caught in their own small festivals. We have already seen how it takes a carnival occurrence to alter Ed Vega's Don Sinforoso Figueroa in such a way that he finds, unexpectedly, true love in a rich woman's garden oasis. Before the "warm summer rain," he has embarked on an "odyssey" in search of his favorite food, a richly seasoned fricassee of "cabrito" or goat meat. This business adventure to buy goats and sell them to the barrio Puerto Ricans turns into a slapstick comedy where Vega mocks the police, the Puerto Rican youth movements and most of all, the vehemence and fervor which people can attach to symbols of their lost past. It is not uncoincidental that the goat winds up in a new paradise within the city, and that Don Sinfo abandons for the moment the impossible task of recreating an Edenic Puerto Rico through the nostalgic dream of eating "cabrito."

An inconclusive attitude on the part of Latino writers toward the meaning of the carnivalesque is part of the larger, non-judgmental, polyphonic quality in the fiction itself. To indulge in the emotional power of these ingredients (and one feels the enjoyment the writer is having recalling smells and sounds and tastes) is not only to escape practicality or to avoid social responsibility, but also to expose the imperfections within official society. Like the festival of the dead, as Gonzalez-Crussi notes, the carnival in general has "the unambiguous aim . . . to ridicule everyone, rich or poor, humbled or exalted, foolish or wise" (39) and to show life less seriously. Establishing the carnival idiom within the fiction directs the reader's perspective and his or her laughter is pointed in either direction from a flexible liminal position between the official and the folk. We laugh at both the nostalgic dreamers and the pragmatism of the American dream.

NOTES

1. From the poem "Tata" by Puerto Rican poet, Pedro Pietri:

2. The inhabitants of this shantytown, "Buckeye Road," bear similarities to those in John Steinbeck's *Cannery Row.* Both novels celebrate the individuality of characters living on the fringes of society.

3. See Jorge Febles's article in *Confluenica: Revista hispanica de cultura y literatura* entitled "Risa, crisis y coronación paródica: lo carnalvalesco en *La vida es un special 1.50 .75." Fall '88 Vol. 3, #1 pp. 123-128.* Mary Vásquez also discusses the "carnivalesque vibrance and color" in Fernández's novel *Raining Backwards.*

4. Though outside the scope of this study, the Puerto Rican scholar Juan Flores, has done extensive work on the relationship between music and Nuyorican culture. See *Divided Borders* and his article "Puerto Rican and Proud, Boyee!: Rap, Roots and Amnesia." published by Ollantay Center for the Arts, 1993. For consideration of Cuban-Americans and music see Perez-Firmat's *Life on the Hyphen.*

5. Miguel Algarín, the Puerto Rican / Nuyorican poet suggests that the idea of fast food is actually worse than the meal itself. Rejecting claims of superiority made by Puerto Ricans on the island, he condemns the place as a US product:

> don't lie to me
> don't fill me full of vain
> disturbing love for an island
> filled with Burger Kings
> for I know there are no cuchifritos
> in Borinquen ("A Mongo Affair")

6. Hijuelos is much less successful in conveying a sense of an era in his later book *Mr. Ives' Christmas* where all the details of the 1960's come from stereotypical TV images: "American hippy records" (160); people smoking marijuana in pipes (128) wearing "love beads" (124); "Columbia University love children" (80). Whereas the richness of *The Mambo Kings Play Songs of Love* lies in his vivid descriptions and ability to capture the flavors of the 1950's, in this work, Hijuelos seems more interested in lazy narration (the point of view is frequently inconsistent), bland imagery and prosaic characterization.

7. A book often alluded to in Martínez's novel: Miguel sees a young teenager "a little older than Lolita (142), and he refers to one woman as a "niña-mujer-hembra," a woman so familiar as to be "like a character out of a novel" (89).

CHAPTER SIX

"Flowers of the Dead:" The Latino Quest for Ancestors

Cristina Garcia's short story "Tito's Good-bye" concerns the last seconds of a man's life in the instant he is hit with a massive heart attack. He isn't given a moment for "the luxury of nostalgia," for remembering his mother's cheek, his father's hands, or his daughter's childhood dance. There isn't time for him to help the desperate immigrants he has defrauded, call the brothers he's ignored or make his estranged wife happy. So, in futile protest, he can utter only the word "Coño." In Spanish the curse refers (with varying degrees of vulgarity, depending upon country) to female genitalia, but here suggests that place where all life begins: Tito's end is his beginning.[1] The story points toward the Latino's desire to avoid Tito's fate, to recapture connections to the past and maintain the bonds of family and culture.

Garcia's first novel, *Dreaming in Cuban,* tells the opposite story, one where families *can* be reunited and the complexities of attitudes toward post-revolutionary Cuba at least partially resolved. If, during that New York City snowstorm, Tito had had the time, he might have embarked on an important Latino quest, a journey toward spiritual identity, a trip through one's grandparents and ancestors toward family ghosts and cultural traditions. Most Latino writers now have round trip tickets[2] between the past and the present, the dead and the living. Like Garcia's Pilar Puente, they seek to "bridge"[3] the gap between the material world and the diversity of folk spirituality, of syncretic religious heritage. All the characters of *Dreaming in Cuban* are thus "going south." What they gather in their travels, their shuttling between cultures, encourages them to balance logical reality with the unexplainable. Treating folk beliefs and faith with reverence and understanding, Latino writers return to their cultural beginnings (literally or imaginatively), and bring back with them to life in the U.S. the foods and sounds of post-colonial or indigenous worlds, and along with tropical fruit, "napolitas," achiote con culantro, salsa, corridos and merengues come the ideas, customs and values of their grandparents to be either discarded as antiquated superstitions or more often molded into some aspect of life in the U.S.

Latino fiction explores the traditions of past generations as protagonists emotionally unite with "abuelas" and "abuelos" [grandmothers and grandfathers] or, venturing one step further, wander among dead ancestors in search of meanings to their own lives. Ron Arias has written of the need to "touch the death" for "in that touch, life is given its truest meaning" ("Mexican Way"), an idea that echoes Eliot's claim that we "die with the dying" and are "born with the dead." Tomás Rivera wrote that Arias's novel *The Road to Tomazunchale* showed readers that "dying as living is a creative ambient and attitude" (*Road* Intro) because the discovery of meaning in death leads to rebirth. Arias, the Chicano, like all Latinos, balances between the Anglo-Protestant "denial of death" (an example of what he sees as the "controlled, mechanistic world of Anglo answers to grief, fear and the unknown"), and the Mexican's Indian-Catholic acceptance of living spirits. Thus the personal, anthropological search for cultural roots constitutes one way Latinos break ranks with U.S. practicality. Octavio Paz claimed in *The Labyrinth of Solitude* that the Mexican is "seduced by death," that he or she "jokes about it, caresses it, sleeps with it, celebrates it" (57-58), and we see similar fascination with the subject in Latino fiction as writers focus on the moment of death, on the close calls, or when they ponder their inability to leave the dead alone. Latinos seem in constant confrontation with their own brand of hybrid spirituality where ghosts share equal time with the business of living. Where the northern European tendency is to separate life and death into distinct compartments or boxes, the walls of the these boxes corrode as one move's south and western systems of classifying cultural truths function less smoothly.

Given the importance of the search for cultural and spiritual identity in Latino fiction, it comes as no surprise that Latinos often structure their works around the classical "descent into the underworld" motif. They send their Latino heroes on symbolic trips into some portion of a Latin American (or Spanish) Hades, and bring them back, all sorts of baggage in hand, to cope with the officials of U.S. customs. "Hell," proclaims La Loca, "is where you go to see yourself" (Castillo *So Far From God* 42). What Latinos discover often disrupts both their U.S. life and their understandings of their cultural heritage. In this way, death serves as an organizing principle for much of Latino fiction as each writer tries to untangle his or her cultural identity. For example, Arturo Islas's *The Rain God* begins with Miguel Chico's recollections of his first trips to the cemetery of his relatives (even before he can understand what the place means—9), and of his friend Leonardo's suicide and funeral. The book is saturated with the deaths (murders, drownings) of his friends and family members. Like many Latino narratives, it is a story about the "sins of fathers" (97) and the coming to terms with divided ancestral heritages. Miguel Chico, as the "central consciousness" or "family analyst" is seeking to understand his family's past (J.D. Saldívar 113). The project of numerous Latino protagonists as they lie upon their deathbeds or in hospital rooms is to reconcile their individual identities with their family's complex memories and experiences. Latin American novels built around flashbacks like Fuentes's *The Death of Artemio Cruz* and García Márquez's *The General in His Labyrinth* provide structural models for these works in which dying men reexamine the paths their lives have taken.[4] Both *The Rain God* and Cecile Pineda's *Face* begin at the point when the central character confronts his need to physically and emotionally rebuild his life. Arias's Fausto, the hero of *The Road to Tomazunchale*, in the opening paragraph, fantasizes that he is peeling off his skin, foreshadowing his mental resurrection. Like the snake, he will renew himself through the process of memory, dream and fantasy which the novel will explore though the hero may never actually leave his deathbed. In Fausto's mind at least, he follows the sound of a Peruvian flute back toward his ancestral indigenous past.[5]

Nash Candelaria's famous *Memories of the Alhambra* opens abruptly with the line: "The Patriarch was dead." The novel then portrays, as Bruce-Novoa explains, an "aging protagonist, José Rafa [who] "fears tradition slipping away and flees to Spain in search of his ancestry" (*Retrospace* 105). José's son, Joe, must confront his own mixed heritage because of his father's departure. Candelaria uses the descent into the underworld pattern to illustrate the beginning of both men's spiritual journeys toward unifying the Latin American and European fragments of their identities. For Jose Rafa, the quest which leads from California to Mexico to Spain is a futile search to begin with. Introduced, as it is, by a phony genealogist significantly named (as we noted above) "Alphonso de Sintierra" (without earth), Jose's journey is frequently characterized as madness, and a "raging compulsion." When he arrives in Spain, in search of his conquistador ancestors, only to find dwarfs, gypsies, statues of Don Quixote ("a madman and his servant fool" -143), and a man of Moorish descent, he is confronted with the futility of his "crazy search . . . at every step nothing but confusion" (166). Candelaria plays upon the motif in order to suggest that José's true heritage lies, not in Spain, but in the indigenous Indian backgrounds he so desperately denies. José, unlike his son, finds it impossible to reconcile the truth of his mixed heritage, and therefore fails in the attempt to organize the scattered pieces of experience and memory, to create order out of chaos, and make sense of the "heap of broken fragments."

Jose Rafa ultimately recognizes that if his heritage is tied to the infamy of Cortés, then it is also linked with the treachery of the Indian Malinche and that he is Indian and Mexican, not pure Spanish as he has always claimed, but a part of the "rainbow of humanity as losers" (181). A similar pattern shapes Guy Garcia's story "La Promesa." Tom Cardona, a middle class, republican Chicano journeys south into Mexico in search of his grandmother's past. He has promised his grandmother to undertake the excursion in much the way the narrator of Rulfo's *Pedro Páramo* promises his mother. The twist here is that Tom Cardona is motivated by his expected inheritance of $30,000, and not an oedipal desire to find his father. Tom crosses the border (the threshold of his adventure) and encounters a haggard old woman with "claw-like fingers" (Soto 133). He journeys down "tangled freeways" (133) through a labyrinthine mansion with a "receding hall of mirrors" (140), and with the guidance of a story telling coffin maker, ventures through the municipal cemetery. He winds up finally in the town's claustrophobic "museum" of mummies, probably that of Guanajuato west of Mexico City. Here he learns that one mummy is presumably his true grandmother, a scorned woman, driven insane by her fiancé's murder of her lover and probably buried alive as a devil figure, a "succubus." Her mummified damaged fingernails recall both the old woman at the border (a sort of haggard Charon figure) as well as "The broken fingernails of dirty hands" in Eliot's "Wasteland," because it is Tom, up to this moment of recognition, who has been able to "connect nothing with nothing," has treated his Mexican origins as a "footnote"

(135) and lived by his motto: "drive fast, don't look back" (136). In addition, the claw-like fingers of the ancient women suggest the famous serpent goddess Coatlicue with her taloned feet symbolizing the "duality" of life, "the digging of graves into the earth as well as the sky-bound eagle" (Anzaldúa *Borderlands* 27, 47). F. Gonzalez-Crussi, the pathologist, reminds us that her "vulturelike claws" tie her to the earth goddess that, like the vulture, feeds upon the dead (51). The discovery of his relative (a sort of "La Llorona"/"La Malinche" figure) is powerful enough to rid him of "pride and worldly pretense" (151) and force him to realize that connecting with the past is a source of renewal, that to deny the dead, to turn your back on the blinding "Aztec sun" is to reject one's true nature.

John Rechy in *The Miraculous Day of Amalia Gómez* uses the descent motif to follow his heroine through LA's Hollywood Boulevard which Amalia sees as a "graveyard for the living dead." Amalia walks toward self-awareness, amid Hollywood's glittering falseness. For nearly half the novel, we follow her through a poverty strewn neighborhood, a "crazy maze" (118) of female wrestlers (115), bible pushers (116), a ragged old woman disappearing into an abandoned building (113) and a humorously typical visit to a fast food restaurant. As Amalia progresses, the illusions she has maintained to protect herself, the enabling fictions of her past are stripped away one by one until, and like a Eugene O'Neill character, she is left with the devastating truth of the failure of her family. She walks through the "glistening palace" of a mall (203), and recognizes herself as being "out of place," existing, like the other poor Chicanos of southern California with "a gun to her head" (77). In the end, when a gun-wielding stranger uses her as a hostage, this expression turns into a literal reality.

Like Amalia, Dagoberto Gilb's Mickey Acuña also passes through a type of Hell, in this case a YMCA, his "last known residence." Mickey is a lost soul wandering amid fringe dwelling losers each with a story to tell. Wearing mirror sunglasses, he stumbles over a blind man (Tiresias?) at the entrance. Yet the similarities between these two unfortunate Chicano protagonists break down as the results of their respective journeys become clear; Amalia's violent experience sends her toward an epiphany which leaves her feeling "resurrected with new life" (Rechy 206), while Mickey walks toward "the border," feeling guilty, confused and still unable "to remember true and real things" (209).

Latina writers twist the "descent into the underworld" motif, not to negate its symbolic significance, but to problematize the effectiveness of such spiritual journeys that endorse unequivocally male traditions. Like previous modernists, Latina writers are less interested in past allegiances (and by extension in traditional, literary patterns of structure and theme) as they are in discovering the present and looking toward the future. Gloria Anzaldúa's short story "People Should not Die in June in South Texas" switches, almost immediately, from the solemn funeral of her father "Urbano, loved by all," to a sarcastic mocking of the entire graveyard ritual: "after two and a half days, her father has begun to smell like a cow whose carcass has been gutted by vultures. People should not die in June in south Texas" (Augenbraum and Stavans 280). Compared to Candelaria's opening, Anzaldúa's story privileges the details of a rotting corpse, the incisions and fluids of the embalming and the price of coffins over the mythical significance of her heroine's growth. In fact, Prietita's growth comes from recognition, four years later, that the dead are simply dead, that the ritual of the wake has little to do with her life (after a few days she is just as "invisible and invincible" in the black of mourning as she was before).

Anzaldúa rejects the power of the dead, the influence of the corpse (the Antigone archetype) over the living, yet in her sheer practicality, she is atypical of Latino writers who, in general, exploit the hazy territory of the spaces between fact and belief, between life and death. The story actually seems to repudiate the famous line from Rulfo's *Pedro Paramo*: "The dead carry more weight than the living." Anzaldúa argues in *Borderlands / La Frontera* that the descent motif is symbolic of the artist's Shamanistic endeavor to understand the oppositions and "duality" in life. Through a hazy mid-state of sickness and health, sleep and waking, the artist can "jump blindfolded into the abyss of her own being and there in the depths confront her face, the face underneath the mask" (74). In her story, however, there is no chance of the little girl's bridging the gap between Mictlán (69) or Miktlán (48), the "region of the dead" and her daily life. Perhaps this is true because the ancestral patriarchal chain of the dead male offers nothing that she as a woman can use. The journey toward the dead is, for Latina writers, often sterile and pointless when it follows the roots of the father. Anzaldúa's stressing the physical deterioration of the deceased father figure indicates that she'd have the young heroine look elsewhere for her identity than in patriarchal tradition.

For Ana Castillo, the journey back to Mexican heritage is problematic, since just as more and more Mexican women cross the border in search of work and then return with mixed ideas about their rights and positions in traditional society, so Teresa in *The Mixquiahuala Letters* finds difficulty with Mexico's age-old attitudes about female behavior and gender roles. Teresa is drawn by her "devotion to the culture that preceded European influence" (49) to the "pre-Columbian village of obscurity" (19) referred to in the title. Her name is perhaps an allusion to Theresa the wife of the autocratic José Rafa since Candelaria's "Chicana flapper," Theresa, embodies the independence, modernity, and rebelliousness that Castillo's Teresa would admire. After all, Theresa Rafa is "a fighter who wanted more" (Candelaria 141) and resents her husband's racism (78). She forces him to escape his stifling autocratic family and is the only character in *Memories of the Alhambra* to recognize "that remnant of their Spanish forebear's' cruelty in the men and in the women that docility that came from the Indian ancestors that they [the rest of the Rafa family] would deny" (62). Castillo's heroine's journey (presumably paralleling the reader's "journey"[6]), recollected piece by piece in the letters that constitute the book is an encounter with both the authenticity of her Mexican-Indian roots and the traps and taboos for women within that culture. Like all Latinas, she must mark herself as an individual without sacrificing the benefits provided by the Latin American communal and family systems. At one point, Castillo's letters speak of returning to "ancient Tenochtitlan, home of my mother, grandmothers, and greatmother, as embracing bosom, to welcome me back and rock my weary body and mind to sleep . . . " (92). Yet moments later, she undercuts the mythic Edenic womb image by recalling her actual arrival and being "shuffled out like excess cargo, placed in a cab and sent away . . . to the family of a friend" (92). "Mexican hospitality did indeed have its limits" (93). Teresa's outsider's perspective allows her to see how Mexico "embraces as it strangulates" (59). She starts to find herself a "snag" in Mexico's societal pattern (59). As Alarcón has argued, Teresa is "forced to recall that she is not as free as she thought" (98) when confronted by the restrictions of Mexican women. Her southern journey, her symbolic descent, "down, down, for days and nights" (60) thus enhances the ambiguities of her identity,[7] ultimately uniting her with other Castillo heroines who embrace the unfixed hybridity of mestizo consciousness. Yvonne Yarbo-Bejarano draws parallels between Teresa's multiple subjectivity (67) and Pastura's (the heroine of Castillo's second novel *Sapogonia*) divided nature whose nickname, Coatlicue, suggests again the "goddess of the union of opposites" (Yarbo-Bejarano 68). In *Sapogonia,* it is the "anti-hero" Maximo Madrigal whose quest is portrayed as he travels south to rescue his Mayan grandmother from revolutionaries. Having only belatedly switched his search for roots from a paternal direction (from which he learns little about himself) to a maternal one, he finds his "abuela" dead and so the search fails. Unlike the semi-revolutionary Sofi, the heroine matriarch in *So Far From God*, Maximo doesn't recognize a need to depart from male tradition, and, in a manner similar to Tom Cardona in the Garcia story, his loss of connection to the abuela leaves him stranded. He "functions," according to Gómez-Vega, "within an intrinsically male-identified culture . . . that values the mythological male hero's separation from the community" (244) while Castillo's articulation of the descent motif clearly emphasizes the positive female side of her Latin American cultural and familial ties. As Maximo journeys "away from communion into solitude" (Gómez-Vega 244), the novel advocates the Latina's need to progress in the opposite direction.

Though Castillo's epistolary novel allows for a "Conformist" reading (the first of three possible orderings of the chapters) such a reading is clearly the least attractive to the ethnographer/author[8] because it confirms what Yarbo-Bejarano calls the "maternal dictates" of traditional Mexican women (67-68). If the past is essential in forming identities, the errors within past traditions must also be understood. According to Sofi, the "conformist" is despicable, or as her daughter Esperanza says, someone "who just didn't give a damn about nothing" (139). To conform is to acquiesce, to bow to the forces of the powers that be. Such is the fate of Sofi's daughter, Fe who, betrayed by her romantic lover, pursues the elusive American financial dream into the Acme weapons plant and dies of cancer from toxic cleaning fluids. As her name suggests, misguided "faith" in her bosses proves fatal, her obedience deadly, and, on an allegorical level, faith in the system dies with her. In fact, Castillo writes: "she did not resurrect . . . Fe just died. And when someone dies that plain dead, it is hard to talk about" (186). Sofi, on the other hand, becomes mayor of Tome and gains a permanent voice to "speak her mind" as a woman and for women (157), positioning herself to *rewrite* the town, to edit the "Tome."

For Cristina Garcia as well, the concept of seeking out one's heritage is valid, provided the journey is properly directed along matrilineal lines. Thus early in the novel, the young heroine, Pilar Puente, travels south by bus to Florida on her way toward Cuba. On the bus, Pilar meets Minnie French, a woman "weirdly old-looking for a young person" (27). Minnie tells Pilar that she is the "last of thirteen children," that her born-again mother died giving birth to her and that she is in route to Florida to get an abortion. If Pilar's journey is to truly result in increased understanding and a symbolic "rebirth" into greater maturity through connection with the past, then this encounter on the bus with its emphasis on death and sterility is inauspicious. In fact, Pilar's trip will end in Florida which, politically at least, is decidedly not Cuba. Moreover, she will wind up trapped in the house of her father's patriarchal family. Abuela Zaida, her father's sister, uses the collective "we" to include only men and to exclude women, and Pilar's grandfather from the old world likes his wife to call him "Don Guillermo." This "blustery caballero's" flagrant macho behavior once led him to kill an innocent dog which had been trying to drag the year and a half old Pilar out of the street where she had wandered. We know early in the novel that Pilar is in search of a fading connection with her grandmother, Abuela Celia, with whom she shares birthdays. Reacting to the falsity of her mother's exaggerated patriotic bakery and her father's adultery, Pilar leaves New York in search of a truth somehow associated with her grandmother's visionary, mystical world. As the character Minnie foreshadows, however, this first Florida trip proves to be a sterile journey in terms of Pilar's psychological development. She winds up getting drenched in the tropical rain, and symbolically locked outside the home of her paternal grandparents. Pilar's genuine journey, the one that will establish the authentic relationship between her and her past will occur eight years later, for six April (i.e. the month of rebirth) days in Cuba, and this experience, rather than the initial bus trip, will restore Pilar to a sense of herself and at the same time bridge (as her name, "Puente," suggests) the gap between the island and the U.S., the past and her present.

For Latina writers in particular, the ties to a homeland are both necessary and problematic. Links with a Mexican heritage, while important, can constitute what Rosaura Sánchez calls a "contradictory inclusion/exclusion trap" ("Discourses" 84) for the Chicana. This is true for Latinas of Cuban or Puerto Rican descent as well, and the tensions involved in confronting male traditions consequently produce works in which the family, the "community" ("collectivity" for Sánchez), becomes divided along gender lines. Whenever Latinos, especially women, as individuals, are pitted against the family social codes, the Latino finds him/herself caught between a refusal to abide by rules of the past and being incapable of living without certain familial bonds. "The family is hostile to the individual" complains Pilar midway through a novel that will demonstrate that the family is also essential to the individual. The father's side of the family is frequently disparaged in stories and novels, often because the male genealogies reveal the line from Latino to Spanish to Conquistador (the ultimate criminal) rather than from Latino to Mestizo to Mexican, Indian or African (the victims). In Castillo's *So Far From God*, the patriarchal lines pass along rare blood diseases (20), while in Lucha Corpi's mystery novel *Eulogy for a Brown Angel*, it is the father's side of the family, a la Hawthorne, that hands down the curse for revenge from Grandfather Soren Bjorgun to the murderer and rapist Paul Cisneros. The latter figure is part of a Brazilian paramilitary group (185-186). Such a heritage, according to Corpi, ultimately leads to a game "where all the main players were men, and the losers were all women and their children (170).

The effort (in Corpi's case, transparent), to validate the female line while discrediting the male is not uncommon in Latina fiction. Alma Villanueva's *The Ultraviolet Sky* even manages to lay the blame for a malamute's violent behavior not on the dog's nature but upon a young boy who has trained it to attack other dogs (373). Eliud Martínez constructs a relationship between a grandfather Don Miguel Velásquez and his grandson, the "voice haunted passenger" who tells the story, which is not entirely built on affection, despite the same name and a "remarkable resemblance" between them. The memory of this grandfather, however, haunts him throughout the book, like his "tocayo" or namesake, allowing the older man to live on through him (121). The sins of the grandfather in this case are handed down to young Miguel who comes from "his grandfather's garden" (190), searches for and discovers him "in the rumors of the family elders" (14) and suffers from the same personality defects. He tells himself that his writings, like his grandfather's notebooks, are "nothing more than a record of a man who was born to bring grief and anguish to loved ones" (228).

Unlike the grandmother figure, generally portrayed in Latino fiction in a positive light, the abuelo and his descendants exert an ambiguous and complicated influence. We see the moving and beneficial relationship between, for instance, a grandson and his shaman, Yaqui grandfather in Alfredo Véa's *La Maravilla*, but also the oedipal struggles of the Velásquez family in Martínez's *Voice-Haunted Journey* or the homophobic machismo of Arturo Islas's male figures. In the story "A Silent Love" by Bejamin Alire Sáenz, a deaf boy and his 73 year old grandfather communicate non-verbally "like dancers" in much the way abuelas and granddaughters do (*Flowers* 21). Their signing turns the old man's hands into "wings" according to the older grandson who sits outside this silent mystical communion between the two. The scene recalls the wing-like hands of Anderson's Wing Biddlebaum not only because the hands express what words cannot, but also because the love between the older man and younger boy is genuinely maternal. At one point, the older brother tells his grandfather that he has "turned into an old woman," become, in effect, an abuela. Though not meant as a compliment from the older brother, the remark is ironically positive to the reader.

Male characters in the works of Sáenz, Véa and Islas seem to generate sympathy in direct proportion to their feminine qualities, while those in Garcia (especially in *The Agúero Sisters*), Cisneros and Castillo invite scorn for lacking these same characteristics. To resemble the abuela is to reject the stereotypical bravado of Latin American fathers and grandfathers, and become aware of the deficiencies of a patriarchal tradition. This is so because the abuela figure usually represents the connection to everything outside the injustice and corruption of institutional controls. She is the "transmitter" of oral, folk culture, and serves as the link between the present, often oppressive world, and the lost past (Rebolledo "Abuelitas" 153). The abuela is often "nurturing, comforting and stable" (156). Though a writer like Roberto Fernández makes fun of the formulaic "abuela" by describing one rather inept grandmother as being "in a trance for a few minutes, rewinding her mind" (*Raining* 147), usually, as Marcienne Rocard notes, the abuelita is sympathetically portrayed as a person "closer to grandchildren . . . [than children] especially granddaughters" and who thus "insures continuity with the past" (153-154). Her intuition is bound up with an oral tradition and she communicates the non-European cultural values otherwise ignored by society.

Perhaps, above all, the grandmother is the conveyor of folk spirituality, the means by which granddaughters and grandsons attach themselves to the world of unorthodox religious beliefs. She has ties to a "knowledge and wisdom identified with magic and old ways" (Rebolledo "Abuelitas" 153). Abuelas are linked to curanderas (healers), seers, and to the rituals of indigenous cultures and the practices of syncretic religions—validated or not by the texts in which they appear.[9] They can even be related to brujas (witches) or the dual goddesses and mythic figures like Coatlicue that suggest both negative and positive aspects of female power. Sometimes, like curanderas, they know of medicinal herbs and homeopathic remedies. Thus, in the Latino search for identity, characters venture through the kitchens[10] and dreams of older women on their way to understanding themselves. Anaya's Ultima, perhaps the most famous curandera figure, leads the young hero on his spiritual quest. The mythic curandera figure combines the strength and power of independence with the wisdom and ability to heal the sick. As Rebolledo notes, she "has control over her own life and destiny as well as that of others" (*Women* 88). When Cristina Garcia's Pilar returns to Cuba, she gathers the folk-spirituality of her independent grandmother at the same time she denounces the male traditions of the old world. In Villanueva's novel, it is Rosa Luján's Grandmother, Luz [light] after whom Rosa names her newborn baby, and not her mother Dolores [pain]. Rosa's "Mamacita" has taught her the prophetic quality of dreams (58) on which she relies extensively and has showed her how notions of God and the Devil could be "lumped together" (89) and seen as masculine vehicles for the repression of women. Near the end of her search for self-identity and independence, Rosa thanks this "dark-skinned, Indian looking woman" (126) "por todo" [for everything] (377). When her husband's grandmother dies, she photographs a series of stark, desert pictures suggesting that the death of an abuela marks a loss of fertility and life. Those grandmothers who rebelled against past convention even acquire heroic status in the eyes of their descendants. Cisneros's Esperanza of *The House on Mango Street* admires her great-grandmother as "a wild horse of a woman, so wild she wouldn't marry until my great-grandfather threw a sack over her head and carried her off" (12). In *Memories of the Alhambra*, Theresa Rafa sees a genuine peace in the home of her storytelling grandmother. Compared to the Rafa women, dressed in black and reminiscent of Islas's elderly, Catholic matriarchs, Theresa's "Nana" is naturally connected to "our mother, the earth" (69), believes deeply in the holy dirt of Chimayo (73) and her home in the mountains has a "nesting quality of comfort and refuge . . . a place in which to be fed and kept warm" (68).

In the effort to explore the past, Latino writers authenticate the grandmother's spirituality, and in so doing, identify themselves with a whole range of unwritten, unorthodox religious traditions. Female lineage encourages a writer to enter a vast world of non-western attitudes toward life and death, and bringing these concepts into Latino fiction raises interesting complications. The trend of documenting non-European religious thought suggests that Latino writers are, like most post-colonial artists, not merely aiming their work at mainstream audiences, but rather guiding readers in new directions. They seem rather to be engaged in an active pursuit of living mixed cultures, and interested in the cross-fertilization going on between the accepted and the taboo, the modern and the "old ways." In this process which is guided not by nostalgia, but by respect, superstitions get reevaluated. We find that Cuban-American, Dominican-American and mainland Puerto Rican writers depict the ritualistic elements of Santería or "the religion of the saints,"[11] while Chicanos incorporate both Native American and Mexican folk spiritual traditions into their stories. What significance these elements contribute to the literature depends on the writer, but their inclusion demonstrates the importance and diversity of Latino spirituality. Latino fiction shows an increasingly pronounced need for Latinos to confront their indigenous, non-western spiritual roots if they are to adequately understand the influences that have shaped their lives, in terms of their culture, race and religion.

Taking a specific example, we see, for instance, the importance of ritual bathing in several works. While typically seen in literature as a symbolic representation of spiritual cleansing (or in Roman Catholicism as baptism or rebirth into the world of God), in Latino fiction, bathing also suggests emotional bonding between characters, particularly between women. A Taino Indian instructs the gypsy Rosa on the precision necessary for magical, ritual bath in Judith Cofer's *In the Line of the Sun.* The out-of-body telepathic connections between a woman and her lost brother in Benjamin Alire Sáenz's *Carry Me Like Water* begin with a bath in clean and hot and seductive water (38). In Helena Viramontes's story "The Moths," both granddaughter and grandmother "nurse" each other and bath in "the waters of the womb" (28). This bath is in direct opposition to institutionalized religious purification for it represents a personal ritual of connecting where the young granddaughter acts "with the sacredness of a priest" though no actual priest is involved. The dying grandmother cannot speak, yet her granddaughter who cradles her in the tub can somehow hear her.

In *Dreaming in Cuban*, Pilar bathes in a tub filled with herbs while her distant grandmother, Celia, swims in the ocean. Somehow, telepathically, the bathing connects Pilar with her abuela. The magic of her herbal baths is derived from the magic of the Santería ritual, the cleansing ceremonial bath known as a "despojo" (González-Wippler 22). "Nine consecutive nights" of herbal bathing (usually, according to González-Wippler "to attract good vibrations and help solve the problems of the consultant" 219) convinces Pilar that she and her mother must go to Cuba and find her abuela. She can, as Ivanito sees, bring her grandmother "back to life" (*Dreaming* 230); she feels her "grandmother's life passing to [her] through her hands. It's a steady electricity, humming and true" (222).[12] Throughout the novel, Garcia refuses to discount the validity of Santería beliefs. In fact, the novel endorses them in as much as Pilar's actions bring her toward her grandmother which is the essential element of her quest for identity. Moreover, the ritual bathing links Pilar to her rebellious aunt Felicia when we recall Felicia's initiation ceremony where sixteen Santeras bathed her in river water (187). Pilar is recognized as a daughter of Changó, the Yoruban deity disguised under the Catholic Santa Barbara [Saint Barbara] and thus associated with power, either "procreative, authoritative, destructive, medicinal, or moral" (González-Wippler 40), suggesting perhaps the power of the artist to unify and gather strength from a complex cultural heritage. In any case, the inclusion of Santería mysticism emphasizes the otherworldly quality of Pilar's relationship with her family. Like Herminia, the black daughter of a Santería priest (90) who lives "on the fringe of life" (184), Pilar is also "connected to another world" (186); part of her spiritual growth depends on her recognizing, like the granddaughter in the Viramontes story, the non-verbal channels of communication, the "languages lost."

Ana Castillo goes to extremes to validate southwestern curandera practices by filling her novel *So Far from God* with information about "limpias" or "sobasos" or cleansings. By declaring that "all who had lived on that tierra of thistle and tumbleweed knew that every cactus and thorn had a purpose and reason, once put into a pot to boil" (233), the narrator authenticates the medicinal beliefs of women over those learned, for example, at "Northwestern University Medical School in the coldest city of the world" (227). The healing women are particularly attractive to Chicano political writers like Castillo since they stack up well against the stereotypical Mexican mother who is always patient and enduring. In contrast, the curandera exhibits a magical strength unknown to others and avenges herself when necessary (Rebolledo *Women* 90).

There are many parallels between the folk religions of African/Cuban practice and the healing rituals of indigenous south westerners, and, in fact, we find mention of Santería itself in *So Far from God.* Two soldiers in Vietnam ponder the differences between Puerto Rican and New Mexican Santería as they wait "to be killed if they didn't kill first" (96). They discover that the details of ritual practice vary, but both men share a respect for the Yoruban tradition. They are, in effect, united on a spiritual level as they fight the U.S. government's war. Francisco el Penitente, the Chicano, is known as "Chico" while his Puerto Rican friend is called "Little Chico," because "to the white and black soldiers all 'Spanish boys' were 'Chico'" (94). Clearly, believing in the syncretic religion provides each Latino with an escape from the prejudice of a world "transforming beyond comprehension" (97).

In a different sort of novel, the detective story *The Killing of the Saints* by Alex Abella, a Marielito's belief in Santería collides with the logic of U.S. law. Two Cuban exiles murder a group of people in a jewelry store and, acting in their own defense, claim they had been possessed by the warrior god Oggun. The store's owner had taken back an object which had been used as a propitiatory offering to the Santería orisha who had therefore retaliated with the ghastly massacre via the two "innocent" men. Though the dust jacket of the novel dismisses the story's religion as mere "voodoo-like cult," Abella relays the importance of these beliefs in several ways. Ramón, one of the accused is an especially articulate speaker. Charlie Morell, the private detective investigating the crime, notes that he had never before "seen someone use his foreignness to such an advantage, to be able to enjoy the benefit of both worlds, the alien and the native, the Hispanic and the Anglo." Ramón argues that "the truth of the matter depends on one's personal interpretation" (260). "Witchcraft," according to this eloquent Cuban exile, "is a pejorative term used by members of one religion against practitioners of another" (282), and thus his innocence or guilt becomes "a question of selective belief" (282). The reader, and the jury, is persuaded by this sort of intelligent logic, and Ramón is acquitted, thanks to what he calls his "cultural defense" (170). Turning to the narrator/detective, we find even more that authenticates beliefs in Santería. Charlie Morell, like many Latino figures, is also investigating his own life, specifically his relationship to his dead father whom he feels he had abandoned. Morell's confrontation with the mystical spiritualism of the Cuban exiles brings him closer to understanding the reasons for the guilt he feels. He seeks to discover the "pieces of [him]self that were scattered among these Caribbean exiles like the arms and legs of a starfish, which, torn from the body, will grow a new center to replace the missing heart" (74). Something in the exposure to the spiritual side of his Cuban past allows him to become reconciled with his father's ghost. Because of the encounter, at the novel's conclusion, he rejoins his estranged wife and begins a new relationship with his son.

Chicana critic Gloria Anzaldúa would argue that Charlie's Morell's enlightenment comes as a result of his "entering into the serpent," by which she means a willingness to believe in other modes of consciousness. She has in mind pre-Colombian serpent goddesses, the powers of mother earth, and the rejection of institutionalized religions like Catholicism and Protestantism which "encourage a split between body and spirit and totally ignore the soul" (*Borderlands* 37). Whatever the name given to these alternative religion systems, Latinos, particularly in recent fiction, are moving toward an embrace of the spirit world. Even writers as focused on concrete realities as Dagoberto Gilb seem unwilling to deny the validity of dreams, intuitions, and visions. This is due in part to dissatisfaction with orthodox religion. The reverend, for example, in Gilb's *The Last Residence of Mickey Acuña*, though "polite," is surely the most "threatening" resident of the YMCA (145). Anzaldúa claims that understanding "La Facultad" [the faculty] or the ability "to see in surface phenomena the meaning of deeper realities" (*Borderlands* 38) will help women understand themselves where organized religions "encourage fear and distrust of life and of the body" (37). Those individuals on the outskirts of society (outcasts or rebels) are sensitized by the natural world and able to escape the confines of society's limited vision. The victims of society (the abused, the raped, the misunderstood) can develop extra perceptions because the standard roles have broken down, and the domestic rigidity given way. Anzaldúa writes: "Those who are pounced on the most have it the strongest—the females, the homosexuals of all races, the darkskinned . . . the persecuted, the marginalized, the foreign" (38) "La Facultad" is "a survival tactic that people caught between the worlds, unknowingly cultivate" (39), and can be brought on by "anything that tears the fabric of our everyday mode of consciousness" (39).

One would expect, by Anzaldúa's reasoning, some degree of acceptance of the occult in fiction about men and women in the margins of U.S. society. Think, for instance, of Garcia's Felicia or Castillo's Caridad, or the narrator and abandoned lover, Inés, of Cisneros's story "Eyes of Zapata." All three are women wronged by an unjust world and all exist in a liminal, otherworldly, haze.[13] Not all Latino writers are as accepting, however. In his first novel, *Our House in the Last World*, Hijuelos offers judgments on Cuban spiritualists whose beliefs Mercedes inflicts on her son Hector (pounding on his stomach "to get the devils out" for instance—93). There is even a brutal edge to Hijuelos's commentary as, for example, when he writes that Mercedes "had the kind of faith in science that the ignorant have: It will do everything. She had a faith like the faith hoods with knife wounds that spill their guts have, who come to the hospitals thinking they won't die. They come walking in nonchalantly and then fall to the floor, dead" (95). These types of authorial judgments are atypical. There are also minor characters who adhere to the rigidity of Pentecostal doctrine (mostly in Mainland Puerto Rican fiction) and old world Catholicism (notably, the New Mexican Hispanos) within Latino stories, but the central figures are rarely people intolerant of non-European beliefs. More often, as in Sáenz novel *Carry Me Like Water*, the fringe dwellers (the gay, poor, abused, deaf and dumb, illegal, criminal—the novel includes them all) find themselves connecting spiritually and miraculously across barriers of time and space. The mixtures and blends of religious thought even take place within individual characters as is the case with Véa's syncretic Josephina who is both Castillian Catholic and a mystical curandera.

In two novels, we find young heroines passing beyond the folk spirituality associated with the adults around them. The rites of passage for Marisol, in Cofer's *The Line of the Sun,* and Estrella, in Viramontes's *Under the Feet of Jesus*, both confirm a young woman's need to assert her independence against any sort of spiritual limitation. Marisol is "in a state of limbo, halfway between two cultures" (222). She is caught between the "organized, sanitized world of school" (220), the "discipline and order" imposed on her by Catholic nuns and the "hidden world of Puerto Rican women and secret "spiritist meetings" (232). Her initiation into the "world of phones, offices, concrete buildings and the English language" (273) comes when the apartment building where she lives burns to the ground. "El Building" is a "parody" of Puerto Rican life in which all the sounds and smells of the island are mimicked by the tenants, and it is destroyed when overzealous Spiritists, in "a mass *despojo,*" offer the god Changó a bit too much lighter fluid. The novel's ending suggests Cofer's attitude that the "silly" (230) folk spirituality is antiquated, and Marisol draws a practical lesson from the experience: she will carry her "island heritage" with her, but she will abide by a "new efficient voice" (276). For Viramontes, the outcome is less unequivocal. Her young heroine never completely discards adult superstitions. Estrella listens to stories of the "evil eye" (24) and knows that "not even a few drops of menstrual blood in [her father's] coffee would keep him from leaving" (23). More than once, she follows her mother's instructions to draw a circle around the dirt house in order to ward off scorpions, while Perfecto, her mother's companion, dreams of ghosts, his memories binding him "to the native soil" (100). He knows the ghosts are "working in the dream world to tell him something" and he believes in the "insect signs" (100-101). The process of Estrella's maturation does not involve outright denial of her family's beliefs, yet in the final scenes when her mother's statue of Jesus is smashed and Perfecto abandons them, Estrella finds her own brand of spiritual connection to the natural world; she climbs up through the barn's loft as if "out of a box" (174) and gazes at the stars, standing "on the verge of faith" (176).

The Latino exploration of Pan-American past or what Ilan Stavans refers to as the "five-hundred-year-old fiesta of miscegenation" that began in 1492 (13) sends writers beneath the Roman Catholic churches toward indigenous pyramids and temples, and past Catholic saints toward African deities. In this way, the syncretic religions neatly accommodate non-European perspectives on human existence, and provide writers with a creative flexibility to ponder their cultural roots from both sides, to value the mixtures and blends that have formed their family's beliefs. "We are all," writes Stavans, "children of lascivious Iberians and raped Indian and African maidens" (32). Writers document the oral rendition of events, blending the legends of Indians and slaves with written accounts. Magical "story" is fused with accepted "history" and neither negates the other.[14] Attitudes about life and death become unfixed, polyphonic and ambiguous. The result of this widening of spiritual guidelines is often a playful rendering of a special Latino spirituality where the ways of the old world combine with the new, where, as a character in *Carry Me Like Water* declares, the modern Latino journeys south "to pick up [his] ghosts" (337).

Spiritualism,[15] by definition, is concerned with the spirits of the dead, and in legitimizing the African-indigenous acceptance of communication with past spirits, the Latino writer slides around within a hazy area condemned by mainstream doctrines as the occult. Yet this richly populated region of belief where the dead exist on "a parallel universe" (Stavans 118) never stops infiltrating Latino practical life, because the marginal, spiritual views of non-orthodox religious traditions make up a part of who Latinos are. This is why, in the fiction, the past literally comes alive as the distinction between the living and the dead is blurred. Equipped with this form of cultural access to the spirit world, Latino writers use it to prove that the ghosts of the past cannot be ignored. Each of the protagonists in Sáenz's first novel, for example, commences a spiritual quest into a troubled personal history, knowing that nothing can "bring down the houses of the past" (352). They travel south (to El Paso) as if "beckoned by something they cannot resist" (368). Latinos, recognizing that they embody their pasts, lean toward those systems of belief that accent the practice of honoring the dead as if they were alive. "The dead do not sleep," thinks a character in *Carry Me Like Water*, "and they do not let the living sleep either" (91). Like "visitors" (381), they do not leave.

Molina, a coffin maker, in the Guy Garcia story "La Promesa" (who is possibly named after the homosexual prisoner in Puig's *Kiss of the Spider Woman*) significantly laments the notion that: "we Mexicans are not very good at burying our dead. They live with us, behind doors, under creaking beds, in the cobwebs that cling to walls, watching, judging . . . " (147). The idea is given graphic emphasis in the story when Tom finds the body of his "succubus" grandmother, her mummified nails broken from a failed attempt to claw her way out of a coffin. As a motif, the difficulty of burying, erasing one's dead (or past) is as old as *Antigone* and prominent in the chain of influence one sees from Faulkner (*As I Lay Dying,* "A Rose for Emily") to García Márquez's *Leaf Storm.*[16] We find it, for example, in Portillo-Trambley's short story "Pay the Criers" where two drunks labor strenuously to bury an old woman. It is integral as well to the García Márquez story "The Handsomest Drowned Man in the World," and this story reverberates through Ron Arias's *The Road to Tomazunchale* when a group of children discover the beautiful body of David the mojado [wetback] in a dried up riverbed near the border. He is "the best looking young man they had ever seen, at least naked" (56). He is a man "so perfect," he "should not be buried" claims Fausto, and the cadaver is restored, cleaned, dressed and left further down the river where others can find him, so great is his power of moving people to better their condition. García Márquez's handsome Esteban (the corpse) provokes the town's people to recognize for the first time the "desolation of their streets" and, in order to maintain their pride in their town where the glorious dead man came ashore, they improve their situation. In Arias, the corpse, "dead, half-dead or alive" (61) pushes Fausto into his fantasy of saving the mojados, and the encapsulated rendition of the story becomes, as Nieto argues, is "the structural apex" of Arias' novel (246). Corpse becomes catalyst as the dead man in each case serves the living who are given "a new sense of purpose through the presence of death" (Nieto 243) and who must therefore ritualistically honor the corpse, and recognize that the dead have meaning for the living.

As we have seen, magical realism encourages the Latino writer's tendency to blur the distinctions between reality and illusion. Thus it fits nicely with the Latino's sense of folk spirituality and his or her refusal to accept that truth lies exclusively in the rational and logical world. Marjorie Agosin argues in the introduction to her collection of fantastic stories by Latin American women, that the fantastic "offers territories and spaces for subversion, disorder and illegality" and "opens possibilities in order to imagine . . . a territory of intuition, magic and the beginnings of language" (13-14). As narrative mode, magical realism (or any form of the fantastic) accentuates the already unfixed ideas of spirituality that Latinos gather from syncretic religious backgrounds. Dissolving the line between the living and the dead becomes therefore both a feature of fantastic narrative and a political statement against the rigidity of European reasoning. To accept the strange is to distance oneself from the norm; "the comfortable familiarity with the preposterous has as its counterpart an alienation from the familiar and everyday" (Vásquez "Parody" 97).

Something in U.S. practical wisdom dictates the need for one to "move beyond" the dead, to "get over with" one's emotional connections to them. In pop psychology, you are "OK" once you "deal" with someone's death and focus on your own life once more. In Latino fiction, however, the dead are always present, and living with them is integral to life. Part of the explanation for this comes from the Catholic tradition of death as "transcendence" (Paz 57), and doctrines of purgatory where one is neither dead nor alive, but caught midway until proper forgiveness allows for the passage of the soul into heaven. The extended family household where the old give up their places to the young encourages a feeling in family members for the cyclical nature of life. For the Latino, encounters with the dead create rebirths, just as voyages into the underworld lead to resurrections and renewed lives. In this way, as Paz claims, death is conceived of as "creation" (61). The well-known Mexican celebration of All Souls Day, the Day of the Dead (All Hallows Eve) when families picnic with dead relatives in cemeteries and bake bread in the shape of skulls is a ritualized way of affirming the value of the relationship between the living and the dead. At the conclusion of *Carry Me Like Water*, three central figures celebrate this November day in "Concordia" cemetery (where all are in concord, in harmony), Maria Elena proclaiming: "I am in love with my rituals, in love with the people who created them, the people who handed them to me" (495). On the Day of the Dead, Sáenz's people do not mourn (495); they celebrate. This is why Mundo, the "vato" gang member dances in the morgue to the displeasure of a police sergeant (300). The Day of the Dead is a "time machine" which "re-creates all times at once and allows all who participate to breath the past" (Véa 98).

In Latino fiction, death inspires not fear, but wonder and fascination. Nearly all the characters of *Carry Me Like Water* desire their own deaths at some point.[17] They seek what Paz calls the "nostalgia for limbo," to feel themselves a part of a timeless "maternal source" (61-62). For Tomás Rivera's boy, the "cemetery isn't scary at all" (93) since the search for the past through the dead is not a negative thing. The "cemetery is real pretty" (94). Within it, "halfway home" (94), he realizes its value: "It's like I can hear all the dead people buried there saying these words and then the sound of these words stays in my mind" (95). The dead wander the earth in order to be remembered, forgiven, respected (through prayer), and written about by the living. The ritual of the "wake" (the reawakening of the soul), makes obvious the belief in the immortality of the soul. This, in part, accounts for those characters throughout Latino fiction who talk to dead people as if they were alive, or make statements that seem ludicrous from the typical Anglo-Protestant point of view. Chasing a ball, a Viramontes's character steps carefully through a cemetery muttering "excuse me, please excuse me, excuse me" (*Moths* "Growing" 37). "To catch even a glimpse of the crosses would be to eavesdrop, to intrude upon the conversation going on beneath . . . [the] soft whispering in Spanish" thinks the protagonist of Véa's *La Maravilla* (173). "People cook food for the dead and invite them into their homes," declares Beto's grandmother, "Mexican graveyards are alive" (Véa 18). In the story "The Idol Worshippers" by Sáenz, a grandmother lies in a "bedroom filled with her past" (125) conversing with Victor, her lover's ghost. Somehow these talks help her to understand the mistakes she has made in her relationship with her daughter, and through them, she learns she can bring her grandson and daughter closer as she and her daughter never were. For her, it is "sane to argue with the dead . . . the most natural thing in the world" (134), and that the practice gives her understanding is clear when she rightly instructs her daughter that arguing with the living makes less sense. The grandfather in "A Silent Love" speaks to his dead wife, then admonishes himself: "I'm just a goddamned fool talking to the dead—sure sign I'll be joining them soon" (22), while another Sáenz character converses with her dead mother because it makes her "feel better" (50). "It's cultural," she explains to her skeptical husband, "Mexicans speak to the dead" (50).

So do the elder Cubans, to the exasperation of the younger generation. The same abuela who claims it sometimes "rains backwards" in Fernandez's novel states categorically that "dead people feel alone too, they have feelings, you know" (143). As in *Our Town,* Martínez's narrator/writer can "feel the presence of invisible people carrying on conversations as they did in life" (*Voice-Haunted Journey* 250). "Even dead uncles want coffee" thinks an old man in the story "The Birthday of Mrs. Pineda" by Alberto Rios in which the coffee "reminds [him] to remember" his past. "Coffee is not a thing a man stops wanting" he decides, as he drifts between an evening conversation with his wife and memories of his energetic youth. It is the coffee that spurs the memory, and the belief that even dead uncles need caffeine that somehow maintains Adolfo's sense of being. He needs to feel conscious of his "lion" self, and attentive to his sexual energy which contrasts so sharply with the "flat" and "dimensionless" pictures of dead Salvadoreaños in his magazine (*Iguana* 115-118).

Disrupting the rigid notion of death's finality serves in these novels and stories as a standard motif. By altering such an obvious and accepted "truth," the Anglo/mainstream reader is thrown into a new and distorted picture of reality, into a distinctly foreign idea about the ordering of time. The desire to create this ambiguous framework gives rise to the supernatural elements in stories that begin with a death and a resurrection. In fiction that so expressly confronts the relationship of the past to questions of cultural heritage and character identity, it is noteworthy how many of these works contain characters who die and appear again. Often, a surrealistic atmosphere is established in the first line that, if nothing else, disturbs the reader's initial attention sufficiently enough to alter traditional, realist expectations—which is often exactly what these writers are attempting to do. *La Maravilla* by Alfredo Véa begins: "I died some time ago. Soy mujer de historia. I passed away. No, no, don't be sad . . . " This ghostly voice belongs to Josephina Valenzuela de Castillo, a curandera, whose ritualistic ceremonies and "ofrendas" (altars raised to the souls of the departed) establish the "unbroken link between the living and the dead" (Gonzalez-Crussi 70). Opening the story with the voice of a ghost, Véa frames his novel in cyclical time so that the chronology of events is displaced by a larger cosmic sense of time that stretches beyond individual lives. In fact, the book is about a young man's learning to time travel from his ancestral past through the present and into the future. The central chapter of Véa's novel is also called "La Maravilla," dividing the book between descriptions of the "backwards" (8) world of Buckeye Road in the first eight chapters from Beto's spiritual journey, the focus of the novel's second half. "La Maravilla," the marvel (thus the allusions to Andrew Marvel—48, 206, 232) can be read as the truth in folk spirituality, the authenticity of what cannot be explained rationally. "Maravillas" or marigolds are the "flowers of the dead" (278) and Beto's initiation ceremony is designed to connect him with his ancestors and to convince him that time and death are relative.

Eliud Martínez's novel begins: "Suddenly Alejandro Velásquez sat up in his coffin. Years later Alejandro's older brother would not remember how many people were there, sitting in the funeral chapel in Austin, Texas." "Even surrounded by decorated chrysanthemums," writes John Rechy in *The Miraculous Day of Amalia Gómez,* "and lying in the coppery coffin with her hands crossed over her rosary on her chest, Teresa had managed to look sternly at her daughter" (90). Ana Castillo's *So Far From God* opens similarly: "La Loca was only three years old when she died." Three pages later, she pushes up the lid of her coffin and sits up "just as sweetly as if she had woken from a nap" (22).[18] La Loca's sister, Esperanza is kidnapped and killed during the gulf war in Iraq, but returns in "transparent" form to converse with her clairvoyant sister. Another woman, Esmeralda, is apparently murdered by Francisco Penitente, the dysfunctional santero priest, yet seems to have returned to her friend's house. There she "said nothing or did nothing but look up at [Maria] occasionally with an expression on her face that also said nada" (209). Castillo cryptically mentions that this ghostly presence "was not afraid because she just was *not*" (emphasis mine 211). Later, she flies off a cliff with a third sister, Caridad, and both disappear forever (to the sounds of wind "like the voice of Tsichtinako") into the deep, soft earth (211).

Early in *Dreaming in Cuban,* the patriarch Jorge Del Pino dies in a New York hospital, only to arise from the ocean near the Cuban shore for a midnight swim with his estranged wife. He frequently visits his daughter Lourdes in those twilight (63, 70) times, that according to the narrator he has "stolen between death and oblivion" (193). In what Ramón Saldívar sees as Ron Arias's use of narrative fantasy "to subvert the closure of history" (129), *The Road to Tomazunchale* often obscures the distinction between life and death. Caught in a movie set, Fausto is mistaken for a dead extra (52). In the liquor store, his streetwise Chicano guide, Mario, claims he is dying of cholera ("No more vida for my dad"—25) in order to get a free quart of milk. A short time later, in a wild turn of events, Fausto is put into a hearse where he hides in another man's coffin, only to resurrect himself later at the funeral to the astonishment of the family: "Oh my God! Is that John? Do something . . . " (29). Further on in the book, Fausto instructs his "mojados" to incongruously look dead if they want to survive (68), that is, its easier for a dead wetback to survive in the U.S. than a live one. A dead man in the play within the novel needs a jacket to keep him warm (85). Finally, Arias's hero has "no funeral, no burial. Instead, Fausto insisted they take him to the beach so he could look at the sea and the women in bikinis for a while" where he fills "his mind with enough bodies to last several lifetimes." He then wants to go to a bookstore because, he claims, "where I'm going, nobody sells books. Maybe I could open a little shop" (99). This entire death fantasy which the reader is never allowed to believe or disbelieve completely simply provokes questions about reality and the construction of it. Where one wants to divide portions of the text between those that are plausible and those that are pure fantasy, Arias, like Rulfo before him, refuses these distinctions, and sanctions neither side in any way. Arias's jumbling of death and life, reality and illusion make his work a metafictional novel whose bits of realism act as points, or grounds from which his irony and parody proceed. Unlike Rulfo, however, there is little of the fatalistic pessimism that enshrouds the haunted town of Comala. If writers like Arias, Rivera and Castillo owe a debt to Rulfo (and they do) they have also managed to treat the themes of death with a light-heartedness unseen in the cynical Mexican writer's macabre work. This is because instead of fatalistically lamenting the deterioration of values and the human condition, they relish the blurring of borders in general.

Jean Franco argues that Latin American writers invert (and "masculinize") the traditional Antigone theme that one's family and timeless rituals outweigh the needs of state. They focus on the unburied Polinices as a marginal figure and commemorate the dead in an effort to insure their survival by metaphorically keeping them alive (130-131). Latino writers have also taken up this task in order to "commemorate" Nash Candelaria's "rainbow of humanity of losers," especially since North America is "strewn with the bodies of losers who [won't] stay dead . . . " (*Memories* 181). One thinks of Arias's dead mojado, David. The townspeople make the outcast come alive and force each other to recognize, as Fausto does, the tragic plight of the illegal alien. This is why they move him down the river so others can also be enlightened. To write the stories of Latinos and thus install them in history has always been a major preoccupation among Latinos. Works like Americo Paredes's *With His Pistol in his Hand* are only the most overt examples of the need to record the mixture that is Latino cultural heritage. Characters themselves struggle to document who they are by communicating (writing and talking), with their dead.

Sandra Cisneros's story "Eleven" concerns a young girl who firmly believes that while she is eleven, she is also ten, and nine and eight, etc. Rachel is her past; she is made of previous experience and the threshold of a birthday while it brings her new life, it doesn't negate the emotions of her younger self. Latino writers trace the past beyond their individual lives and back through their multicultural ancestry. In *Dreaming in Cuban*, the chapter that reveals Lourdes Puente's tragic past (her rape by Cuban Revolutionary soldiers and the subsequent loss of her second child) is framed by twilight visits from her deceased father (64-74). The traumatic event has shaped her adult life in numerous ways, and somehow, it must be left to the dead to reveal its meaning to her so that she can escape its power. The dead can teach us. On The Day of the Dead, writes Viramontes, "all the veins of memories are filled with the blood of resurrection" (*Moths* 89). The journey to the underworld thus reveals Latino hybridity because resurrection depends on the understanding of the diverse forces working on Latino memory and that understanding governs and strengthens the ability to cope with practical reality. The artist struggles to fix what Díaz-Quiñones called the broken memory (*La memoria rota*), to reestablish ties to *all* his or her past, no matter how strange elements of it may seem, to reconnect with the mythic island on the other side of the "charco."[19] Alfredo Véa's wise man, Ted For Short, in the final passage of Véa's second novel, *The*

Silver Cloud Café, argues that U.S. systems encourage people to "deny their pasts," to the degree that "each person here believes that he has succeeded on his own, without help from anyone . . . If you don't share a past or a culture, you don't have to share your labor or your earnings or your future." The resulting decay of community – "People who share buy less" – reveals that "America's conscience *is* the market" (337-338). Puerto Rican poet Martín Espada writes: "We survive here [in the U.S.] because of the strength we have gathered from that island" ("Culture" 88).

Latino fiction is a manifestation of the continuous struggle to look simultaneously both north and south, to hover somewhere over a real or figurative border. In Véa's words to survive the "anticultural" U.S., a "land of amnesiacs who pretend there is no past" (*Silver* 125). Gloria Anzaldúa speaks of "being" a crossroads, living "sin fronteras" [without borders]. Aurora Morales declares herself "whole" though "born at the crossroads." For Gina Valdés's Portillo family, "crossing the border [is] a continuous ritual," and the border "invisible" (85). The stories and novels by Latinos display the mixtures of influence on narrative craftsmanship, the blendings and experimentations of Spanish and English, the subversiveness of alternative political and social perspectives, and the celebrations of cultural hybridity from food to music to spirituality. Each time the writer's imaginative round trip is completed, Latino cultural differences assert themselves and are authenticated within the mainstream literary world. And as the process of "circulatory migration" is on going, and "La Carreta" makes another U-turn, literary cross-fertilization continues to feed those in the position to appreciate both worlds.

NOTES

1. The story recalls the Colombian writer Gustavo Alvarez Gardeazábal's tale of La Violencia (during the 1940's and 1950's), "Donaldo Arieto," in which a man, dying on the street, relives in the seconds before he dies, the events leading up to his murder. Both stories disconnect their characters' minds from chronological time and linear recollection in such a way as to expand the instant into a detailed narrative. It is the technique of Ambrose Bierce's famous story "Occurrence at Owl Creek Bridge," as well as Latin American stories like Julio Cortázar's "The Night Face Up" and Horacio Quiroga's "The Dead Man." Though time stops for a character, the reader (unlike the hero) begins a vicarious (possibly cathartic) journey into the past

2. Tickets for example on "the flying bus" between New York and Puerto Rico. See Luis Rafael Sanchez's article of that name in *Images and Identities: The Puerto Rican in Two World Contexts.* Ed. Asela Rodríguez de Laguna. New Brunswick, New Jersey: Transaction Books, 1987.

3. "Puente" in Spanish means "bridge."

4. Sergio Elizondo's novel, *Muerte en una estrella* (1984), based on an actual case in Austin, Texas, also deals with the last fragmented memories of two dying Chicanos in the 1960's (Sánchez "Discourses" 86).

5. Fausto's name may suggest that up until the time of his death for reasons never made clear in the novel, he has avoided such a personal investigation, and thereby sacrificed the essence of his soul in a futile attempt to deny his Latin American heritage.

6. The three part Table of Contents for the novel is followed by the following comment: "For the reader committed to nothing but short fiction, all letters read as separate entities. Good luck whichever journey you choose!"

7. Perhaps Castillo's use of the small "i" throughout the novel for the first person singular signals an uncertainty of the subject.

8. The critic Alvina E. Quintana calls Ana Castillo an ethnographer novelist because Castillo's novel incorporates observations and descriptions of Mexican and Chicano culture as seen through Teresa's eyes.

9. Rosaura Sánchez argues that while critics sometimes view these figures as exaggerated, one-dimensional, "formulaic images of Chicano/Mexican women" (84), they are also portrayed as complex individuals who nevertheless embody a common set of positive characteristics.

10. See the preceding chapter for more on the role of food in Latino fiction.

11. Santería is defined rather succinctly (by a murderer) in Max Abella's *The Killing of the Saints* as "a syncretic religion . . . it has fused together two separate strands to from a new one. It is a combination of West African religion and Catholicism, wherein the old Nigerian Yoruba pantheon of gods is identified with the saints of the Catholic church. It was born during the times of slavery, when African slaves had to hide their religion from their white masters" (281). To which we might add that the practice began in Cuba though now spans throughout Puerto Rico, The Dominican Republic, and along the South American coast. See Gonzalez-Wippler's *Santería: the Religion* for further information.

12. The final scene of the novel suggests as well the death of Virginia Woolf (who advocated looking back "through our mothers"—which is what Pilar is literally doing by skipping her mother). It evokes as well the "awakening" of Kate Chopin's Edna Pontellier. The allusions go deeper still.

Thinking of Eliot, the reader knows that in Pilar (who loves "pearls and the sea"—176) the artist figure will be born again, as Celia drops her pearls to the fertility god, the eyeless dead Phoenician soldier in "Wasteland." The allusive quality of the final scene is strong enough to bring in Joyce as well when one remembers the "strange and beautiful seabird" woman, half in the water, half out from *Portrait* and the epiphanic result to Stephen's artistic mind, the symbolic initiation of the artist creator. Celia, the lyrical letter writer (one is even written in blank verse – 51) will be reborn in the younger woman painter—a fact Celia recognizes: Pilar "will remember everything" she tells her lover Gustavo in her last letter (245). This kind of rebirth is understood as well by the narrator of "The Moths" in her conclusion that "endings are inevitable. They are necessary for rebirths" (27). The ocean swim is a frequent motif in Latina writing. In Alma Luz Villanueva's *The Ultraviolet Sky,* Rosa's swimming (in the ocean, in a whirlpool, and later in dark mountain lakes) signals her communing with the natural world and her Jungian psychic integration with her own darker side, with "something they couldn't name: fear chaos, raw power"(83). In her story "Golden Glass" a mother "too naked, somehow" (thinks her son) swims "out into the water, at night, as though trying to touch the moon" (*Growing Up Latino* 261). Discussing Villanueva's poetry, Ordóñez sees this theme of "the interconnectedness of all living things" and "the self as an integrated union of opposites" as something prevalent throughout her work ("Body, Spirit" in *Criticism in the Borderlands* 62).

13. See Jeff Thomson's article on the liminality of Inés and her ability to see two sides of the world: "both the physically violent world of Zapata's revolution and the emotionally violent world of love" (415).

14. In fact, in Spanish the same word, historia, is used for both "story" (or tale) and "history."

15. González-Wippler explains that Spiritualism should not be confused with Spiritism. The former focuses primarily on a "medium's psychic powers and his or her abilities to communicate with the dead, while the latter "has loftier ideals" (275). Spiritism, espiritismo (in Latin American) is a mixture of Spiritualism and the writings of a 19th century French philosopher and includes Santería.

16. One thinks also of Donald Barthelme's *The Dead Father* and of numerous other Latin American writers (noted in Jean Franco's *Plotting Women: Gender and Representation in Mexico* (130), and of modern Latino writers struggling with a Latin American / North American literary tradition.

17. Sáenz's, at sometimes, overt symbolism presents a mixture of Christian and Mexican beliefs. A dying Aids patient named Jesus Salvador [Savior] Aguila [meaning eagle and symbolizing Mexico] gives his gift of

clairvoyance to his sister, Maria de Lourdes Aguila. Salvador's ashes are given back to Mount Cristo Rey [Christ the King Mts.]. Lizzie, or Maria de Lourdes, becomes the catalyst for a series of reunions between lost family members, one of whom is a deaf mute named Juan Diego Ramirez, the only person able to see the value in a street woman claiming to be the Virgin Mary. A character named Luz [light] suddenly appears to Juan on the streets of El Paso, "out of nowhere, like a vision, like the Virgin of Guadalupe" (386). Christian names and Indian legend mesh throughout the book, generally suggesting the need for all to return south, to the desert, to ancient Mexican heritage (i.e. the ruins of Casas Grandes), to religious ritual, and to be "carried" like water toward kindness and faith.

18. Castillo's description is possibly inspired by García Márquez's short story "La Santa" in which a father journeys to Italy to seek the canonization of his daughter whose body has remained in tact after years in a grave.

19. "Charco" means puddle or pool. The phrase is sometimes used by Puerto Ricans to describe the distance (or lack of distance) between Puerto Rico and the mainland.

Works Cited

Abella, Alex. *The Killing of the Saints.* New York: Penguin Books, 1991.

Agüeros, Jack. *Dominos and Other Stories from the Puerto Rican.* Willimantic, Ct.: Curbstone Press, 1993.

Agosin, Margorie, ed. *Secret Weavers: Stories of the Fantastic by Women Writers of Argentina and Chile.* Fredonia, New York: White Pine Press, 1992.

Akers, John C. "Fragmentation in the Chicano Novel: Literary Technique and Cultural Identity." *Revista Chicano-Riqueña.* 13.3-4 (1985): 121-135

Alarcón, Norma. "The Sardonic Powers of the Erotic in the Work of Ana Castillo." Horno-Delgado 94-107.

Alcalá, Kathleen. *Mrs. Vargas and the Dead Naturalist.* Corvallis, Oregon: Calyx Books, 1992.

———. *Spirits of the Ordinary.* San Francisco: Chronicle Books, 1997.

Alegría, Fernando. *Nueva historia de la novela hispanoamericana.* Hanover, NH: Ediciones del Norte, 1986.

———, and Jorge Ruffinelli, eds. *Paradise Lost or Gained?: The Literature of Hispanic Exile.* Houston: Arte Publico Press, 1990.

Alexander, Marguerite. *Flights from Realism: Themes and Strategies in Postmodernist British and American Fiction.* London: Edward Arnold, 1990.

Alvarez, Julia. *How the García Girls Lost Their Accents.* New York: Penguin, 1991.

———. *In the Time of the Butterflies.* Chapel Hill: Algonquin Books, 1994.

———. *Yo.* New York: Penguin/Plume, 1997.

Anaya, Rudolfo A. *Bless Me, Ultima.* Berkeley, CA: Tonatiuuh-Quinto Sol, 1972.

———, and Antonio Márquez, eds. *Cuentos Chicanos.* Albuquerque: University of New Mexico Press, 1984.

Anzaldúa, Gloria. *Borderlands / La Frontera: The New Mestiza.* San Francisco: Spinsters Aunt Lute Book Company, 1987.

———. "Ghost Trap." Tatum 40-42.

———, ed. *Making Face, Making Soul Haciendo Caras: Creative and Critical Perspectives by Women of Color.* San Francisco: Spinsters Aunt Lute Book Company, 1990.

———. "People Should not Die in June in South Texas." Augenbraum and Stavans 280-287.

———, and Cherrie Moraga, eds. *This Bridge Called My Back: Writings By Radical Women of Color.* New York: Kitchen Table: Women of Color Press, 1981.

Aparicio, Frances R.. "On Sub-versive Signifiers: U.S. Latina/o Writers Tropicalize English." *American Literature.* 66 (1994): 795-801.

Arias, Ron. Interview. *Chicano Authors: Inquiry by Interview.* Ed. Juan Bruce-Novoa. Austin and London: University of Texas Press, 1980.

———. "The Mexican Way of Death: Celebrate it, Play with it, Challenge it." Los Angeles Times 17 Nov. 1981. B2.

———. *The Road to Tamazunchale.* New York: Doubleday Anchor Books, 1987.

Ashcroft, Bill, Gareth Griffiths and Helen Tiffin. *The Empire Writes Back.* London and New York: Routledge, 1989.

———, Gareth Griffiths and Helen Tiffin, eds. *The Post-Colonial Studies Reader.* London and New York: Routledge, 1995.

Augenbraum, Harold and Ilan Stavans, eds. *Growing Up Latino: Memoires and Stories.* Boston: Houghton Mifflin Co., 1993.

Baker, Houston A., Jr., ed. *Three American Literatures: Essays in Chicano, Native American, and Asian-American Literature for Teachers of American Literature.* New York: MLA, 1982.

Bakhtin, Mikhail. *The Dialogic Imagination.* Trans. Caryl Emerson and Michael Holquist. Ed. Michael Holquist. Austin: University of Texas Press, 1981.

———. *Problems of Dostoyevsky's Poetics* Trans. and Ed. Caryl Emerson. Minneapolis: University of Minnesota Press, 1984.

———. *Rabelais and His World.* Trans. Helene Iswolsky. Bloomington: Indiana University Press, 1984.

———. *Speech Genres and Other Later Essays.* Trans. Vern W. McGee. Ed. Caryl Emerson and Michael Holquist. Austin: University of Texas Press, 1986.

Bauer, Dale and Jaret McKinstry, eds. *Feminism, Bakhtin, and the Dialogic.* New York: State University of New York Press, 1991.

Bevan, David, ed. *Literature and Exile.* Amsterdam and Atlanta, GA: Rodopi, 1990.

Bhabha, Homi, ed. Introduction. *Nation and Narration.* By Bhabha. London and New York: Routledge, 1990.

Benítez, Sandra. *A Place Where the Sea Remembers.* Minneapolis: Coffee House Press, 1993.

Borges, Jorge Luis. "Narrative Art and Magic." *Borges A Reader: A Selection from the Writings of Jorge Luis Borges.* Ed. Emir Rodriguez Monegal and Alastair Reid. New York: E.P. Dutton, 1981. 34-38.

Bradbury, Malcolm, and James McFarlane, eds. *Modernism: A Guide to European Literature 1890-1930.* 1976. New Preface. London: Penguin, 1991.

Brathwaite, Edward Kamau. "Nation Language." *The Post-Colonial Studies Reader.* Ed. Bill Ashcroft, Gareth Griffiths and Helen Tiffin. London and New York: Routledge, 1995.

Bruce-Novoa, Juan. *Chicano Authors: Inquiry by Interview.* Austin and London: University of Texas Press, 1980.

———. "Deconstructing the Dominant Patriarchal Text: Cecile Pineda's Narratives." Horno-Delgado 72-81.

———. *Retrospace: Collected Essays on Chicano Literature.* Houston: Arte Publico Press, 1990.

Brushwood, John S. "Reality and Imagination in the Novels of García Márquez." *Latin American Literary Review.* 13 (1985): 9-14.

Calderón, Héctor, and José David Saldívar, eds. *Criticism in the Borderlands: Studies in Chicano Literature, Culture, and Ideology.* Durham and London: Duke University Press, 1991.

———. "Rudolfo Anaya's *Bless Me, Ultima:* A Chicano Romance of the Southwest." *Critica* 1.3 (1986): 21-47.

Candelaria, Nash. *Memories of the Alhambra.* Tempe, Arizona: Bilingual Press/Editorial Bilingüe, 1977.

Carpentier, Alejo. Prologue. *The Kingdom of this World.* By Carpentier. Trans. Harriet de Onís. London: Andre Deutsch, 1990.

Castedo, Elena. *Paradise.* New York: Grove Weidenfeld, 1990.

Castellanos, Rosario. *The Nine Guardians.* Trans. Irene Nicholson. London: Faber and Faber Limited, 1959.

Castillo, Ana. *The Mixquiahuala Letters.* Binghamton New York: Bilingual Press/Editorial Bilingüe, 1986.

———. *Sapogonia.* Tempe, Arizona: Bilingual Press/Editorial Bilingüe, 1990.

———. *So Far From God.* New York: Norton, 1993.

Castillo, Debra A. *Talking Back: Toward a Latin American Feminist Literary Criticism.* Ithaca and London: Cornell University Press, 1992.

Castro-Klarén, Sara, Sylvia Molloy and Beatriz Sarlo, eds. *Women's Writing in Latin America: An Anthology.* Boulder: Westview Press, 1991.

Chanady, Amaryll Beatrice. "Latin American Discourses of Identity and the Appropriation of the Amerindian Other." *Sociocriticism* 6.1-2 (1990): 33-48.

———. *Magical Realism and the Fantastic: Resolved Versus Unresolved Antinomy.* New York & London: Garland Publishing, Inc., 1985.

Chapman, Seymour. *Story and Discourse: Narrative Structure in Fiction and Film.* Ithaca and London: Cornell University Press, 1978.

Chávez, Denise. *Face of an Angel.* New York: Farrar, Straus and Giroux, 1994.

———. *The Last of the Menu Girls.* Houston: Arte Publico Press, 1986.

Christian, Karen. "Will the 'Real Chicano' Please Stand Up? The Challenge of John Rechy and Sheila Ortiz Taylor to Chicano Essentialism." *America's Review.* 20.2 (1992): 89-104.

Cisneros, Sandra. *The House on Mango Street.* Houston: Arte Publico Press, 1984.

———. *Women Hollering Creek and Other Stories.* New York: Random, 1991.

Clark, Katrina and Michael Holquist. *Mikhail Bakhtin.* Cambridge, Mass: Harvard University Press, 1984.

Clayton, Jay. *The Pleasures of Babel: Contemporary American Literary Theory.* New York and Oxford: Oxford University Press, 1993.

Cofer, Judith Ortiz. *The Latin Deli.* Athens and London: University of Georgia Press, 1993.

———. *The Line of the Sun.* Athens and London: University of Georgia Press, 1989.

———. *Silent Dancing.* Houston: Arte Publico Press, 1990.

Corpi, Lucha. *Delia's Song.* Houston: Arte Publico Press, 1989.

———. *Eulogy for a Brown Angel: A Mystery Novel.* Houston: Arte Publico Press, 1992.

Cypess, Sandra Messinger. *La Malinche in Mexican Literature: From History to Myth.* Texas Pan American Series. Austin: University of Texas Press, 1991.

Davidson, Ned J. *The Concept of Modernism in Hispanic Criticism.* Boulder: Pruett Press, Inc., 1966.

Deaver, William O. Jr. "*Raining Backwards*: Colonization and the Death of a Culture." *America's Review.* 21.1 (1993): 112-118

Díaz, Junot. *Drown.* New York: Riverhead Books, 1996.

Díaz-Quiñones, Arcadio. *La memoria rota.* Rio Piedras, Puerto Rico: Ediciones Huracán, Inc., 1993.

Dorfman, Ariel and Armand Mattelart. *How to Read Donald Duck.* Trans. David Kunzle. New York: International General, 1984.

Doyle, Jacqueline. "More Room of Her Own: Sandra Cisneros's *The House on Mango Street. Melus* 19.4 (Winter 1994): 5-35.

DuPlessis, Rachel Blau. "For the Etruscans." *The New Feminist Criticism.* Ed. Elaine Schowalter. New York: Pantheon Books, 1985. 271-291.

Durán, Richard P. ed. *Latino Language and Communicative Behavior.* Advances in Discourse Processes 6. Norwood, New Jersey: ABLEX Publishing Corporation, 1981.

Eliot, T.S. *The Sacred Wood.* London and New York: Methuen, 1920.

Eliade, Mircea. *Myths, Dreams, and Mysteries. Trans.* Philip Mairet. New York: Harper and Row, 1960.

Espada, Martín. "Culture and Independence in Puerto Rico." *Being América.*" Ed. Rachel Weiss and Alan West. Fredonia, New York: White Pine Press, 1991.

Estes, Clarissa Pinkola. *Women Who Run with the Wolves.* New York: Ballantine Books, 1992.

Faulkner, William. "Dry September." *Selected Short Stories of William Faulkner.* New York: Random House, 1930. 62-77.

Febles, Jorge. "English and Spanish Pop Songs as Part of Character Speech: Cultural Hybridity in Roberto G. Fernández's *Raining Backwards.*" *Imagination, Emblems and Expressions: Essays on Latin American, Caribbean, and Continental Culture and Identity.* Ed. Helen Ryan-Ranson. Bowling Green, Ohio: Bowling Green State University Popular Press, 1993. 99-108.

———. "El pretexto de la parodia o la parodia del pre-texto: en turno a un capitulo de *Raining Backwards.*" *Hispania.* 75.1 (1992): 69-77.

———. "Risa, crisis y cornonación paródica: lo carnavalesco en *La vida es un special $1.50 .75.*" *Confluencia: Revista Hispanica de Cultura y Literatura.* Vol. 3.1 (1988): 123-128.

Fernández, Roberta. "'The Cariboo Cafe:' Helena Maria Viramontes Discourses with her Social and Cultural Contexts." *Women's Studies.* 17.1-2 (1989): 71-85.

———. *Intaglio.* Houston: Arte Publico Press, 1990.

———. ed. *In Other Words: Literature by Latinas of the United States.* Houston: Arte Publico Press, 1994.

Fernández, Roberto G. *Raining Backwards.* Houston: Arte Publico Press, 1988.

Fernandez, Ronald. *Prisoners of Colonialism: The Struggle for Justice in Puerto Rico.* Monroe, Maine: Common Courage Press, 1994.

Flores, Angel. "Magical Realism in Spanish American Fiction." *Hispania* 38 2 (May 1955): 187-192.

Flores, Juan. *Divided Borders: Essays on Puerto Rican Identity.* Houston: Arte Publico Press, 1993.

———, and George Yúdice. "Living Borders/Buscando America: Languages of the Latino Self-Formation." *Social Text* 24 (1990): 57-84. Rpt. in *Divided Borders: Essays on Puerto Rican Identity.* Houston: Arte Publico Press, 1993. 199-224.

Fontes, Montserrat. *Dreams of the Centaur.* New York: W.W. Norton & Co., 1996.

Foster, David William, ed. *Handbook of Latin American Literature.* 2nd ed. New York and London: Garland Publishing Inc., 1992.

Franco, Jean. *Plotting Women: Gender and Representation in Mexico. Gender and Culture Series.* New York: Columbia University Press, 1989.

Franklet, Duane. "Social Language: Bakhtin and Viramontes." *America's Review.* 17.2 (1989): 110-114.

Friedman, Ellen G. "Where are the Missing Contents? (Post) Modernism, Gender, and the Canon." PLMA. 108 (March): 1993.

Fuentes, Carlos. *La nueva novela hispanomericana.* Mexico City: Joaquín Mortiz, 1969.

Fusco, Coco. *English is Broken Here: Notes on Cultural Fusion in the Americas.* New York: The New Press, 1995.

Garcia, Guy. *Obsidian Sky.* New York: Simon and Schuster, 1994.

———. "La Promesa." Soto 133-151.

Garcia, Cristina. *The Agüero Sisters. New York*: Knopf, 1997.

———. Dreaming *in Cuban.* New York: Knopf, 1992.

———. "Tito's Good-bye." *Iguana Dreams: New Latino Fiction.* Ed. Delia Poey and Virgil Suárez. New York: HarperPerennial, 1992.

García Márquez, Gabriel. "Big Mama's Funeral." *Collected Stories.* Trans. J.S. Bernstein. New York: Harper, 1984. 184-200.

———. *One Hundred Years of Solitude.* Trans. Gregory Rabassa. New York: Harper & Row, Publishers, 1970

Genishi, Celia. "Codeswitching in Chicano Six-Year-Olds." Durán 133-152.

Gilb, Dagoberto. *The Last Known Residence of Mickey Acuña.* New York: Grove Press, 1994.

———. *The Magic of Blood.* Albuquerque: University of New Mexico Press, 1993.

Gilbert, Sandra M. and Susan Gubar. "The Female Imagination and the Modernist Aesthetic." Intro. *Women's Studies.* Vol. 13, 1986, 1-10.

Giordano, Jaime. "Hacia una definición del realismo en la novela hispanomericana contemporánea." *Nueva narrativa hispanoamericana* 1 (1971): 127-132.

Goldman, Francisco. *The Long Night of White Chickens.* New York: Atlantic Monthly Press, 1992.

———. *The Ordinary Seaman.* New York: Atlantic Monthly Press, 1997.

Gómez, Alma, Cherríe Moraga, and Mariana Romo-Carmona, eds. *Cuentos: Stories by Latinas.* New York: Kitchen Table: Women of Color Press, 1983.

Gómez-Vega, Ibis. "Debunking Myths: The Hero's Role in Ana Castillo's *Sapogonia. Americas Review.* 22.1-2 (1994): 244-258.

Gonzales-Berry, Erlinda and Tey Diana Rebolledo. "Growing up Chicano: Tomás Rivera and Sandra Cisneros." *Revista Chicano-Riqueña.* 13.3-4 (1985): 109-119. New York and London: Garland Publishing Inc., 1992.

———. and Santa Arias. "Latino Writing in the United States." *Handbook of Latin American Literature.* Ed. David William Foster. 2nd ed. New York and London: Garland Pub. Co., 1992. 649-645.

———. Rev. of *Face,* by Cecile Pineda. *Americas Review* 15.2 (1987): 107-109.

Gonzalez, Ray. ed. *Mirrors Beneath the Earth: Short Fiction by Chicano Writers.* Willimantic: Curbstone Press, 1992.

———, ed. *Currents from the Dancing River: Contemporary Latino Fiction, Nonfiction and Poetry.* San Diego, New York, London: Harcourt Brace & Co., 1994.

González Echevarría, Roberto. *Alejo Carpentier: The Pilgrim at Home.* Austin: University of Texas Press, 1977.

Gonzalez-Crussi, F. *The Day of the Dead and other Mortal Reflections.* New York: Harcourt Brace and Co., 1993.

González-Wippler, Migene. *Santería: The Religion.* 2nd. ed. St. Paul: Llewellyn Publications, 1994.

Guerra Cunningham, Lucía. ed. *Splintering Darkness: Latin American Women Writers in Search of Themselves.* Pittsburgh, PA: Latin American Literary Review Press, 1990.

Guizado, Eduardo Camacho. "Notas sobre la nueva novela hispanoamericana." *Nueva narrativa hispanoamericana* 1 (1971): 133-135.

Harper, Phillip Brian. *Framing the Margins: The Social Logic of Postmodern Culture.* New York, Oxford: Oxford University Press, 1994.

Hemingway, Ernest. *Death in the Afternoon.* New York: Charles Scriber's Sons, 1932.

Hernández, Guillermo E. *Chicano Satire: A Study in Literary Culture.* Austin: University of Texas Press, 1991.

Hernández Cruz, Victor. "Mountains in the North: Hispanic Writing in the USA. *Americas Review.* 14. 3-4 (1986): 110-114.

Hererra-Sobek, María. ed. *Beyond Stereotypes: Critical Analysis of Chicana Literature.* Binghamton, New York: Bilingual Press/Editorial Bilingüe, 1985.

———, and Helena María Viramontes, eds. *Chicana Creativity and Criticism: Charting New Frontiers in American Literature.* Houston: Arte Publico Press, 1988.

Heyck, Denis Lynn Daly. *Barrios and Borderlands: Cultures of Latinos and Latinas in the United States.* New York: Routledge, 1994.

Hicks, Emily. *Border Writing: The Multidimensional Text.* Theory and History of Literature Series 80. Minneapolis and Oxford: University of Minnesota Press, 1991.

Hijuelos, Oscar. *The Fourteen Sisters of Emilio Montez O'Brien.* New York: Farrar, Straus & Giroux, 1993.

———. *The Mambo Kings Play Songs of Love.* New York: Harper and Row, 1989.

———. *Our House in the Last World.* New York. Washington Square Press, 1983.

Hinojosa, Rolando. *Klail City.* Houston: Arte Publico Press, 1987.

Horno-Delgado, Asunción, et al., eds. *Breaking Boundaries: Latina Writings and Critical Readings.* Amherst: University of Massachusetts Press, 1989.

Huerta-Macias, Ana. "Code-Switching: All in the Family." Durán 153-168.

Ibieta, Gabriella. "Transcending the Culture of Exile: *Raining Backwards.*" *Literature and Exile.* Ed. David Bevan. Amsterdam and Atlanta, GA: Rodopi, 1990. 67-76.

Islas, Arturo. *Migrant Souls.* New York, Avon Books, 1990.

———. *The Rain God.* New York, Avon Books, 1984.

Iyer, Pico. *Cuba and the Night.* New York: Alfred A. Knopf, 1995.

Jefferson, Margo. "Dancing into the Dream." Rev. of *The Mambo Kings Play Songs of Love*, by Oscar Hijuelos. *The New York Times Book Review* 27 Aug. 1989: 1.

Johnson, David. "Face Value (An Essay on Cecile Pineda's *Face*)." *Americas Review* 19.2 (1991): 73-93,

Kanellos, Nicolás. "Orality and Hispanic Literature of the United States." in *Redefining American Literary History.* Ed. A. LaVonne Brown Ruoff and

Jerry W. Ward, Jr. New York: Modern Language Association of America, 1990. 115-123.

———, ed. *Short Fiction by Hispanic Writers of the United States*. Houston: Arte Publico, 1993.

Kenner, Hugh. *The Pound Era*. Berkeley and Los Angeles: University of California Press, 1971.

Kloepfer, Deborah Kelly. *The Unspeakable Mother: Forbidden Discourse in Jean Rhys and H.D.* Ithaca and London: Cornell University Press, 1989.

Kolmar, Wendy K. "'Dialectics of Connectedness:' Supernatural Elements in Novels by Bambara, Cisneros, Grahn, and Erdrich." *Haunting the House of Fiction: Feminist Perspectives on Ghost Stories by American Women.* Knoxville, TN: University of Tennessee Press, 1991. 236-249.

Lattin, Vernon E., ed. *Contemporary Chicano Fiction: A Critical Survey.* Binghamton, NY: Bilingual Press / Editorial Bilingüe, 1986.

Leal, Luis. *Aztlán y México: Perfiles literarios e históricos.* Binghamton, N.Y.: Bilingual press/Editorial Bilingüe, 1985.

———, and Pepe Barrón. "Chicano Literature: An Overview." *Three American Literatures: Essays in Chicano, Native American, and Asian-American Literature for Teachers of American Literature.* Ed. Houston A. Baker, Jr. New York: Modern Language Association of America, 1982. 9-32.

Levine, Suzanne Jill. *The Subversive Scribe: Translating Latin American Fiction.* Saint Paul: Graywolf Press, 1991.

Lindstrom, Naomi. *Twentieth-Century Spanish American Fiction.* Austin: University of Texas Press, 1994.

Little, Judy. "(En)gendering Laughter: Woolf's *Orlando* as Contraband in the Age of Joyce." *Last Laughs: Perspectives on Women and Comedy.* Ed. Regina Barreca. Studies in Gender and Culture 2. New York and London: Gordon and Breach, 1988. 179-191.

Lodge, David. *After Bakhtin: Essays on Fiction and Criticism.* London and New York: Routledge, 1990.

McCracken, Ellen. "Latina Narrative and the Politics of Signification: Articulation, Antagonism, and Populist Rupture." *Critica: A Journal of Critical Essays.* 2.2 (1990): 202-207.

———. "Sandra Cisneros' *The House on Mango Street*: Community-Oriented Introspection and the Demystification of Patriarchal Violence." Horno-Delgado 62-71.

Martínez, Eliud. Intro. *The Road to Tamazunchale.* By Ron Arias. Tempe, Arizona: Bilingual Press/Editorial Bilingüe, 1987.

———. "Ron Arias' *The Road to Tamazunchale*: A Chicano Novel of the New Reality." *Latin American Literary Review* 5 (1977): 51-63. (Rpt. in Lattin 226-238.)

———. *Voice-Haunted Journey*. Tempe, Arizona: Bilingual Press/Editorial Bilingüe, 1990.

Mohr, Nicholasa. *El Bronx, Remembered: a Novela and Stories*. Houston: Arte Publico Press, 1986.

———. *In Nueva York*. Houston: Arte Publico Press, 1988.

———. *Nilda*. Houston: Arte Publico Press, 1986.

———. "On Being Authentic." *Americas Review*. 14.3-4 (1986): 106-109.

———. "Puerto Rican Writers in the U.S., Puerto Rican Writers in Puerto Rico: A Separation Beyond Language." Horno-Delgado 111-121.

———. *Rituals of Survival: A Woman's Portfolio*. Houston: Arte Publico Press, 1986.

———. "The Journey Toward a Common Ground: Struggle and Identity of Hispanics in the USA." *Americas Review*. 18.1 (1990): 81-85.

Monegal, Emir Rodríguez. ed. *The Borzoi Anthology of Latin American Literature*. Vol. I. New York: Knopf, 1977.

———, ed. *The Borzoi Anthology of Latin American Literature*. Vol. II. New York: Knopf, 1977.

Morales, Aurora Levins, and Rosario Morales. *Getting Home Alive*. Ithaca, New York: Firebrand Books, 1986.

Moraga, Cherríe, and Gloria Anzaldúa, eds. *This Bridge Called My Back: Writings By Radical Women of Color*. New York: Kitchen Table: Women of Color Press, 1981.

Nabokov, Vladimir. *Lolita*. New York: Vintage International, 1955.

Nieto, Eva Margarita. "The Dialectics of Textual Interpolation in Ron Arias' *The Road to Tamazunchale*. Lattin 239-46.

Ortega, Eliana. "Poetic Discourse of the Puerto Rican Woman in the U.S.: New Voices of Anacaonian Liberation." Horno-Delgado 122-135.

Ortega, Julio. "La primera página de *Cien años de soledad." En el punto de mira: Gabriel García Márquez*. Ed. Ana María Hernández. Madrid: Editorial Pliegos, 1985. 137-149.

Ortiz, Rafael Cancel. "The Language Conflict in Puerto Rican Literature." *Americas Review*. 18.2 (1990): 103-113.

Paredes, Américo. *With his Pistol in his Hand*. Austin: University of Texas Press, 1958.

Paz, Octavio. *The Labyrinth of Solitude*. Trans. Lysander Kemp. New York: Grove Press, 1961.

Pérez Firmat, Gustavo. *Life on the Hyphen: The Cuban-American Way*. Austin: University of Texas Press, 1994.

———. *Literature and Liminality: Festive Readings in the Hispanic Tradition.* Durham: Duke University Press, 1986.

Pineda, Cecile. *Face*. New York: Viking Penguin, 1985.

———. *Frieze*. New York, Viking Penguin, 1986.

———. *The Love Queen of the Amazon*. Boston: Little, Brown and Co., 1992.

Poey, Delia and Virgil Suárez, eds. *Iguana Dreams: New Latino Fiction.* New York: HarperPerennial, 1992.

Ponce, Mary Helen. *Taking Control.* Houston: Arte Publico Press, 1987.

———. *The Wedding*. Houston: Arte Publico Press, 1989.

Portillo-Trambley, Estelle. *"Pay the Criers." The Third Woman: Minority Women Writers of the U.S.* Ed. Dexter Fisher. Boston: Houghton Mifflin, 1980. 361-376.

———. *Trini.* Binghamton, New York: Bilingual Press, 1986.

Pound, Ezra. *Literary Essays of Ezra Pound.* 1918. New York: New Directions, 1968.

Quintana, Alvina E. "Ana Castillo's *The Mixquiahuala Letters*: The Novelist as Ethnographer." *Criticism in the Borderlands: Studies in Chicano Literature, Culture, and Ideology*. Eds. Héctor Calderón and José David Saldívar. Durham and London: Duke University Press, 1991. 72-83.

Rebolledo, Tey Diana. "Abuelitas: Mythology and Integration in Chicana Literature." *Woman of her Word: Hispanic Women Write.* Ed. Evangelina Vigil. Houston: Arte Publico Press, 1987. 148-158.

———, and Eliana S. Rivero. eds. *Infinite Divisions: An Anthology of Chicana Literature.* Tucson and London: University of Arizona Press, 1993.

———. *Women Singing in the Snow*. Tucson / London: University of Arizona Press, 1995.

Rechy, John. *The Miraculous Day of Amalia Gómez*. New York: Arcade Publishing, 1991.

Rios, Alberto. *The Iguana Killer: Twelve Stories of the Heart.* New York: Kampmann & Co., Inc., 1984.

———. *Pig Cookies and Other Stories*. San Francisco: Chronicle Books, 1995.

Rivera, Tomás. *. . . And the Earth did not Devour Him.* Trans. Evangelina Vigil-Piñón. Houston: Arte Publico Press, 1992.

Rivero, Eliana S. "From Immigrants to Ethnics: Cuban Women Writers in the U.S." *Breaking Boundaries: Latina Writings and Critical Readings*. Horno-Delgado 189-200.

———. "Hispanic Literature in the United States: Self-Image and Conflict." *Americas Review*. 13 (1985): 173 -192.

———. (Re)Writing Sugarcane Memories: Cuban Americans and Literature." *Paradise Lost or Gained?: The Literature of Hispanic Exile.* Eds. Fernando Alegría and Jorge Ruffinelli. Houston: Arte Publico Press, 1990. 164-182.

Robbe-Grillet, Alain. "A Future for the Novel." *For a New Novel.* Trans. R. Howard. New York: Grove Press, 1965. Rpt in *Twentieth-Century Literary Criticism.* Ed. David Lodge. London and New York: Longman, 1972. 467-472.

Robinson, Louie Garcia. *The Devil, Delfina Varela & the used Chevy.* New York: Anchor Books, 1993.

Rocard, Marcienne. "The Remembering Voice in Chicana Literature." *Americas Review.* 14.3-4 (1986): 153-154.

Rodriguez, Abraham Jr. *The Boy Without a Flag: Tales of the South Bronx.* Minneapolis: Milkweed Editions, 1992.

———. *Spidertown.* New York: Hyperion, 1993

Rodriguez, Richard. *Hunger of Memory.* New York: David R. Godine, 1982.

Rogers, Jane. "The Function of the La Llorona Motif in Anaya's *Bless Me, Ultima.*" Lattin 269-277.

Rulfo, Juan. *Pedro Pararro.* Trans. Lyander Kemp. New york: Grove Press, 1959.

Ruoff, A. LaVonne Brown and Jerry W. Ward, Jr. eds. *Redefining American Literary History.* New York: Modern Language Association of America, 1990.

Sáenz, Benjamin Alire. *Carry Me Like Water.* New York: Hyperion, 1995.

———. *Flowers for the Broken.* Seattle: Broken Moon Press, 1992.

———. "I Want to Write an American Poem: On Being a Chicano Poet in Post-Columbian America." *Currents From the Dancing River: Contemporary Latino Fiction, Nonfiction, and Poetry.* Ed. Ray Gonzalez. San Diego, New York, London: Harcourt Brace & Co., 1994. 522-536.

Said, Edward. *Culture and Imperialism.* New York: Knopf, 1993.

Saldívar, José David. *Dialectics of Our America: Genealogy, Cultural Critique, and Literary History.* Durham and London: Duke University Press, 1991.

Saldívar, Ramón. *Chicano Narrative: The Dialectics of Difference.* Madison, WI: University of Wisconsin Press, 1990.

Sánchez, Rosaura. *Chicano Discourse: Socio-historic Perspectives.* Rowley, MA: Newbury House Publishers, 1983.

———. "Chicano Prose Writers." Herrera-Sobek 61-70.

———. "Discourses of Gender, Ethnicity and Class in Chicano Literature." *Americas Review.* 20 (1992): 72-88.

———. "Ideological Discourses in Islas's *The Rain God.*" Calderón and Saldívar 114-126.

———. "Postmodernism and Chicano Literature." *Aztlán* 18.2 (1987): 1-14.

Sandoval, Alberto. "Dolores Prida's *Coser y cantar*: Mapping the Dialectics of Ethnic Identity and Assimilation." Horno-Delgado 201-220.

Scott, Nina M. "The Politics of Language: Latina Writers in United States Literature and Curricula." *Melus* 19.1 (1994): 57-71.

Soto, Gary, ed. *Pieces of the Heart: New Chicano Fiction.* San Francisco: Chronicle Books, 1993.

Shorris, Earl. *Latinos: A Biography of a People.* New York: Norton, 1992.

Stavans, Ilan. *The Hispanic Condition.* New York: Harper Collins Publishers, 1995.

Stockton, Sharon. "ReReading the Maternal Body: Viramontes' *The Moths* and the Construction of the New Chicana." *Americas Review.* 22.1-2 (1994): 212-229.

Suárez, Virgil. *Welcome to the Oasis and Other Stories.* Houston: Arte Publico Press, 1992.

Tanner, Toby. *The City of Words: A Study of American Fiction in the Mid-Twentieth Century.* London: Jonathan Cape, 1971.

Tatum, Charles M. ed. *New Chicana/Chicano Writing.* Tucson and London: University of Arizona Press, 1992.

Thomson, Jeff. "'What is Called Heaven': Identity in Sandra Cisneros's *Women Hollering Creek.*" *Studies in Short Fiction.* 31. (1994): 415-424.

Thurston, Kay. "Barriers to the Self-Definition of the Chicana: Gina Valdés and *There are no Madmen Here.*" *Melus* 19.4 (Winter 1994): 61-73.

Todorov, Tvetan. *The Fantastic: A Structural Approach to a Literary Genre.* Ithaca, NY: Cornell University Press, 1973.

———. *Mikhail Bakhtin: The Dialogical Principle.* Minneapolis: University of Minnesota Press, 1984.

Torres, J. L. "My Father's Flag." Augenbraum and Stavans 264-273.

Valdés, Gina. *There are no Madmen Here.* San Diego: Maize Press, 1981.

Vallejos, Tomás. "Estela Portillo-Trambley's Fictive Search for Paradise." *Frontiers.* 5.2 (1980): 54-58. (Rpt. in Lattin 269-277.)

Vásquez, Mary S. "Family, Generation, and Gender in Two Novels of Cuban Exile: Into the Mainstream?" *The Bilingual Review / La Revista Bilingüe.* 26.1 (1991): 23-34.

———. "The Fantastic and the Grotesque in the Fiction of Roberto Fernández: The Case of *Raining Backwards. Confluencia* 1 (1990): 75-84.

———. "Gender in Exile: Mothers and Daughters in Roberto G. Fernández's *Raining Backwards.*" *The Literature of Emigration and Exile.* Ed James

Whitlock and Wendell Ayrock. Lubbock, Texas: Texas Technical University Press, 1992. 79-85.
———. "Parody, Intertextuality and Cultural Values in Roberto G. Fernández's *Raining Backwards*." *Americas Review*. 18.2 (1990): 92-102.
Véa, Alfredo Jr. *La Maravilla*. New York: Plume, 1993.
———. *The Silver Cloud Café*. New York: Dutton, 1996.
Vega, Ed. *Casualty Report*. Houston: Arte Publico Press, 1991.
———. *The Comeback*, Houston: Arte Publico Press, 1987.
———. *Mendoza's Dreams*. Houston: Arte Publico Press, 1985.
Villanueva, Alma Luz. *The Ultraviolet Sky*. Bilingual Press/Editorial Bilingüe, 1988.
Vigil, Evangelina, ed. *Woman of her Word. Hispanic Women Write*. Houston: Arte Publico Press, 1987.
Viramontes, Helena Maria. "Miss Clairol" Hererra-Sobek 101-105.
———. *The Moths*. Houston: Arte Publico Press, 1985.
———. "Tears on My Pillow. " Tatum 110-115.
———. *Under the Feet of Jesus*. New York: Dutton, 1995
Waugh, Patricia. *Metafiction*. London and New York: Methuen, 1984.
Weiss, Rachel and Alan West, eds. *Being América: Essays on Art, Literature and Identity from Latin America*. New York: White Wine Press, 1991.
Williams, Raymond L. *The Postmodern Novel in Latin America: Politics, Culture, and the Crisis of Truth*. New York: St. Martin's Press, 1995.
Williams, William Carlos. *Selected Essays of William Carlos Williams*. New York: Random House, 1954.
Woolf, Virginia. "Mr. Bennet and Mrs. Brown." *Captain's Death Bed and Other Essays*. 1950. New York and London: Harcourt Brace Jovanovich, Publishers, 1978.
———. *Orlando*. New York: Harcourt Brace Jovanovich, Inc., 1928.
Yarbo-Bejarano, Yvonne. "The Multiple Subject in the Writing of Ana Castillo." *America's Review*. 20.1 (1992): 65-72.
Young, David and Keith Hollaman. eds. *Magical Realist Fiction: An Anthology*. New York & London: Longman, Inc., 1984.
Zentella, Ana Celia. "Tá bien, You Could Answer Me en cualquier idioma: Puerto Rican Codeswitching in Bilingual Classrooms." Durán 169-178.
Zimmerman, Marc. *U.S. Latino Literature: An Essay and Annotated Bibliography*. Chicago: MARCH/Abrazo Press, 1992.

Index

www.ingramcontent.com/pod-product-compliance
Lightning Source LLC
Chambersburg PA
CBHW071526110726
47908CB00003B/962

* 9 7 8 1 1 3 8 0 0 1 8 0 0 *